JKTPY
(Jar)

THE TEACHING OF VALUES

Through the ages, schools have typically played a part in the instruction of morals and ethics, sometimes in a heavy-handed, indoctrinating way, sometimes more indirectly and subtly. Nevertheless, the purpose of schools has typically been described in cognitive terms, as the teaching of thinking and problem solving, and the transmitting of bodies of fact and theory. Yet knowledge is itself grounded in value, since the knowledge that is taught in schools is the knowledge that society accords the greatest value.

The Teaching of Values reorientates thinking about what schools should consider their *raison d'être*, arguing that schools are better conceived as institutions for instruction in values than as purveyors of knowledge. Based on the author's twenty years of teaching on the place of values in schools, the book demonstrates that schools have always had, and properly should have, a great deal to do with matters of value, such as the development of humane feelings, aesthetic taste, an active concern for the rights and duties of a citizen, participation in family life, and appropriate attitudes towards nation, community, work and friendship.

Written for teachers, administrators, counselors, and all those who are caught up in the public debate about how schools and colleges can best educate, the book examines the principal kinds of values, particularly ethical and aesthetic values, and shows how they relate to each other and how they can be taught. Setting its discussion within a philosophical, psychological and social framework, it seeks to demonstrate how teachers can help to equip their pupils to enjoy—and help others to enjoy—a life rich in values.

James L. Jarrett is Professor Emeritus at the Graduate School of Education, University of California, Berkeley. He started his teaching career in a small town high school five decades ago. He has published seven books in philosophy, professional education and analytical psychology, and has lectured widely throughout North America, and in Europe, the Middle East and South America.

THE TEACHING OF VALUES

Caring and appreciation

James L. Jarrett

London and New York

First published 1991
by Routledge
11 New Fetter Lane, London EC4P 4EE

Simultaneously published in the USA and Canada
by Routledge
a division of Routledge, Chapman and Hall, Inc.
29 West 35th Street, New York, NY 10001

Typeset in Garamond by
Michael Mepham, Frome, Somerset
Printed in Great Britain by Mackays of Chatham PLC, Kent.

British Library Cataloging in Publication Data

Has been applied for.

Library of Congress Cataloging in Publication Data

Has been applied for.

CONTENTS

PREFACE

This book about value is intended to be *of* value to teachers and other educators in their endeavor to broaden and deepen the value-rich experience of students' lives.

The work is not a theoretical treatise, nor a 'how-to' manual. Instead it moves back and forth between theory and classroom practise, paying more attention to the opening up of new possibilities for consideration than to establishing a tightly drawn position.

In the broad scope of ethical values, the emphasis here is upon the attitude and practise of caring along with the obligation to continue development toward an ever higher level of consciousness of self, one's own and others'. In the realm of aesthetic values it is appreciation that gets particular attention here, as well as the intuitive aspects of that impulse toward meaningful novelty that is called creativity.

My own disciplinary affiliation is with philosophy, a fact that will be apparent from drawing so much upon, among others, Plato, Aristotle, Dewey, Whitehead, Buber, and Langer. But psychologists are drawn upon too, both empirical developmentalists and depth psychologists, with a notable tilt toward C. G. Jung. Sociologists and other social scientists have their say here too, along with critics, poets, and story-tellers.

Much is owed to the cited authorities, but even more to my students, over a long span of years, up to the present. Many of these are now teachers. A few—good heavens!—are retired teachers.

Special thanks are owing to my research assistant, Karen Benson, who has worked on every part of the book, bringing to it both library resources and those of her own experience as teacher and parent. Valerie Solheim gave important help with ideas and criticism as well as with work on the manuscript. Peter Kahn and Ravenna Helson gave needed guidance in developmental psychology. Carol Page, Éowyn Mader, Rosemary Lackey, and Wendy Wayman all contributed to the word processing. And my seven children continue to teach me in all sorts of ways.

James L. Jarrett
Berkeley, California

1

INTRODUCTION: THE PRIMARY CONCERN OF THE SCHOOL

"All men by nature desire to know." Such is the first sentence in Aristotle's *Metaphysics*. Not just a few, such as the philosophers and scientists, the intellectuals and heavy inquirers—but *all*, all persons. And by *nature*: it is inborn, not an accidental acquisition, this wanting to know, to find out, to understand. It is not that we are born knowing but that we want to come to know: such is our human need and desire. But if we think that Aristotle meant knowing in a purely thinking, reasoning sense, the sentences that come after the first one tell us otherwise:

> An indication of this is the delight we take in our senses; for even apart from their usefulness, they are loved for themselves; and above all others the sense of sight. For not only with a view to action, but even when we are not going to do anything, we prefer seeing (one might say) to everything else. The reason is that this, most of all the senses, makes us know and brings to light many differences between things.
>
> (*Metaphysics*, A 980a)

Not all teachers have been that impressed with the human desire to know, though perhaps those who teach the five- and six-year-olds more than those whose pupils are older. Sometimes 15- or 17-year-olds may even seem to have used up their curiosity and so be bored with practically all attempts to tell them something new. But schools seem to have been generally founded to promote knowledge. We are born ignorant and we need to know: hence the necessity of teachers and books and writing materials. And human beings need to acquire—if they do not have it already, "by nature"—the desire to know, the taking delight in seeing and bringing to light.

Our culture in this "age of information" is dominated by the "input/output" image. Put meat into the machine, which then makes certain noises and puts out sausages. Put money into the bank and your output is more money. Put abysmally ignorant five-year-olds into school and in time retrieve the 18-year-olds full of knowledge. Ah, the critics carp, but it is not so, the output is disappointing: even after all those years, many of the students don't know

1

their own language, much less any other; don't know mathematics and biology and chemistry; scandalously lack knowledge of the history of their own country, let alone others. Something is wrong with the machine: it is not, as it promised, stuffing the children with knowledge. So the advice comes: get better teachers, add computers, make the teachers accountable, build better schoolhouses, get more efficient administrators. But the desired end is the same, to abolish ignorance, to promulgate knowledge. Knowledge is what schools are about, what they exist to teach.

Yet suppose some mischievous person asked: what's so important about knowledge? (Certainly, the early school leavers implicitly ask this, along with many who stay in school, but show a remarkable capacity for resisting the motivations of their teachers.) Back to Aristotle one more time to notice that he makes *desire* more basic than *knowing* or *coming to know*. Perhaps he exaggerates the human desire to know, but we cannot disagree that *only* if we so desire are we likely to gain much in the way of knowledge.

So our question shifts: what is it to desire, to want? We can safely shorten the sentence to: "All men by nature desire." The newborn infant who does not desire (however unconsciously) to breathe will not live. Early learning may be said to consist in part in expanding the most basic desires with which we are born, those essential for mere survival. The two-year-old is a virtual bundle of desires: for cuddling, bouncing, running, throwing, building, smashing, eating sweets. And yes, finding out about things, coming to know. But in the beginning was desire, even if one comes to realize that some desires are futile (like reaching for the moon) and some are quickly extinguished by getting what one wanted (like a bite of a mud pie). We come to say, "I used to think I wanted —— but . . . . " Apparently things (states, etc.) that one initially desires constitute values—at least provisionally. But the child soon knows that she values her dolly, no doubt about that, though the word "values" is unlikely to be a part of her vocabulary.

Suppose, then, we rethink what schools are for, now in terms of desires, wants and values—or *goods*. Even when we were thinking in terms of knowledge, we tried to imagine someone impishly asking what is important (good, valuable, worthwhile) about knowledge. To justify knowledge and its pursuit, then, is to assign it a value, or perhaps several kinds of value. Taking this new tack, it will be quickly apparent that just as schools have had much to do with knowledge, so have they had much to do with values, and not just the cognitive values either. When in the whole long history of education has there been a school unconcerned about changing the child-as-valuer? Here comes the boy who obviously loves to shout whenever the urge arises, without respect to what else is going on at the time. But that will not do. There are times when shouting is bad, disallowed. Yet the teacher very much wants her charges to learn to enjoy—unless they do already, in which case to learn to enjoy *more*—hearing, and later reading, stories. The teacher wants her charges to come to prize drawing and singing and also to

2

see why it's good to await one's turn and at times to be quiet, and not to snatch or hit out, but to help another in need. What could be more obvious than that the school is a molder and modifier and reinforcer and extinguisher of values. Reminiscing, the adult will say, "It was then that I first learned to like —— . . . to care about ——"—such an experience makes an important addition to one's being.

But of course it is not necessary to decide whether knowledge or value is primary. For anyone thinking more than a little about the matter, it will quickly turn out that they have a great deal to do with each other. But in this work, emphasis will be upon value, valuing, coming to value, evaluating, and what teachers (in and out of school settings) can do to enhance value.

Sometimes philosophers and scientists give us the impression that values like *good* or *attractive* are more or less dispensable additions to reality-as-it-is-given, that there are first of all things, objects, states of affairs, relations, processes, conglomerates, and then, under very special circumstances, sometimes—almost to say *occasionally*—they come to have, for someone, a certain kind of worth or value. But it is worth noticing that, to the contrary, it typically takes a certain amount of effort to disengage things from values, to set aside the value aspects in favor of bare, raw, unadulterated facts. The teacher asks, "Who knows what is half of a fourth?" and hears the response, "I hate fractions. They're yucky." But the teacher patiently explains that her question was about a fact, not a value.

Anything or any sort of thing that can have qualities can have that kind of quality called a *value*. Values are sometimes found in and sometimes attributed to things. The difference between these two has to do with the degree of confidence we feel in our belief that the value is, somehow, present in the object. If God, having created the world, found it to be good, there can be no doubt that it *was* (and perhaps still is) good. A child tasting an ice cream cone immediately lights up and says, "Good!" There is no hesitation or doubt present. But often enough a more jaded adult will express various sorts of reservations about his attributions of value: "I suppose it is . . . ." "I guess, for the most part . . . ." Perhaps, probably, maybe, right on to some such extremely cautious remarks as "Possibly somebody might conceivably under certain circumstances . . . ."

But we all know (very likely without being able to say exactly how we know) that we can change our minds, change our evaluations, after an initial response. We can grow surer of our judgment, whether it be for good or ill. It would not be too much to say that we often accumulate evidence in support of our original judgment, or of some modification (including flat reversal) thereof. Having pronounced a new ball point pen a good one, imagine somebody's challenging us to say why we think so. We had only vague expectations, and yet a moment's reflection will produce an answer like this: "I like the feel of it, the way it fits into my fingers. It gives me a steady line, without skips, of a breadth I like, and without being excessively light or heavy, or inky. Also the color pleases me." Now, "pleases" and "likes" are left vague and they could be sharpened a little, on demand. But they also seem to be general ingredients in value judgments of perhaps any sort—that is, directed to any kind of object.

But "object" and "think" are not to be thought to embrace only physical entities, like ice cream and pens; they may be institutions like schools and tax bureaus; laws or statutes like those prohibiting littering, events like noon swims; works of art like Picasso's "The Lovers", scientific accounts like Hawking's description of black holes; intentions like that of soothing someone's wounded feelings; or even a whole life or a large stretch of a life. Margaret Fuller is purported to have said, "I accept the universe," thereby generalizing her approval about as much as possible.

Commonsensically we all often imagine this or that value as just as much a definite attribute of an object as its color (taken now as just a fact) or length or solidity. Perhaps values differ only in being somewhat more difficult to measure, but even this is not always true; sometimes we have in mind very precise criteria, for, say, what makes a steak "prime" rather than "choice." God is good by definition, so that the question does not even come up as to whether the deity could be unjust or unkind. (At least in the Hebrew/Christian/Muslim traditions; Eastern gods are recognized to have their evil aspects.) Such ways of thinking make value an *objective* characteristic, one that belongs to the object, and is therefore there to be missed or discovered by any individual, including lower animals. But from as long ago as the fifth century B.C. Sophists, there have been those who deny any objectivity to values, saying that instead values are always *relative* to somebody. The founding Sophist, Protagoras, made this pronouncement: "Man is the measure of all things . . . . " It is not clear whether he meant mankind or each individual person. But there is an intermediate position that bears the name of Cultural Relativism, made famous by anthropologists. It argues that our tastes (values) are rarely idiosyncratic, but commonly the result of a process of socialization. We come to approve and disapprove what "our people" approve and disapprove. If this says that there are no cross-cultural or non-cultural standards, then that seems to imply that there is no sense in talking about good and bad, better or worse, cultures, except as this registers the judgment taken by one culture of another.

But a more subjective position says that as civilizations develop, heterogeneity proliferates, so that in modern-day Japan, Scotland, Italy, or the United States, a great many people rather pride themselves on having values that are quite contrary to those that are said to be the normal or traditional ones—and then they go on to say that indeed there is nothing but statistical normality or rightness anyway, since each person must be the final court of appeal with respect to his or her own values. This way of thinking (to which we will often return in a variety of contexts) sometimes gets elaborated into a more complex theory which in broad outline holds that values have their locus not in objects at all, but in experiences.

A good experience, one that is satisfying in some respect, may be said to testify to the worth of that which afforded the experience or was its object. Thus "I had a very interesting experience yesterday" prompts our companion to ask what it was, what it had to do with.

"I was looking at the lake in Central Park, and all of a sudden a great bevy of mallard ducks swooped in and landed in front of me. It was breathtaking—just beautiful."

The *it* can refer either to the experience or what the experience was of, the landing of the ducks. Either one may be said to have the kind of value in question—in this case, beauty.

The name commonly given to the kind of value an experience has in and of itself is *intrinsic*. This contrasts with an instrumental value, illustrated by my saying: "I'm glad I went to the dentist!"

"Oh, you mean you had a good time there?"

"Hardly! But he caught just in time a tooth that was in danger of breaking off."

The value or the good of what happened in such a case lies in its preventing some negative value occurring. Very often objects, notably tools, are found good for something they accomplish for us. I don't particularly enjoy pounding nails, but the hammer I use is a good one for the purpose to which I put it. And the nails will prevent the hinge from falling off and causing the door to fall, perhaps break: a *disvalue*.

Or again, I take satisfaction in having a good long talk with a friend. It is both very enjoyable in the process, and at the end I perhaps have a sense of having learned something too—thus an instance of something that is both intrinsically and instrumentally of worth or value.

Hence it is apparent that we humans (and other animals as well) are very much involved in increasing the amount of value in our lives. Saying "amount" is not meant to imply some definite quantity or clear measurement, yet we all know what we mean by preferring chocolate to strawberry ice cream, Rodin to Brancusi, swimming to badminton, a clever sitcom to a sentimental soap opera, this companion to that, and so on. We know the difference, too, between having a fairly good time, a fine time, and a wonderful time. In short, we have ways of assessing values that come our way, or having some grounds for making choices among them. And we know quite a lot about the negative values or disvalues that lurk in our path. But if a value is something prized, cherished, wanted—in some degree or another—what is to be said about the other side of the coin?

Generic value has two kinds of opposite. The first and most dramatic opposite is negative value or disvalue: such words as *bad, wicked, evil, wrong, ugly, unhealthy, revolting, disgusting, vile*—the list could go on and on—come to mind. It might seem as if, between them, *value* and *disvalue*

5

blanket the universe, especially given the indefinitely large number of gradations between the extremes of the value-opposites. That is, obviously not everything is either marvelous or awful (though occasionally one meets people who talk as if these are the only possibilities), but if one includes all the ways of being good short of the greatest superlative, and the same at the other end of the scale, a lot of ground has been taken in. But another kind of opposite to any of the sorts of GOOD is that which is simply lacking in value, negative or positive. Put in terms of the experiencer or the one asked to make a value judgment, there are surely at least as many things in the world that we are indifferent to as there are those we feel attracted to or repulsed by. Sometimes we say, "I just don't care, one way or another; I'm neutral on that." Yet to be sure, there's a pathological state of general indifference. This is a point to be returned to later, so suffice it to say for now that the name "alienation" is sometimes given (for instance by Friedrich Nietzsche) to that state in which virtually nothing seems worth bothering about, a general torpor that is symbolized by a general shrug. But even the healthy-minded person will find no room in his accepting/rejecting psyche for a great many objects, events, relations. This is perhaps best seen when we are reminded that, at any given time, each of us is simply not noticing an immense number of potential stimuli in our neighborhood: we screen them out or perhaps simply fail to screen them in. But then, too, there are other matters about which, even when our attention is drawn to them, we feel almost wholly unmoved, oblivious of the merits or demerits of the case.

For those who have a bent for visualization, then, a triangle may be drawn.

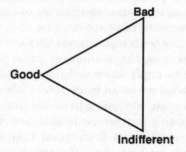

Figure 1.

Here "Good" and "Bad" are used in the generic sense, not necessarily having any moral overtones. And each of the lines may be conceived as highly graded, for there are degrees of indifference too. Thus we speak of an excellent pen, a beautiful sunset, a comfortable chair, an effective teacher, a wonderful car, an interesting article. Or these same objects may be said to have the opposite, negative quality. Even the indifferent may seem to be an attribute of the object, as in the case of a tasteless salad or a so-so film. Yet there are those who will quickly point out that these are all necessarily cases of attribution. You or I endow the object with these value qualities. This latter way of talking puts the emphasis upon somebody's experience (and not necessarily human either, for chimpanzees, cats, oysters, even rose bushes may be noticed to "express a value judgment" of something or other and perhaps thus, at least implicitly, to give or project the value onto the thing. This way of thinking seems to locate value in some sentient being's experience. But different people have different experiences of what we are pleased to call the same thing and thus the attributions may vary all over the map—say the triangular map above.

Often enough we agree to differ, even with our closest friends, associates, lovers: I prefer the house thermometer to read about 68° F, you like it much warmer, say high 70s. My political opinions are on the whole liberal, yours conservative. I have an amateur's interest in archaeology, but you are bored by the subject. We can accept these differences and not worry about them. Or one may try to persuade the other. Or the disagreement may amount to a quarrel, even a parting of ways.

But to what extent do we realize that we are all educable with respect to values? I'm bored walking through the National Gallery, but you begin to point out some features of the paintings I hadn't noticed, perhaps tell me something about this or that artist; and I begin to enjoy myself, begin to see the value that is, somehow, *there* and which I had missed. I had always thought coin collecting a total waste of time until I came across an article which showed how much you can learn about an old civilization by examining its coins—and my interest was whetted. Someone who had been a casual acquaintance turned out to be somebody I now like a lot, a real friend, but first I had to learn to prize his particular qualities.

This is the single most important thing about coming to see values as utterly central to the whole educative process: how else does one come to enjoy life more, live a better life, than by gaining new or deeper access to values? The teacher of six-year-olds has herself the satisfaction of realizing how much she will be able to add to the lives of her charges by teaching them to read. She thinks with satisfaction of how, now, they open eagerly a new book to discover the tale it tells, the information it provides. Whether for the sake of something that lies beyond the reading experience or for something that is contained within it, the reading is (often) of value, and the ability to read is precisely the means of access to values that before had been, quite literally, a closed book.

As the teacher imagines her pupils five or ten or fifteen years from now, she may take satisfaction in imagining them to have become very knowledgable—but even more important is just this: that they have had opened up to them whole rich worlds of experienceable values.

7

As John Dewey put it, "Since education is not a means to living, but is identical with the operation of living a life which is fruitful and inherently significant, the only ultimate value which can be set up is just the process of living itself" (Dewey 1916: 281). This being so, we need to think again—and again—what sorts of qualities and capacities we might best cultivate in our students in order to enhance that ultimate value of living, what kind of experience we should help provide and conduce toward. Dewey answers this challenge by a list of traits and values that are central to the school's very nature:

> The kind of experience to which the work of the schools should contribute is one marked by executive competency in the management of resources and obstacles encountered (efficiency); by sociability, or interest in the direct companionship of others; by aesthetic taste or capacity to appreciate artistic excellence in at least some of its classic forms; by trained intellectual method, or interest in scientific achievement; and by sensitiveness to the rights and claims of others—conscientiousness.
>
> (pp. 285–6)

This is a typology of values: efficiency, sociability, the aesthetic, the intellectual, and conscientiousness (or what will here be later called *moral*), though to be sure he is limiting himself in this context to the values thought to be relevant to schooling—which in turn makes us wonder: which values are *not* so relevant? We will be returning to the matter of value typologies, but let us for the present raise again the question of the distinction between instrumental and intrinsic kinds of value.

About any of the sorts of values listed above, say efficiency, the question may be raised of why it is valued as an outcome of teaching and learning. The answer would probably come in such a way as this: efficiency in the organizing of our energies enables us to get things done, tasks accomplished, effectively and with dispatch. That sounds like a perfect instance of instrumental value: its real value lying in something beyond itself, so that the efficient work is a means to something else. The aesthetic kind of value, on the other hand, would no doubt be classified by us as intrinsic, for the simple satisfaction taken in looking at the waves break against a cliff is not obviously good for anything else, but is, instead, good in and of itself.

Or suppose we think of Dewey's emphasis upon the importance of gaining skills in communication, which he justifies as a means (instrument) toward the end (intrinsic value) of "a widening and deepening of conscious life . . . a realization of meanings." If one should say, "What, in turn, is the good, the value of *that*?" there is no answer—surely no satisfying answer. Which is to say that unless one understands that that is a value in and for itself, nothing more can be said or understood.

And yet Dewey, that debunker of dichotomies, was particularly critical of the sharp distinction between means and ends, and perhaps this point is easier to take in, for only a moment's thought is necessary to see that in education (particularly but not exclusively) the means one uses to reach one's ends are themselves going in some measure to determine the nature of those ends. Those who don't see that are invited to ponder a teacher's decision to set up his room in such a way as to be able, by pressing a button, to give a pupil committing an antisocial act an electrical shock. If this proves effective in inducing a prosocial (or let us now say compassionate) behavior, the means is "justified." A less violent counter-example might be drawn from another passage from Dewey: that that method of learning from books for recitation does indeed *teach* but what it turns out to teach is something not probably consciously aimed at, to reproduce "statements at the demand of others."

But Dewey was there to remind us that there can be a vast difference between impulsive and reflective valuation. How often it happens that something we took an instant delight in turns out on revisiting to be something we find quite dispensable?

Furthermore, as far back as Plato, philosophers have discussed how some things (acts, etc.) are both valuable in themselves and *for* some other end. To read a fine poem may yield immediate gratification and at the same time inspire a new course of worthwhile action.

Whatever has been the case in remote times and cultures, in our times and cultures the school is the chief instrumentality for making the lives it can touch rich in values. Understanding this to be the principal purpose and justification of formal education is the first and most important step in improving the lot of humankind.

Yet the other side of this coin—not yet the coin of the realm—is the reduction of disvalue, for in the lives of an enormous percentage of the world's population "richness of values" seems like a hopeless luxury in the face of present, gnawing want. Therefore we must say too that education aims or should aim at working toward reducing pain, ugliness, and impoverishment of body and spirit in the world. But such endeavors to reduce evil presuppose caring. Only when we care for others—truly desire the alleviation of their woes to make way for growth—can we become effective moral agents.

Part I

THE MORAL AND THE ETHICAL

2

THE MORAL KIND OF VALUE

Values come in kinds. (So does knowledge.) Here for quick reference are the outlines of two typologies of value.

Paul W. Taylor (1961: 299) calls the types "points of view," or "realms," and says there are eight of them to be found in all civilized cultures. These points of view correspond to certain institutions and activities. They are:

the moral
the aesthetic
the intellectual
the religious
the economic
the political
the legal
etiquette or custom

DeWitt H. Parker (1931) divides his types of value into those of "Real Life" and of "Imagination." In the first category are:

health and comfort
ambition
love and friendship
ethical or moral
knowledge
technological (efficiency)

the values of Imagination are:

play
art
religion

It is somewhat curious that these typologies overlap only with respect to the moral, the aesthetic (art), the intellectual (knowledge), and the religious. Perhaps even more curious is that neither of them includes sensual value.

In this work primary attention will be paid to the moral/ethical and the

13

aesthetic, but with some attention also to the intellectual, the political, and the value of love and friendship, and work; and a glance at play, the religious, and the sensual.

In the West, the philosophical study of values begins with Ethical value among the Greeks, but Socrates is the first to do much at all with this, so that something like two hundred years of philosophic or quasi-philosophic activity took place before this branch of philosophy got invented.

Both Plato and Aristotle also raised and discussed certain questions about the arts, especially poetry (which had also been of some concern with earlier Sophists), but also a little with the visual arts and music; yet a separate study of Aesthetics, having to do with the special kind of value associated with the experience of works of art and with perception and meditation upon aspects of nature, had to wait until the 18th century for emergence into the light of day. Axiologists or theorists of value-in-general (and of the relations of the types of value) arrived on the philosophic scene only late in the 19th century.

There is still no established distinction between the moral and the ethical. Frequently the two are regarded as synonymous. Sometimes the first is considered in terms of conventional norms, the mores or prevailing codes of forbidden and allowable or praiseworthy conduct, with ethics having to do with more reflective norms and judgments. A variant of this would have morality inclined toward casuistry, the specification of dos and don'ts, with ethics concentrating on the principles which may be cited in decision-making, employing terms like *good*, *evil* and *bad*. But in this work, ethics is thought to ask Kant's question, "How shall we live?" and the moral (and morality) will be considered as an aspect of the ethical, namely that which particularly concentrates on obligation, the ought and ought-not, on duty and conscience and human virtues, whereas the ethical will also include consideration of the good life, happiness, well-being, admirable conduct over and above the call of duty, and the place in life for such kinds of value as the aesthetic, cognitive, *et al*. But to emphasize the *ought* as a particular moral concern is not yet definitional, since we do sometimes say such things as "You ought to see the play that just opened," when no moral obligation is called into consideration. (This is sometimes called "the prudential" or the "hypothetical" ought.) We must add, therefore, some such modification of the *ought*, to indicate its moral nature, as "with respect to our consideration for the welfare of others, or the requirements of our duty"; and with the further addition to *ethical* concerns, of "that for our own development and fulfillment."

This said, let us now undertake some account both of moral theory and (in the next chapter) of moral education. Moral theory, whether considered historically or analytically, is of course an enormous subject, with respect to both its complexity and the extensive publication on the subject. For present purposes, we will put rather severe constraints on our treatment of the theoretical portion of the study, hardly more than noticing a few of the historical landmarks (though leaping about chronologically) and a small sampling of current writing.

In philosophic consideration, as distinct from the prophetic tradition, the story begins in the West, as we have said, with Socrates, who seems to have had two chief concerns: morality and logic. (Since Plato used Socrates as the chief protagonist in most of his dialogues, whether or not he was espousing his own views or those of his chief disciple, it is not always clear where Socrates stops and Plato begins.) But for Socrates, logic and morality were much closer to each other than might be supposed. In the first place, Socrates practiced his logic on the definition of such terms as *piety*, *friendship*, *courage*, *moderation* (*sophrosyne*) and on such questions as whether one should try to escape from prison where one has been unjustly incarcerated, or whether virtue can be taught. Both directly and indirectly (that is, by demonstrating the best way of dealing with such moral subjects—logical argument), Socrates took the position that immoral conduct is invariably a matter of mistaken thinking. We all want the good, but we get confused or we do not take the pains to get clear about the meanings of central terms, and end up advocating, and also doing, what we should not do. The prophylactic then is to clarify and sharpen our thinking. Famously, Socrates professed himself to be ignorant of the answers to the questions he propounded, with perhaps only one exception: the dependence of virtue upon logical reasoning. (A possible second exception—depending upon whether this is something that Socrates really believed or was simply attributed to him by Plato—is love, for in the *Symposium*, Socrates is represented as saying that that *is* a matter he understands, by virtue of having been instructed by the priestess Diotima.) Socrates had faith that if we continue to raise serious moral questions and do our best to think our way through them, we will be doing everything we can to reduce our ignorance and, at the same time, our tendencies toward vice.

It is apparent too from Plato's depiction of his teacher that Socrates also found thinking and thoughtful conversation to be *intrinsically* valuable. He makes the point in his defense against his prosecutors by saying in the latter part of the *Apology* that he is not distressed by his conviction and sentence to drink the hemlock, because of his believing that death is no evil, for either it is like a profoundly deep sleep or it is, as we have been told, an escape from the bounds of body, space, and time to be able to carry on his conversations, but now with the heroes of old, like Achilles.

Socrates is also represented as an almost wholly admirable man: kind, friendly, serious and exceedingly persistent in the search for truth, yet with a delightful sense of humor, moderate in his habits, courageous (in battle as well as in his bucking the Athenian conventions and authorities), and exceptional in other ways, such as in his almost total disregard for material advantage, much less luxury.

Aristotle concentrated his attention in the *Nichomachean Ethics* upon the moral virtues, such as courage, temperance, pride, ambition, good temper, friendliness, truthfulness, ready wit, and justice. His great point was that it is generally possible to arrive at a virtuous stand by understanding what the opposite extremes are and then taking some appropriate middle position. Thus it is right to have a sense of shame instead of falling into either bashfulness or shamelessness; to be liberal rather than prodigal or stingy; to be courageous rather than timorous or foolhardy. Beyond *moral* virtues, there is, he insisted, intellectual virtue; that is, it is more god-like to think and meditate than to be always concerned with the mundane activities of life.

But as Socrates, Plato, and Aristotle knew and deplored, there was a powerful hedonistic strain to moral thinking just then. Again in the 19th century, hedonism became a popular way of thinking about morality or values more generally. One form of hedonism is not moral at all, in that it claims to be simply a psychological fact that everyone all the time acts in that way which he believes will maximize pleasure for himself. Although Socrates was certainly no hedonist, this theory too makes failures to do "the right thing" for yourself just a matter of mistake. But in addition to egoistic hedonism there is that kind that says, with Jeremy Bentham: act in behalf of the greatest possible happiness (pleasure) for the greatest number of people. Obviously acting in this way may sometimes entail a forfeit of your own chances of pleasure, thus meaning an abandonment of psychological hedonism.

Still another twist on hedonism is that introduced by—back to the ancient Greeks—Epicurus, namely that the best way to get a favorable balance of pleasure over pain is to avoid the likelihood of pain. This meant for him the great advantage of an ascetic life. One final modification of hedonism may be mentioned, that of John Stuart Mill, who argued that pleasures differ not so importantly in a quantitative way (as Jeremy Bentham believed) but qualitatively, so that there are higher and lower pleasures. For him the test of whether a pleasure is qualitatively better is to consult someone who can know both kinds and see what she chooses. His famous example is that Socrates and a pig would disagree about whether piggish pleasures or Socratic pleasures are the best, but only Socrates can know both kinds.

Monotheistic religions (usually anti-hedonistic) have not typically tried to justify the moral requirements learned through revelation, for God, in his or her wisdom knows that, and presumably why—if there is a why—such-and-such an act or attitude is best. For Christians, it was on the authority of Jesus that communicants professed love of God and love of fellow humans to be the greatest of commandments. But St Paul listed faith, hope, and charity (*caritas*) as the three highest virtues. If faith overlaps with love of God and charity with love of neighbor, the only addition is that of hope.

In the late 17th and 18th centuries, there grew up a new emphasis upon intuition, sentiment, and sympathy in theories of morality. Thus Shaftesbury posited a capacity of the mind to make a direct discernment of the good and the ill, though he admitted the possibility of a corruption of this faculty requiring correction by reasoning.

Friedrich Nietzsche blasted virtually all moral theory and practice of his time and previous centuries, clear back to the Persian sage Zarathustra, who had a bifurcated world of light and darkness, each with its presiding deity, and so established his oughts on a metaphysical foundation. Nietzsche was particularly critical of Christian emphasis upon the "soft" virtues like mercy, love, and propensity for returning good for evil; instead, he propounded acceptance of what for him was a fact, that at the basis of human nature is a "will to power," but from of old those who are relatively deficient in this will, or have corrupted it by false doctrine, gain their power indirectly by banding together the weak, although (as Marx proclaimed just a little earlier) the strong may often sustain their power by preaching acquiescence as a virtue: hence "religion as the opiate of the people." Nietzsche's was an attempt to liberate potentially strong and especially creative persons from the shackles of a morality that extolls weakness: in short, one ought to be strong.

But in the latter part of the previous century Immanuel Kant had gone in a direction entirely different from that of hedonists (including utilitarians), Christians (and also Jews and Buddhists), and contrary to what was to be Nietzsche's advocacy. Kant's was an attempt to build a duty-centered doctrine. He argued that since we can never know for sure what effect or consequence our actions are going to have, we need to look rather toward the motivations for our acts. The only totally good and reliable thing is, Kant held, the good will. But for him this is not at all the good intentions that pave the way to hell. What *good will* means is that we should be able in all matters of decision to act in such a way that we could consistently make a universally applicable law for others to employ the same principle in their actions. Kant was especially impressed with the importance of never counting ourselves an exception. Just as in mathematics and the sciences we want to find principles which apply to all situations alike, so too, he felt, this should prevail in the moral realm.

One of his principles, which he stated as "So act as to treat all people as ends, never as means only," has been found appealing even to those who do not go along with his universalistic, rationally grounded theory. And a great many philosophers and a number of psychologists in the 20th century who have sought a close connection between knowledge and moral principle have followed Kant's lead in the strongest sense. This is notably true of Lawrence Kohlberg, whose proposals for moral development we will presently look at.

As the natural sciences steadily gained power and importance, supported by technological advances that were grounded in empirical discoveries, and with mathematics increasingly considered to be cut off entirely, except adventitiously, from the space/time universe, the Western world was ripe for a new wave of positivism in the early years of the 20th century. Building atop a growing assumption that the realm of fact and value are entirely separate, increasingly it came to be believed that knowledge is confined to fact. The positivists, centering in Vienna and then spreading out to Berlin, England, France, and the United States, laid down the dogmatic claim that (1) only propositions are either true or false; (2) meaningful propositions are those which admit of confirmation by approved empirical means, like those employed in physics and the other hard sciences, and (3) truth is confined to those propositions that are either proved as in mathematics and formal logic or empirically verified as in scientific law. Since this ruled out all value judgments, morality, ethics, aesthetics, and other value realms were assigned a non-cognitive status. The hard-liners said that this meant that statements about values (unless they were purely descriptive, as "93.6 percent of Scotsmen believe that it is divinely ordained that we should honor our fathers and mothers"), are, strictly speaking, meaningless or nonsense. Instead, value judgments are assigned to the realm of emotion.

This gave rise to a school of *emotivism* (though not all members thereof were positivists in other respects), which declared as a basic principle that though moral and other value judgments are typically cast to sound like statements or propositions, in fact, properly analyzed, they only signify the utterer's feeling of approval or disapproval of something. Or, in a slightly more refined version (that of C. L. Stevenson), all value judgments come down to an emotional expression plus an imperative; as when "Justice is the noblest of virtues" is interpreted to mean, on the part of the one who proclaims it, "I like (or have a good, positive feeling toward) justice; please do so as well."

This way of thinking held considerable sway for a time, but gradually gave way before a steady attack, though many thinkers continue to believe that value judgments lie outside the realm of fact, truth, reason, and knowledge.

In the last thirty years or so, in philosophy and psychology, moral theory has focused upon the centrality of moral *judgments*, usually with great emphasis upon the rational scrutiny thereof in the interest of coherence and clarity, whether or not there is any claim that in any important sense such judgments can be called true or false. Sociologists have for the most part concentrated on descriptive studies of the importance of the process of socialization, not merely of the young, but of the entire population, in determining moral and other value preferences. Emile Durkheim has taken a particularly leading role in showing how morality

> is not a system of abstract truth which can be derived from some fundamental notion, posited as self-evident . . . . It belongs to the realm of conduct, of practical imperatives which have grown up historically under the influence of specific social necessities.
>
> (Durkheim 1970: 34)

Social psychologists have taken a similar approach, but often looking at narrower groups within society. Developmental psychologists have often concentrated, as in the case of Piaget, upon how a child's moral conceptions change as she develops from highly concrete ways of thinking to ever more abstract ways, which in morality means more emphasis upon principles.

Recent philosophy has tended to follow Kant in emphasizing principle-based judgments, and the utilitarians in putting emphasis upon consequences of acts as determinative of their worth, though it is now rarer to speak of pleasure or happiness as the desired result; rather, something more general such as "the best available outcomes overall." Or they have followed Aristotle and others in developing a theory of human virtues in answer to a change of the central question from "What ought I to do?" to "What kind of person ought I to be?"

Following this rapid survey of some main currents in thinking about morality over the ages, we may now turn for a slightly more detailed look at some recent ideas about moral judgments, attitudes, and action.

Theorists about moral questions and topics have had a tendency toward the either/or, all/nothing way of thinking. For instance, morality is altogether a matter of motivation or intention or altogether a matter of consequence, and intention doesn't count. But the law knows better than that, making a very important distinction between a crime committed with and a crime committed without malice aforethought. Still, consequences are essential: having the bad thought but not doing anything about it is not illegal, even though Jesus said that the thought of lust is already a sin. Furthermore, it matters a lot what the result of doing something about it is: if one is angry, hits out with an intent to do grievous injury, but lands only a glancing blow, chances are the offender will go scot-free, both in law and in public opinion. It would seem, then, that intention, act, and consequence all have to be taken into account if we are trying to decide on the right or wrong of the situation.

Why must we think, cynically, either that human nature is wholly self-serving and that only in the fortunate instance where my interests and another's coincide do we do something that could possibly be praised, or that the morally perfect being would be one who constantly denied his own interests in being taken up with others' welfare, as in the case of the self-confessing mother who "lives for my children"? There are excellent reasons for believing that though humans obviously differ with respect to propensity for helpfulness and beneficence, all of us—even Scrooge—have at least a streak of altruism in our make-up. Indeed, today we are likely to look upon that unusual person who is very largely malevolent as mentally ill, which is to say someone whose deviation from the normal can to a degree be explained by natural causes, and who is susceptible to psychological help toward a much more normal way of being.

One ethicist who likes to use the word "flourishing" to describe a generally benign state argues that not just the human but:

a wide range of creatures deserve moral consideration and are capable of flourishing; and benevolence in their regard would consist either in letting them be, so that they flourish without impediment, or in the active promotion of their flourishing. But whether creatures flourish is not wholly, or most importantly, a matter of pleasure attained or of pain avoided; indeed the painless stunting of a creature's growth (as in an accident involving both concussion and brain damage) could be worse than pain, and the unfolding of anyone's powers is a benefit and a blessing whether or not the person concerned is happy or in any other way self-aware.

(Attfield 1987: 40)

Or again, the value/fact distinction often gets made in a black/white manner. Yet it is uncommon for facts to be utterly neutral to everybody involved – remembering that the presence even of interest is already a sign of the presence of value. The other way around, it would be a very odd value indeed that had no factual basis: for instance, my needs, wants, interests—all of which are typically involved in value situations—are, taken as conditions of the body and psyche, from one point of view simply given, facts. The nerve ends of my stomach are exposed, the nutrient having moved along, and I notice the feeling and say I am hungry. This is probably simply a fact—*probably* being slipped in here to allow for the possibility of hysterical hunger! Hunger makes me interested in the sandwich which is awaiting me (or someone) in the refrigerator. I value that sandwich in anticipation, and if all goes well, in the eating thereof, and even perhaps afterwards for a moment of recollection of its deliciousness. All of that has to do with experienced value. Even the weightiest moral situations are structurally similar to this minor sequence.

Or yet again, shall we say that we have knowledge of values, or only of feelings, emotions? Why the choice? There are obligations that I do indeed have, such as those of providing food and shelter to my children. Unless I am a very crass person, I will *feel* these obligations, and probably act accordingly. Belief, truth, knowledge, feelings are all present, typically involving a combination or sequence of persisting beliefs, reflections thereupon, considerations of possibilities, imagining the likely results, reconsidering my initial intentions, taking first steps and so on and on. Commandments and absolute universal pronouncements or eternal verities are rare in every dimension of life, but so is the complete absence of beliefs that admit of a degree of validation or invalidation. Doubtless Moses himself knew when he read out to the Israelites, HONOR THY FATHER AND THY MOTHER, that there are occasions when honoring is not exactly appropriate, and that one may even neglect this attitude with impunity.

Bernard Williams puts such things, and more, more elegantly:

One ethical belief might be said to be in its own right an object of

20

knowledge at the reflective level, to the effect that a certain kind of life was best for human beings. But this will not yield other ethical truths directly. The reason ... is that the excellence or satisfactoriness of a life does not stand to beliefs involved in that life as premise stands to conclusion. Rather, an agent's excellent life is characterized by *having* those beliefs, and most of the beliefs will not be about that agent's dispositions or life, or about other people's dispositions, but about the social world.

(Williams 1985: 154)

Is morality subjective or objective? Dare we risk saying both? Only someone kept curiously isolated will in our times fail to realize that societies and cultures differ, sometimes quite significantly, in what acts are permitted, condemned, or praised. However, there is far more commonness than is sometimes admitted by those who delight in cultural relativity. But within a culture, individuals differ too, and legitimately so, with respect to their favorite charity, whether lying to one's parents about one's whereabouts after school is a mortal or a venial sin, or—remembering the Muslim condemnation of a recent novel by Salman Rushdie—assassination is an appropriate punishment, even a required punishment, for one guilty of what is deemed flagrant blasphemy.

While people of good will tend to tolerate a considerable amount of diversity in moral matters, there are limits to such tolerance, even among the most understanding of people. For instance, that both Hitler and Stalin were repeatedly and flagrantly guilty of ghastly crimes against humanity is asserted by a large group of people who differ in many other respects, and furthermore these people are not at all moved by the Nazis and Stalinists who disagree, but would say and believe fervently that the latter are plain wrong and misguided.

But another approach to this matter of possible objectivity in moral judgments has to do with the ways in which one might go about trying to be objective. The main point in this respect is that human beings are capable of and are often morally required to practice reflectiveness. Although we are motivated instinctually, we have the capacity to resist acting on instinct or impulse and instead to consider, ponder, and generally be reasonable, in deciding on a moral question, whether it be a matter of one's own action or of coming to some judgment about another's. We can and usually should consider—or reconsider. Henry D. Aiken has made the point in this way:

The only principle of objectivity is ... essentially a principle of reconsideration. What it demands, when a question about the objectivity of a particular judgment or principle arises, is that we consider whether such a judgment or principle, as it stands, can be

21

consistently upheld in the face of whatever other moral considerations might be thought, in conscience, to defeat it.

(Aiken 1965: 97)

However, conventional wisdom and collective common sense do not
always provide us with all we need to know in order to lead a relatively moral
life. For instance, it very well may not have occurred to us that we have any
obligation to someone who lives on the other side of the world—until we
read in the newspapers of the suffering of starving and homeless Sudanese,
when we are moved to send in a check. It is even more unlikely that we will
continually have in mind our obligation to those who will live on this planet
a hundred years from now, but reflection may reveal this obligation when
we begin to imagine what it might be like for them to be born into a world
denuded of its rain forests and all that that means about the ecology. It may
even occur to us—though this is harder yet—that we have a kind of
obligation to those who are long dead and gone, as when a historian
unearths a noble deed long forgotten and we agree that a monument ought
to be erected to the distant hero. Or, of course, our felt obligation may go
the other way, as when, having recently come to realize the enormity of
Stalin's crimes, we retroactively resent the honor paid him, even by such
democratic leaders as Roosevelt and Churchill.

A human being without a feeling and sense of obligation, responsibility,
a feeling of the need to do something as a result of this realization, or to
refrain from doing, would be someone bordering on the edge of not
deserving to be called human. Nietzsche called man the "animal with red
cheeks" to signify the commonness of embarrassment, shame, and finally
guilt. If therapists have often noticed the unfortunate results of excessive or
misplaced guilt feelings, this is far from implying that guilt is *ipso facto* a
symptom of psychic unhealthiness.

If we read in fiction or history of a time and place where highwaymen
preyed upon travelers, pirates menaced seagoing vessels, brigands roamed
the streets and broke into houses, soldiers descended upon towns to rape
and pillage, or the secret police of dictatorships made dawn raids on
innocent and unsuspecting families and carried out instant executions, we
realize (however much we still deplore the extent of crime in our cities) to
what a high degree we rely upon a safe, orderly, dependable social environment, one in which—though we probably lock our doors at night and put
chains on our bicycles—we do not have to live in constant fear and suspicion.
And if our city streets have become places in which we feel unsafe in walking
at night, we are certain that this should not be, and that "something ought
to be done."

An infant's freedom from responsibility does not last very long at all. Soon
we feel the need to help the young child see the difference between an
accidental and a deliberate breaking or hurting. The child will for a while be

able to get away with "It broke", attributing a mischievousness to inanimate objects, but soon we stop smiling and point out that a more accurate statement for the child to make is "I broke it." Without this realization it is not even possible to exercise the virtue of forgiveness.

So we as children (and later) learn something—never enough?—about duties that we *have* that are *ours*. And yet are we required, with Kant, to say that an act will count as morally good only if it is done from a realization of duty—or even more severely, that if there is even a speck of pleasure taken in the doing, it automatically gets excluded from the moral province? Surely not, though his very severity may help us realize that there are duties in addition to those more tolerable acts which we quite enjoy doing although they happen to be our duty.

Even more generally, pleasure has seemed to many theorists to have everything or nothing to do with morality. Yet here again an in-between position recommends itself very strongly. Although there is something particularly beguiling about those situations in which we are thoroughly enjoying ourselves at the same time as we are affording pleasure to others, yet there are other times when we feel we must do something quite unpleasant, our only (slight?) reward being that we *have* done our duty. It was Jeremy Bentham, the high priest of quantitative hedonism, who when asked why, given his theory, he spent so much time in doing his social duty, like engaging in prison reform, said, in effect, "That's one of my ways of getting pleasure."

Oftentimes, the chief obligation falling upon us is to do something rather than nothing. Put otherwise, indolence, laziness, a constitutional fear of getting involved, a reluctance, springing sometimes out of a basic shyness, to step forward, to take a stand—such failures are perhaps commoner sources of evils in our social contexts than downright malice, hatefulness, or perversity. Edmund Burke put it this way: "All that is necessary for forces of evil to prevail is that good men do nothing." And what would we have them do? From ancient times it has been recognized that one of the most comprehensive obligations humans have is that for the prevalence of justice in society.

> No account of rightness or obligation is adequate which allows minorities or the weak to be downtrodden, which is indifferent about how goods are distributed in society, or which fails to prohibit unfair practices.
>
> (Attfield 1987: 135)

Moral theorists have been often fascinated with the subject of promises, for here is an explicit instance of an accepted obligation, and the one disappointed in another's act has a stronger case if able to say, "But you *promised*." A promissory note or any other kind of contract inscribes a promise in such a way as to be "actionable" in law. Nevertheless, life is notably replete with broken promises, including those to oneself, which is an odd kind of obligation: "I promised myself that I would not eat any more chocolate, but then . . . ." But such a case is not yet quite moral, so we need to invoke something like "I promised myself that I would stop stealing wash cloths from hotel rooms, but. . . ." Or, if one wants to be a little less self-punishing, instead of the harsh word "stealing" we will say "taking," "lifting," even "swiping."

But a child has to *learn* the difference between a promise and some weaker indication of intent such as "If the day's fine, I'll come" or "I'll probably . . ." or "If I'm still in the mood . . . ." But the promiser cannot foresee changes that do in fact occur. The woman who promises to love her husband forever finds that she has fallen out of love, or stopped loving, or even come to hate, and may even take refuge in the observation that love cannot be forced, or even the continuation of love, for that matter. Or, if she has taken the (now old-fashioned?) vow to "love, honor, and obey . . . so long as we both may live" she may, having become better instructed in the equal rights of the sexes, not only regret this promise but revoke it, not simply (or even at all) because of a change of heart, but because of a change of abstract belief, a matter of principle.

Having experienced such changes, one may easily grow chary about making promises at all, but there is no way, within the human condition, of avoiding the incurring of obligation, whether or not any such gets categorically confirmed in a promise. Both tacitly or otherwise, we incur responsibilities of a bewildering variety of kinds, ranging from those wherein a failure to live up to a declaration or pledge amounts to treason to those in which the matter becomes moral at all only because a promise has been made, as when one is reminded that "You did say on the very next holiday we would go to the shore." But we require that others live up to their responsibility in order that our lives have a degree of order, predictability, safety.

> People must rely as far as possible on not being killed or used as a resource, and on having some space and objects and relations with other people they can count as their own. It also serves their interests if, to some extent at least, they can count on not being lied to.
>
> (Williams 1985: 185)

And yet of course others disappoint us, turning out to be greedy when we would have them be generous, self-serving when we want them to be helpful, brutal when we ask for gentleness, and inconsiderate when we think it our basic right to be treated with consideration. This concept, indeed, covers a lot of the ground of parents' and teachers' efforts to improve their charges morally. The teacher at the end of a trying day may think or say, "If *only* I could get them to give some thought to what they're doing, how it affects other people, and become considerate of others' feelings." And, given at

24

least a normal amount of good will in one's make-up, it often does seem to be more a matter of consciousness-raising than anything else:

"Think of the poor custodian having to clean up your mess."

"Put yourself in the place of the other when you yell out, 'I don't want *him* on my side'."

"Wouldn't it be nice to send along a letter to the hospital? Mightn't Doris be feeling a bit lonesome, away from all of us?"

This is the considerate part of caring: how can we become more disposed to consider others' perspectives and the plights they bring into view.

But with these latter considerations we are obviously already over into *moral education*, to which topic we more fully come around in the following chapters, where we take notice of how humans develop morally and of certain schemes and programs for learning to be more moral.

3

A NOTE ON THE SCHOOL ETHOS OF YESTERYEAR

To set the cause above reason,
To love the game beyond the prize,
To honour while you strike him down,
The foe that comes with fearless eye,
To count the life of battle good,
And dear the land that gave you birth,
And dearer yet the brotherhood
That binds the brave of all the earth.
(Sir Henry Newbolt, "Rugby Chapel")

These lines from a poem of 1912 afford us a vivid reminder that in the course of the century conceptions of life and duty have changed! To be sure, this is an expression of some portion of a small, highly privileged segment of society, the English public school—Rugby, Eton, Harrow, Winchester and the rest. It was a highly visible segment, one which produced to quite an exceptional extent the leaders in government, the civil service, the army and navy, business, finance, and industry, and even the cultural and intellectual elite. Since *Tom Brown's Schooldays* (Hughes 1857) novels had poured forth detailing life within such institutions, in many respects a miserable one, even in the eyes of those who more than a little envied the elite few who enjoyed such privileges. With only minor variations, the schools seem to have been bastions of conservatism. The curriculum was rigorously classical, the faculty was educated at Oxford and Cambridge (except perhaps for the art and French masters), the pedagogy was teacher- and book-centered, with exceptional emphasis upon the memorization of large quantities of facts, rules, and literary passages and stanzas, and the whole regimen was ruled over by a headmaster whose power is perhaps best symbolized in more recent times by that of the conductor of a symphony orchestra, or of course, then and now, by the commander-in-chief of an army. These were residential schools that were, to a degree almost inconceivable in our times, acting *in loco parentis*. Indeed, the parents seem to have faded so much into the background of the pupils' lives as to have become those who were visited during holidays. The ruling assumptions were: a great deal of work in the way of lessons and the preparation thereof, inflexible rigidity of schedule, militaristic hierarchy of authority, quick and severe punishment for violations of the rules, enforced discomfort, including, according to many accounts, unbelievably uninviting food, insistence upon full participation in highly competitive sports, with equal emphasis upon winning, glory, and unstintingly sportsmanlike attitudes, uniformity in clothing, curriculum, games, reading, and almost everything else, and a nearly total isolation from female company, except that of the Head's wife, the nurse, and a retinue of servants.

The moral code was—no surprise—as rigid as every other aspect of the regimen. The verse above is a fair if incomplete summary: school, class, and national loyalty, jingoistic patriotism, dauntless courage in battle (from athletic fields to inevitable war), and solidarity with one's classmates—which is to say, those of like age, for those senior to oneself were as officers to enlisted men, and those junior were there to be sneered at and kept in their place. Bertrand Russell's story (1932:61) illustrates the latter point. Reprimanding a boy seen bullying a smaller boy, Russell was told by the oppressor: "The bigger ones hit me and I hit the babies. That's fair."

The irony of the conspicuous place within such schools, of at least the *formalities* of religious observance celebrating the gospel of love, has not been wasted on novelists.

Important as were the Head (and other administrators, though they were few), and the faculty, much the greatest part of the ubiquitous discipline was in the hands of the prefects. Alasdair MacIntyre (1967:38–43) has gone so far as to say that in the upper middle class at the end of the 19th century "the morality of the public school prefect" was dominant. This meant loyalty to group and the "bearers of the essential past", with no limits to what one could do to outsiders, and the conviction that insiders had a "right to a certain sort of job." He goes on to say that the prevailing mores of the middle class at that time were those of the businessman: thrift, hard work, self-help, self-advancement, and a future-looking attitude. The labor class, he claims, was governed by a trade union morality, workers being linked to fellow workers. Religion was important right across class lines, though doubtless in somewhat different ways.

From a school document of 1905 one learns something of the ethos of the period. Manliness was idolized, a trait symbolized by keeping a stiff upper lip during immersion in a morning cold bath. Character training was of course thought essential. Teachers were told:

> The everyday incidents of school life will enable the teachers to impress upon the scholars the importance of punctuality, of good manners and language, of cleanliness and neatness, of cheerful

obedience to duty, of a consideration and respect for others, and of honour and truthfulness in word and act.

(Handbook of Suggestions for the Consideration of Teachers and others concerned in the Work of the Public Elementary Schools,
1905, p. 8, as cited in Musgrove 1978:67)

Very much less has been written about the public schooling for girls, but in 1927 the report of the chief medical officer of the Board of Education made a distinction of genders: "The girls must learn the foundations of Motherhood; the boys must acquire the strength and skill for manual labour and understanding of the spirit and methods of cooperation" (cited in Musgrove 1978:68).

By the 1960s important changes had set in. Feminists were beginning to modify the sharp distinction between the genders, but more generally there began to appear an acknowledgment of a moral pluralism—which of course appeared to some as a-moralism or immoralism. This was in part a recognition that there were built-in class, religious, and ethnic differences which the school could not any longer simply override by its explicit or (more generally) implicit avowal of a received way. But beyond that, cutting across these groupings, it was increasingly recognized that boys and girls had choices to make and that the school's place was—perhaps!—to "help the young to choose from the available moralities or perhaps even to help them create for themselves a new morality" (Musgrove 1978: 82–3). One of the signs of these new times was the endorsement by a growing minority of liberal church-people of a "situational ethic" as in John Robinson's *Honest to God.* This split in the ranks of institutional orthodoxy was viewed, differentially, with alarm, relief, and amusement, but there can be no doubt that it made available a new outlook for those who still took their cue from the church. Inevitably, there appeared a very popular answer to this heterodoxy, *The New Morality* by Arnold Lunn and Garth Lean (Catholic and Anglican) (1964). Yet that number too was waning; on many sides people were beginning to argue, or at least to assume, that it is not necessary to have divine sanction for one's moral code; but also that there are other religions available than that one has grown up in and with.

A second force for change was the increasing move toward relating morality to mental health. One form this took was that of asserting the importance of personal worth, of self-esteem. This often took the form of recognizing that one is not bound by the opinions of authorities, more especially the authority parents exercise over children. Thus *The Little Red School Book* of 1971 addresses itself to teenagers: "Grownups do have a lot of power over you: they are real tigers. But in the long run they can never control you completely: they are paper tigers." This went on with the assurance that "you are a person in your own right. In the end you're accountable only to yourself. You're as good as anybody else" (cited in

Musgrove 1978: 74). Adults in turn were urged to see deviancy as maladjustment, and to take a mental health approach in dealing with it. This way of thinking may legitimize the pluralism of moralities so that the teacher or parent is seen less as imposing a morality than as assisting the young to find their own from a ready stock of possibilities.

Even as early as the late 1930s there had appeared "lifeline" materials to help 13–16-year-olds "adopt a considerate form of life", with role-playing exercises designed to increase sensitivity to others, first in local situations, but in the advanced lessons working up to a "one-world" approach (see McPhail *et al.*, 1972). Concomitantly, religious education in the schools increasingly became eclectic and ecumenical.

In the United States, a somewhat similar history had different beginnings in that from the 18th century there had lingered a strong belief, built into the Constitution, in the separation of church and state. The proliferation of Protestant sects and the massive immigration from Europe and Asia in the last half of the 19th century, though accommodated by a "melting pot" ideal, meant in fact the diversification of religious and moral realities in many (especially big city) classrooms. School prayers were commonly said and the strength of "the moral majority" (as it later began to call itself) was evidenced by legislation to insert the phrase "under God" in the pledge of allegiance to the flag: "One nation, under God, with liberty and justice for all . . . ." which was typically intoned by pupils standing with hand over heart.

Nevertheless, secularization continued apace. Courts upheld a ban on "released time" for children to get sectarian religious instruction outside—or sometimes even inside or right next door to—the school plant. Roman Catholics were in some places successful in extirpating aspects of school practice that smacked of Protestantism, and those pronouncing blessings on various occasions were reminded that references to Jesus excluded the Jews present. So, too, Christmas pageants and celebrations began to disappear, again under the rubric of "separation of church and state," the schools now acknowledging that—certainly in their financial support—they were "state."

This went so far that, inevitably, but quietly, one began to hear laments over an exclusion of religious content from the curriculum that was so thorough as to give students little knowledge at all of the place of churches, mosques, and temples in the lives of people worldwide and throughout history—to say nothing of the study of comparative religious beliefs and philosophies. One investigator combed the contents of ten sets of social studies textbooks designed for the elementary grades of American schools and found that:

Serious Christian or Jewish religious motivation is featured nowhere. References to Christianity or Judaism are uncommon and typically superficial. In particular, Protestantism is excluded, at least for whites. Patriotism is close to nonexistent in the sample . . . .

Traditional roles for both men and women receive virtually no support, while role-reversal feminist stories are common.

(Vitz 1986: 90)

But secular moral teaching, already perfunctory by the 20th century, was given a setback by the widely publicized Hartshorne and May experiment of 1928–30 wherein teachers were given some support from social psychology for their strong suspicions that, whatever be its justification or the lack thereof, explicit moral education was wholly futile. This experiment showed that students who had been given lessons in morality were not a whit less inclined to cheat during examinations than those who had been deprived of such edification.

Needless to say, teachers, as of old, continued to caution pupils to keep their eyes on their own paper, not to copy from books without explicit acknowledgement of the source, not to take others' pencils and sandwiches, and to give an honest answer to teachers' questions, but even those who continued to believe that explicit moral lessons had a place in the school day increasingly felt guilty about this breach in school rules and accepted procedures.

Despite this strong de-emphasis upon moral and religious instruction— the religious, after all, being in large measure moral in nature—in American schools at mid-century stirrings were felt of a new interest in school-based social and personal moral instruction. In small part, this seems to have been stimulated by reports that American students had become less knowledgeable about and appreciative of their own ways of government than those of totalitarian regimes, and far less influential in establishing a unified conception of the nation. After all, American schools, given the 19th century massive immigration from Europe and Asia, had been widely held to be a major agency in building a unified country with so many diverse elements ("E pluribus unum," the motto stamped on American coins). For instance, in 1884, the Rhode Island School Board in its annual report said:

The heterogeneous masses must be made homogeneous. Those who inherit the traditions of other and hostile nations; those who are bred under diverse influences and hold foreign ideas; those who are supported by national inspirations not American must be assimilated and Americanized. The chief agency to this end has been the public school and popular education. No better agency has ever been devised by men.

(Cited in Hersh et al. 1980: 18.)

More recently there appeared a book by U. Bronfenbrenner, *Two Worlds of Childhood*, which showed that Soviet education, based upon Makarenko's long studies in pedagogy, inculcated a love of the fatherland beyond anything comparable in the Western democracies, but also that Soviet children are much less inclined toward antisocial behavior than their same-age mates in the United States, England, or Germany (1969: 78).

Public opinion polls began to show a surge of opinion, not previously suspected by school authorities, that it was the duty of schools to counter the immense rise of vandalism, theft of school and private property, bringing weapons to school, threats directed toward teachers, along with increasing instances of real violence. A Gallop poll conducted in 1980 showed that more than two-thirds of the American public favored instruction in ethics, ranking it at or near the top of educational goals. It can hardly be doubted that it was the increase of antisocial behavior in and around school grounds that prompted this judgment, but school administrators and teachers were by no means stampeded by public opinion in this regard. Very likely teachers were still unconvinced that moral instruction could be effective, and, besides, their own strong inclination in many instances toward a moral relativism made them disinclined to abandon their largely neutral stance. A horror of indoctrination, which rose to a new height in the 1960s as the public became increasingly aware of the insidious powers of advertising, and of the influence of "the military/industrial establishment" on all branches of government, including the courts, largely countered any feeling that the schools ought once again to take a moral stand. A rapidly growing awareness of the rights of minorities in the schools led not only to the outlawing of "separate but equal" schools but also to a fear on the part of many conscientious teachers of even their own power subliminally to reflect class and ethnic bias.

Far more than in Great Britain, Americans began to take to the courts, suing teachers and school districts for alleged discriminatory behavior and denials of people's right to dissent in word and practice from established opinion. Teachers became increasingly nervous, fearing that even the most innocuous moral lesson might be reported to parents and found at odds with the ethos of the home. Thus teachers began even to wonder if they had the right to insist upon the peaceful solution of quarrels in school, lest a pupil cite his mother who always urged him to stand up for himself, or his father who himself practiced corporal punishment in the home and was known to fight in the street.

Nevertheless the tide began to turn. Social theorists began to show that value neutrality is utterly impossible in a school setting: "It Goes With The Territory", as one article on the inevitability of school inculcation of a moral code put it. Others began to argue that teachers who refuse to take a stand are simply making way for others, with perhaps far less understanding, to exercise moral authority over children. Philosophers, psychologists, and sociologists began again to take an interest in these matters, and programs for moral and, more generally, values teaching and learning began to appear—and, soon, to proliferate.

In America, the most popular of these programs was "Values

31

Clarification," first developed by Louis E. Raths. More recently the influence of Jean Piaget has been felt, mainly through the six-stage theory of moral development devised by Lawrence Kohlberg. In Britain John Wilson began in the early 1960s what was to become a major effort in theory building for moral education and more recently Peter McPhail and associates developed a kit of materials for pupils, along with a teacher's guide, within the Schools Moral Education Curriculum Project. Some of these and other programs for moral and values education will be discussed in the following chapter.

But by way of summary it is fair to say that in Britain and America alike, with a different history in each instance, there has emerged in the century's last decade a new interest in value, and especially moral, education, one that is by contrast with 19th and early 20th century theory and practice:

1 sophisticated in the way of reflecting an analytical acquaintance with philosophical, psychological, sociological, and pedagogical work;
2 Liberal and non-doctrinaire in the sense of trying to take account of human diversity, both personological and cultural, and allowing for— often even encouraging—a pluralistic society, with a very considerable amount of departure from any prevailing ethos and at the same time being open about the tentativeness and fallibility of judgment in a field so bafflingly complex;
3 secular and naturalistic in not presupposing any particular theological or religiously institutional position, but proceeding instead by rational and empirical inquiry into man and society as a basis for and a way of arriving at a theory;
4 with a new concern for and sensitivity toward groups who have so often in the past (continuing into the present) been left out of account or even systematically discriminated against: girls and women, ethnic minorities (some much more than others), political and religious minorities, the economically poor, those at both extremes of the life span, and the mentally, emotionally, and physically handicapped;
5 and showing a new degree of concern for the physical environment (not excluding outer space), animal rights, and the rights of future genera- tions of human beings.

To all of this, in the way of praise for advancement, must be added that the most "advanced" civilizations are now characterized by incredible degrees of mass alienation, brutality, and crass insensitivity.

4

A LOOK AT RESEARCH ON EARLY MORAL DEVELOPMENT

Everyone knows, if only from memory, that early childhood is a time for learning rules of behavior, but recently developmentalists have conducted a great many sustained and close observational studies on exactly how this is done. One of the most respected workers in this vineyard is Judy Dunn, who records (1989) such dialogues as these:

> *Child (16 months) throws biscuit on the floor.*
> *Mother*: What's that? Biscuit on the floor? Where biscuits aren't supposed to be, isn't it?
> *Child looks at mother and nods.*
> *Mother*: Yes . . . . Now what's all this? (*Points to toothbrush and toothpaste on kitchen table*.) Who brought that downstairs?
> *Child looks at mother and smiles.*
> *Mother*: Yes, you did. Where does this live?
> *Child*: Bath.

Such loaded questioning style was found in these investigations to be very common, at least among middle-class families. Generally, this way, the actual rule is arrived at inductively: "Put things where they really belong." Not, one will notice, precisely a deep moral issue, and yet such instruction in rules is continuous with those weightier matters like "Don't hurt others" and "Do not take things not your own."

Of course it is not only parents who teach and enforce rules; siblings do too, sometimes taking particular pleasure in exposing and correcting the misdemeanors of their younger (or even older) brothers and sisters. One way and another, all children by school age "know" a great many rules—and in school there are new ones to master.

Like teachers, parents naturally vary considerably in the attitude they convey as to the rules, and very early, children monitor their parents' faces for clues about how serious that attitude is, or, since some parents are highly punitive, what is likely to happen if they do not mind.

The question of the effects upon character of parental attitudes toward children's behavior continues to be studied. One important piece of research that dates back to the 1940s by Alfred Baldwin:

> compared families who conducted their affairs "democratically" (frequently communicating about family rules and policy decisions) with families who were more closed, secretive, and arbitrary about decisions. He also looked at the extent to which these parents effectively controlled their children's conduct. He found that children from families with democracy *without* control were often cruel and disobedient, while children in families with control *without* democracy often lacked initiative and an inner sense of responsibility. The combination of democracy *and* control in the family led to an optimal pattern of assertive kindliness on the part of the child.
>
> (Damon 1988: 57)

Although sociologists remind themselves and each other from time to time that care must be taken in making generalizations about the stratified classes, as if to say that all middle class people are one way and all working class people another, yet class distinction continues to be extremely prominent in their research. Often they seem caught in an uncomfortable bind, in that, being themselves middle class (whatever their origins), they understandably try to guard against imposing their own class biases on their observations and are especially diligent about avoiding words like "disadvantaged" which stigmatize lower class people. Those who are both relatively poor and from an ethnic minority are especially treated with great care in social scientists' research. And yet, very often, they find themselves approving what they take to be characteristic middle class traits and attitudes and deploring those more common in working class groups. Thus in a review of a group of books in the 1970s about social stratification, the reviewer finds one sociologist characterizing middle-class values as "industry, thrift, responsibility, independence, toughness and perpetual advancement . . . ." But the working class got characterized as "resistant to change, implacably wedded to their traditional roles, and fiercely defensive. . ." (Kay 1974: 186).

Catherine Snow (1987) also cites evidence that working class parents tend to appeal to authority (theirs) and threats of punishment, whereas middle class parents more often cite reasons for their rules and regulations and appeal to feeling, as in telling a child that her father will be upset if she does . . . .

The typical way beyond this is to point out that much improvement in the effectiveness of teaching poor people in these and other respects depends upon their rising above poverty level. Many attempts to increase literacy in various parts of the world have dismally failed, apparently because so many of the illiterates were far more interested in finding a way to eat more regularly than in gaining the ability to read and write. It is now widely argued, similarly, that programs designed to educate young children away from the use and selling of drugs will remain ineffective until their conditions of life are improved enough to let them see the possibilities and advantages of other ways. As William Kay concludes his article review (apparently ignoring drug use and other deviancy among the affluent):

> It appears to be a matter of fact that we shall not have a truly moral society until all citizens are able to enjoy those benefits which currently accrue only to the privileged few. Morality, it seems is contingent upon the elimination of inequity in every phase of national life.
>
> (Kay 1974: 187)

Yet since we cannot sensibly wait for that eventuality, we need as soon as possible to know what there is to be known about the early beginnings of moral development—and then later developments, of course.

Since the time of Freud, who was deeply concerned with early childhood in his search for the genesis of neuroses, psychological investigators have become increasingly detailed in their discoveries. Whereas Freud largely depended upon adults' memories of what happened in their first five years, now researchers spend hundreds of hours watching and listening to children in their own home settings as well as in pre-school rooms and playgrounds. It seems that with every new report—as with those of archaeologists probing the origins of *homo sapiens*—the dates get pushed further back. Even an eight-month-old has been known to feed the dog and three months later may play at feeding a doll, instructing it, showing it objects. By three the child may teach the doll words, but also be of considerable help to other children. A 32-month-old has been known to volunteer toys to a child who had none (Stent 1980: 15–16). Lawrence Blum cites the example of two girls, Sarah, 12 months, and Clara, 15 months, on a mother's lap: "Clara is holding a plastic cup which she drops on the floor, cries, and points to. Sarah climbs out of Clara's mother's lap, gets the cup, and gives it to Clara" (Blum 1987: 310). In another example, two 15-month-olds are struggling over a toy, but when one starts to cry, his friend lets go; when the crying continues, the friend gives up his own teddy bear, and finally goes to find a security blanket to present as a peace offering. This works: the crying stops.

A very large number of such observations have been made, including, by the way, those that report unusually early instances of children's sense of humor, as when a two year-old drinking a glass of milk in his high chair, suddenly points at his glass, saying, "Beer!" and bursts into loud laughter (Dunn 1987).

William Damon writes of some of the early tensions in children's lives: "Shame and doubt, which first appear at the toddler stage, are the natural enemies of self-control, and threaten the young child's growing sense of free will" (Damon 1988: 23). Later he says that "Like empathy, shame and guilt have precursory roots in the earliest infant behavior. They derive from affective processes within the infant's natural constitution . . . ." (p. 26). The emotional basis for moral development is also emphasized by one of the acknowledged authorities in the field, Jerome Kagan, who has written that ". . . beneath the extraordinary variety in surface behavior and consciously articulated ideas, there is a set of emotional states that form the basis for a limited number of universal moral categories that transcend time and locality" (cited in Damon, 1988: 13).

Whatever the degree of universality, child behavior takes on distinctive coloration both because of cognitive development and because of socialization processes. Although each culture naturally has its distinctive ways, it is common to make a larger distinction between shame cultures and guilt cultures. Richard Schweder finds that these in turn are associated with the importantly different ways of regarding the individual person: in those in which the individual is mainly seen as part of a group, there tends to be a heavy emphasis upon social roles, rules, and rituals, such that children are anxious over disapproval and react with shame; whereas in those cultures in which humans are seen as—at least potentially—autonomous agents, there is a corresponding emphasis upon moving children toward ever freer behavior, wherein their rights are respected and a sense of justice is cultivated and exemplified—but with a corresponding guilt reaction in its members (Schweder 1987).

But of course such distinctions between cultures are by no means absolute, and the children of the more democratic cultures are obviously not free from shame and anxiety. Children in their second year of life already demonstrate an endeavor to understand adult standards of behavior and when they see their own and siblings' acts as aberrant, they very often react not only with anxiety, shame, and guilt but also by joking, teasing,[1] and laughing—thus helping, as it were, the adult task of correcting and instructing. Furthermore, the emotion generated by adult and peer disapproval may often heighten cognitive awareness so that the child, quite simply, thinks harder about the matter (Dunn 1987: 103).

Jerome Kagan has written:

> A self seems to emerge around the second year of life. A set of abilities indicates this sense of self as five different competencies mature: recognition of the past, retrieval of prior schemata, inference, awareness of one's potentiality for action, and awareness of self as an entity with symbolic attributes.

> (Kagan 1984: 26)

Kagan claims that a two-year-old's empathy with (say) another's distress and anxiety over a task failure indicates a biological preparedness to judge acts right or wrong—analogous to the neural preparedness for speaking—and indeed the coincidence, developmentally, of language, these emotional acquisitions, and the acquisition of such sensitivities as are named by "empathy" is by no means accidental.

If, then, one believes with Kagan that "The ideas of good and bad appear to originate in feelings linked to acts, or the contemplation of acts, . . . rather than the power of rational argument," this seems to call for some revision of the heavy emphasis most philosophers and many psychologists have put upon reason, with a corresponding neglect of feeling. (Yet as far back as the 18th century, both Rousseau and Hume were anti-rational in this regard.[2])

But these generalizations about children's early behavior are given finer tuning by empirical investigators, who notice differences among and within families in these respects. For instance, gender differences: mothers and girls talk more about feelings than do mothers and boys or fathers with either gender children. And this kind of talk seems to make a difference in child development. Thus Catherine Snow (1987: 115) notes that Judy Dunn has found that mother feeling-talk to 18-month-olds highly correlates with the tendency of 24-month-olds to engage in feeling-talk.

Sharing begins early in life too—sharing of toys, food, and favors; but children also do a lot of negotiating with other children and adults about expectations and fairness. Apparently more is learned from peers than most adults recognize, perhaps in part because of a power differential. Damon (1988: 86) has noticed that whereas with other children there is helping and sharing, with adults there is—*cooperation*.

Blum employs the term "responsiveness" to name a characteristic that begins in early childhood; he means by this not just such a response as smiling at an approaching adult, but also and more particularly an altruistic act such as the one previously noticed when a 15-month-old returns a cup her younger playmate had dropped, or when a three and a half year-old boy picks up and gives to his mother an open safety pin lest it hurt his younger sister.

Clearly this "ability to grasp another's condition is a more fundamental cognitive process that more specialized uses of inference can only build upon but not replace" (Blum 1987: 315). That is, there must first be something that one sees, takes in, understands before a moral response is possible, though with youngsters of course this is hardly an intellectual matter. This is a point that has been forcibly made with respect to adults of all ages by Iris Murdoch, notably in her work *The Sovereignty of the Good* (1970). There and elsewhere (including her novels) she demonstrates the tendency of people to fail to see, to take in, the realities of human situations, so blinded are they (we) by sentimentality and illusion.

Developmentalists seem to agree that parental lectures and more generally hortatory lessons have little effect on attitudes and behavior, but if a child spontaneously or with help from an adult becomes engaged in genuine service to another, expressed praise and appreciation of such, or for a job well done, can strengthen these altruistic impulses (see Damon, in Kagan 1987: 118, 130).

Theorists continue to disagree about how distinctly convention-governed behavior and fully moral attitudes and acts constitute different "domains" (a very popular metaphor with Piagetians and others), and about the extent of universal principles of morality. Elliot Turiel (1983), for instance, takes the position that even quite young children, in various cultures, can understand the difference between acts which are all right—even if they seem strange—because they can legitimately differ in different settings—as, for instance, matters of appropriate clothing—and those acts which are just plain wrong, even if there should be a rule in a given place which permits them, as in the case of one child willfully hurting another.

Kagan, however, holds that "The content of moral standards seems to be a product of history, culture, family values, and the individual's personal reconstruction of his or her past experience" (1987: xi).

In any case, the evidence that the prerequisites for moral behavior, such as empathy, sensitivity to others' distress, and being able to understand what kind of help is needed, have their origins early along. But of course development continues. For instance, White and Dunn agree "that the issues of *good* and *bad*, *should* and *shouldn't* continue to occupy the child in increasingly sophisticated ways and to generate input from both parents and siblings throughout the school years" (Kagan 1987: 120). White continues:

> The children, by becoming interested in "rightness," "completeness," "wholeness," and "goodness," as a problem space provoke many occasions for the negotiation of the meaning of words and of acts. During such negotiations, parents exercise the right to define child behaviors as good or bad and to relate their goodness or badness to the intentions behind and the consequences of the acts. The effectiveness of the negotiations in producing a child who shares the parent's views on morality presupposes, in my opinion, the empathy, the likemindedness, established earlier. In the absence of a basically trusting relationship with the parent there is no reason for the child to let the adult arbitrate the meanings of his words or acts.
>
> (White in Kagan 1987: 120–1)

The exceptional importance of trust will again be emphasized as we turn to developmental theories that extend well beyond childhood. But as a bridge, we may glance at an instance of survey research on older children.

In 1989 a study was commissioned by the Girl Scouts of America to explore the meanings of a national survey of 5,000 young people in grades 4–12 (ages 9–18). Many of the results were anything but surprising, for instance that poor children feel very much more pressured by their environment to go in a gang, try out drugs, disobey authority, have sex, and even to consider suicide; but it was surprising to many that in making the moral decisions that they do they are apparently more influenced by "their assumptions and beliefs about the foundations of moral truth" than by socio-economic realities. The surveyors identified five types of moral orientation among this population which they gave the following labels to, here listed in descending order of frequency:

1 *Civic Humanist*, decisions based on what will serve the common good.
2 *Conventionalist*, following authority and accepted moral practice.
3 *Expressivist*, "going with the flow" of feeling and needs.
4 *Theistic*, obeying religious admonitions.
5 *Utilitarian*, deciding on the basis of their own interests.

A few of the differences were: (1) whereas 61 per cent of those in the Theistic group say they would not cheat, in those called Utilitarian the number drops to 38 per cent; (2) among Expressivists 54 per cent say they would have sex with a loved one if opportunity presented itself, 27 per cent of the Conventionalists agree. (In this category girls were found to be only half as likely to be permissive as boys—and indeed, in a number of other respects, girls came out as more moral, according to usual conceptions, than boys.) Another surprising finding was that the children surveyed seemed not to be as concerned with teenage pregnancy, suicide, and school violence as they were with pressures from adults to get good grades, prepare for the future, and earn money (Coles *et al.* 1989).

It is not to be forgotten, once again, that no one knows what the correlation is between what such respondents say and what they do or would do. And this in turn is only a tithe of what we do not know and need to know to do a better job in our efforts to educate for value. But it is becoming ever more apparent that educators of all kinds stand to profit from the work of humanistic and social scientific researchers into human development.

5

RECENT MORAL
EDUCATION

Nowadays, the very mention of the word "morality" (and its variants) often draws a kind of groan or depressed sigh from selected hearers. The response, however dismaying, is easily understandable, though it may be inspired by any of several feelings.

To many, the word conjures up visions of an oppressive parent or institution (especially a religious one) or more generally and vaguely "society"—this society. The two-year-old child is a great nay-sayer, testing out the limits of a newly if dimly seen individuality. Years later, after an intervening time of some degree of compliance, this child may again edge up on rebelliousness. "Immorality" then comes to be seen as a realm of Forbidden Pleasures—or at least of Promising Possibilities. Morality may come to appear as a stick to beat others with, especially the young and relatively helpless, or to shame them into forgoing an unconventional way. "Immoral" or "wrong" or "shameful" come to sound like signs stuck almost arbitrarily onto various acts and ways of being, not so much (perhaps) because of their real iniquity, but as an exercise of power, authority. Thus, if one person by applying such a label can influence another's act, this can at once be a reward for the one, a defeat for the other. The power is greater, of course, if sanctions can be imposed, backing up the name-calling. The young person may be "grounded" by parents, given a black mark on his record, held up to obloquy by others, something especially galling if those others are one's admired peers.

Lawmakers may and sometimes do fall into a rash of proscriptiveness, multiplying beyond reason the number of punishable acts. It has been well said that, in a dictatorship, everything that is not required is forbidden. But even a relatively democratic society may be led into such excess until some reformer like John Stuart Mill or more recent "libertarians" will argue that it is time to reinstate the freedom to govern one's own actions, excepting only those acts that harm another or restrict his own freedom. Of course the attempt to proclaim yet another act as out of bounds is always held to be in the interest of those who are so tempted, and this may well be true both in intention and in consequence. Yet a young person may also make out a case

40

for being allowed considerable leeway to find her own way, even if it means "learning the hard way."

Often enough, too, it is not so much a present authority that is held to blame for moral prohibitions as custom and tradition. Such may not even be enshrined in specific rules and regulations, punishable in prescribed ways. Few cultures have been without some such prescriptions as "Honor thine Elders," which the non-elders may consider far too inclusive and vague. "Why not say, rather, honor those who merit honor or perhaps even those who are themselves honorable?" a youthful critic may ask. Or again if one is told that " *We* do not do that sort of thing," the irreverent reply may be, "Who said so?" and "Why not?" or even "Who's this *we*?"

If divine authority is cited on behalf of a commandment, objections may be indefinitely forestalled, yet there always remains the question of what are the grounds for ascribing any such prohibition to divinity. At a higher level of sophistication, it might be questioned—and today frequently is—whether a wholly beneficent god *would* indeed say any such thing.

Yet even in a society that permits, perhaps even encourages, such criticism in the young, there will inevitably be a sizable group of conformists as well, so that the young rebel cannot by any means claim to speak for the whole of his age group. Work on the psychological/sociological phenomenon of "the authoritarian personality" has shown the parallelism of desire to dominate and desire to be dominated, the latter being an even commoner (because more passive) manifestation of the basic impulse. Has there ever been a time when a large part of the population—any population—has not taken considerable satisfaction in having the rules laid out, the limits clearly set, the rules made explicit? Such realizations are the more maddening to those fired by skeptical and critical propensities.

By these and other means, then, "morality" acquires a gray, burdensome visage, a scowling face, a scolding tongue. And people turn away, saying, "All that is past—or ought to be. Deliver me. Away with Good and Evil—let's, with Nietzsche, go beyond those conventions, those pseudo-authorities, those dulling habits, those confining and joy-denying ways."

But the concept has another negative connotation for many people, that of an oppressive dogmatism and absolutism. "You say, 'morality'—whose morality?" Such a question, asked in a certain tone of voice, is not a question at all but a negative evaluation. It may suggest that any moral position is an imposition of someone's or some group's particular point of view upon others of a possibly very different persuasion. Often this antipathy to *any* moral commitment, unless it be carefully hedged as relative to this or that religious body or ethnic group, is itself grounded in the belief that moral standards and judgments are necessarily matters of faith, disposition, habituation, or socialization, and thus beyond evidential support or rational argument. Thus it will be asserted that any teaching of any morality represents a possible infringement of pupils' (and their parents') right to believe

41

otherwise. Often this is put in such a way as to make it appear that, with the dubious exception of purely descriptive assertions ("The Kapsolutus believe in human sacrifice"), moral teaching is a kind of indoctrination and thus an illegitimate (or immoral) endorsement of a doctrine that is very likely alien to some members of a class. If this can be forgiven, say, in a school wholly supported by a certain religious sect, the point is frequently made, at least implicitly, that in a professed democratic and pluralistic culture, instruction in morals is inconsistent with the very ethos itself. In these days in which a great many schools, more especially in big cities with sizable immigrant populations, have a diverse student population in terms of national origin, ethnicity, religious background, or social class membership, it is frequently maintained that, just as there must be a strict separation of church and state, so moral topics are best left entirely alone, and teachers should be schooled to remain aloofly neutral whenever ideas of faith or morals are broached.

Of course, it requires only a moment's reflection to understand that it is quite impossible for a teacher to maintain an a-moral stance, for can the teacher be passive and neutral toward one who disrupts a class—even if it is maintained that such an act represents a moral commitment to disruption? Or suppose that it is argued that the classing of plagiarism as a vice is nothing but a bourgeois prejudice.

But it may be somewhat more plausibly maintained that the teacher is treading upon dangerous ground in, say, condemning the settling of personal disputes by lashing out against an opponent, for may not this be, in the homes of some of the pupils, the accepted ways of discipline? It is by no means unknown, indeed, for a parent to advise the teacher to be rough with a child who does not obey the rules. But in these instances, what we have is a conflict of moralities in which neutrality can hardly be the solution.

The topics of cultural and personal relativism will be returned to in other contexts, but for the present, the question is whether morality must be seen as necessarily tyrannical, narrowly partisan, and therefore (say) kept as much out of the picture as possible. Or can the image of morality be refurbished?

Nature red in tooth and claw has turned out in our time to be as little dependable a generalized account as that of the peaceable kingdom where lions lie down with lambs and the fierce unicorn rests his obedient head on the lap of a virgin. Zoologists know better. Konrad Lorenz (1967) most notably has told about behavioral analogies to morality. The discovery that many animals have built-in biological mechanisms that work against a fight ending in the death of the vanquished one doubtless brings a warm glow to the heart of gentle and peace-loving humans, but the fond hope of some socio-biologists of finding a number of analogues in the lower animals for the elaborate moral codes of the higher has yielded little fruit. To be sure, within the bounds of a naturalistic morality,

it becomes quite plausible to envisage human behavior and moral behavior in particular [to be] the product of selective evolutionary forces. Thus not only the existence of a moral code but also its actual content would be justifiable by discovering what adaptive value, or fitness, it brought to the human species in the evolutionary struggle for survival.

(Stent 1980: 2)

So-called social evolution can doubtless be invoked to show that the lengthening life span for humans has *something* to do with the development of the civil law and other means of ordering human conduct (forgetting for the moment the increase in the destructive power of modern warfare), but biological evolution pays little attention to the survival of creatures beyond their reproductive period, and no attention at all to the survival of individuals. For a dramatic example of the latter fact one has only to think of the alarm call of certain birds, one which serves to save the species (notably young birds) by endangering the life of the caller.

Still, whatever their survival value, one cannot fail to be cheered by evidence in humans of streaks of altruism that seem to be grounded in biology. Thus witness recent studies of early childhood that show children who as early as two years of age distinguish between intentional and accidental harm, saying things like "I didn't *mean* to." And only a little later children often manifest a sense of responsibility, worry about harm to others, and give justifications for their actions.

But this is not the place to re-raise the thorny issues that pit sociologists against biologists in assigning origins of human traits. If even quite young children have unselfish as well as selfish dispositions, feel sympathy for as well as animosity toward their peers, it remains for parents and other caring adults to nourish whatever exists in the way of natural propensities, even though, as Rousseau labored to show, oftentimes we need to be at pains to avoid subjecting youngsters to the most repressive mores of a corrupt society.

But no culture has ever existed (or will exist) that has not given moral instruction to the young, socializing them in the dos and don'ts of "our people." Of course schoolteachers in due course lend their weight to this process, for the most part continuing the socialization, but in diverse and complex societies this teaching is not always describable as socialization. For instance, teachers often become aware that there is a possible conflict between the school aim of autonomy of the individual and conformity to the mores.

But schools differ considerably in different places and times as to explicit moral instruction. Concern about indoctrination is a relatively recent phenomenon, but what the content of the doctrine is obviously varies. Varied too are the ways children themselves are conceived of, a subject historians such as Phillipe Aries (1972) have in our own times explored more deeply

43

than ever before: whether for instance as "little adults," as anarchic and willful creatures that require heavy catechism, as wild and unruly beasts that need taming (much as colts need breaking in), as docile and nearly helpless beings whose main need is for nurturing, and so on. Except for the most general folkways, it is religious doctrine and state patriotism that have dominated the indoctrinative teaching down through the centuries. Except for the occasional disputatious voice of a Rousseau, we have to look to recent times to find any criticism of the place of morality in the school curriculum.

Probably the chief opposition to overt moral instruction in tax-supported schools has come from those who believe that it is futile. As noted above, in a much-publicized study in 1928 Hartshorne and May tried to find out whether moral instruction is effective in reducing cheating. The long and short of the matter is, at least within the obvious constraints of this experiment, that the "morally instructed" group were not distinguishable in their cheating behavior from those who underwent no such instruction.

Who knows how much direct effect publicity of this experiment had, but at the very least, it supported what a lot of teachers and administrators already believed. Furthermore, there was an increasing amount of suspicion among Roman Catholics, Jews, and various sects of Protestants as to whether school moralizing was not unduly slanted toward one or another of their rival religious doctrines. Furthermore, in the United States, the constitutional requirements of the separation of church and state were increasingly invoked on behalf of the "elimination" of moral instruction in public schools. Later the issue was further complicated as various ethnic minorities began to suspect that there was some tension between home and school instruction along moral lines.

One way and another, teachers began to decrease their explicit moral teaching and more and more began to be heard about the necessity of a kind of moral neutrality on the part of the teacher. School prayers came under the critical scrutiny of the American Supreme Court, the rights of such religious sects as Jehovah's Witnesses to excuse their children from the taking of any oaths or pledges (such as a "pledge of allegiance" to flag and country) were protected. In fine, for some decades moral instruction was on the wane.

But of course the tide turned once again after mid-century. According to a recent survey, in the latter part of this century, worldwide, about 1 per cent of instructional time has been allocated to moral education, and only half that much to civic, as against 4.5 percent to religion. Yet in the 1980s there has been renewed interest in moral education in the United Kingdom, the United States, the Netherlands, Denmark, and the Federal Republic of Germany (Cummings *et al.* 1988). In such societies, distinctions began to be more sharply drawn between indoctrinative and liberal teaching. It was noticed that teachers had never given up trying to discourage cheating, class disruption, playground violence, and other antisocial activity in the school.

There began to be a rise, at least in certain parts of large cities, of threats and violence toward teachers. And whether coincidentally or not, various educational researchers began to take a new interest in the possible development of programs of moral instruction, or, as the educational psychologists tended to put it, with the rise of that branch of their field known as Developmental Psychology and Moral Development. For three decades now this resurgence of interest in America and Britain has been manifest and continues unabated today. Indeed, in very recent years, there has been a surprisingly large interest expressed both by the general public and by legislative bodies in stepping up the amount and quality of this part of the curriculum.

By now, a round dozen—perhaps more—fairly elaborate *programs* of moral education have been described in print, been criticized, revised, and are being employed in at least a few schools somewhere. The best known of these have been so extensively described (and criticized) that we may here content ourselves with rather brief accounts.

"Values Clarification" is the oldest and still most commonly employed of these programs. Part of the reason for its widespread use is that it may be quite minimally employed; in the sense not just that virtually every teacher clarifies values, but that even some of its more specific provisions are easily adapted to a wide variety of classroom situations, and indeed to groups of summer campers, girl and boy scout meetings, etc.

As its name implies, this is not specifically a moral education program, for values of many kinds are included in its expositions. But the moral components bulk sufficiently large to warrant inclusion here.

This movement began in the early 1960s under the leadership of Louis E. Raths, a John Dewey disciple. In 1966 Raths, in collaboration with Merrill Harmin and Sidney B. Simon, brought out the first substantial work, *Values and Teaching: Working with Values in the Classroom*. Early on a definition of "values" is offered: "those elements that show how a person has decided to put his life . . . ." (p. 6). This is a rather vague and odd statement, but it is the basis for declaring the need for new work in the field, namely that "there are far too many children in the schools today who do not seem to learn as well as they might because they simply are not clear about what their lives are for, what is worth working for" (p. 12).

Certain requirements are then laid down for a value truly to exist, having to do with choosing, prizing, and acting upon choices. We are said to be in a genuine value situation when we choose freely, from among alternatives, and after thoughtful consideration of the consequences of each alternative. When we value something we prize, cherish, esteem, respect it, and hold it dear—and will upon occasion affirm our choice. Finally we *act* upon the choice—for it is not enough merely verbally to choose and prize; indeed, we repeat acting upon our choice in different circumstances. This list was in the mid–1970s amplified to include the requirements of thinking, feeling (the

45

above-named cherishing, but also feeling good about oneself) and communicating. These additions and extensions are mainly the work of Howard Kirschenbaum, culminating in his *Advanced Values Clarification* (1977).

A basic assumption of Values Clarification is that values are personal and since persons obviously differ, so do their values. There are, on virtually every issue and occasion, a number of possible, relevant values. Thus the emphasis is upon the recognition of many possibilities, along with an eschewing of any attempt to "give children an absolute set of values . . ." (Simon and Olds 1976: 17).[3]

What Values Clarification does right from the beginning is to justify value judgments. That they need some justification is evident from how often one hears said, in an almost accusatory tone, "But isn't that a value judgment?" which sounds like at least a venial sin. Value judgments are, according to this program's way of thinking, ubiquitous, necessary, and important. The ideal, then, is not to eliminate or even reduce the making of such judgments, but to improve their quality, especially as to their clarity. In effect, the lesson of the teacher is: once you clarify what it is you do value (announce it, act on it, etc.), then you are fully entitled to your value. Some critics feel that this approach is excessively, even dangerously, relativistic, and though this objection has been replied to, the objection still carries weight. The main defense of the position is that it is not conducive to clear, critical thinking for the teacher or another to set herself up as an authority, or to pretend that there are absolute standards, instead of encouraging continuing exploration and reflection, wholly without anything that smacks of indoctrination.

Emphasis in this exposition upon value *judgments* may be a bit misleading, however, for in a time when the forming of cognitively sound judgments is the hallmark of a number of programs—and even more of philosophical and psychological theory on the subject—Values Clarification puts an unusual amount of emphasis upon the feeling or emotional aspects of the process, thus asking questions like "How do you *feel* about world government (non-segregated dormitories, repealing the law against marijuana possession or use, etc.)?"

The extensive publications within this movement are mainly pedagogical in nature: no other program has done so much in providing teachers with materials, suggestions, procedures. But finally it is all in the interest of eliciting, probing, and comparing values.

By contrast, the program of moral development associated with Lawrence Kohlberg is grounded in a theory of cognitive development, namely that of Piaget, with modifications for the moral equivalents by one who is perhaps as much influenced by Socrates, Kant, and Dewey as by the Swiss developmentalist.

In *The Moral Development of the Child* (Piaget 1965), describing what he calls "the two moralities of the child," Piaget announces an impressive parallelism between intellectual and moral development. Of course no parent fails to be aware of this to some degree, in that the pre-verbal child is not supposed to have yet the wherewithal to understand, much less make, moral judgments, yet when the child has learned to understand the rule against appropriating another's property he may be held responsible for any infractions in that domain. But of course Piaget goes well beyond this common sense, proclaiming that "Logic is the morality of thought, just as morality is the logic of action" (p. 398). In the "sensorimotor" stage of cognitive development, the child is said to be highly egocentric; but this stage gives way to the operations of assimilation and construction which in logic correlate with the recognition of classes and relations, and in moral terms correspond to the recognition of regarding the mother or other authoritative adult as the infallible arbiter of prescription of what to do and refrain from doing. When the child leaves behind that stage in which he simply believes every idea that enters his head, he comes instead to be submissive to the word of his parents "and to believe without question everything he is told, instead of perceiving the element of uncertainty and search in adult thought. The self's good pleasure is simply replaced by the good pleasure of a supreme authority" (p. 402). But with attainment of increasing control over language, the child is ready to discuss, consider, and perhaps criticize moral pronouncements. In a yet earlier stage of language, Piaget shows that often what looks like the live give-and-take of discussion with a peer is in children simply a polite taking-of-turns in egocentric pronouncements. Gradually the child:

> is led to judge objectively the acts and commands of other people, including adults, hence the decline of unilateral respect and the primacy of personal judgment. But in consequence of this, cooperation suppresses both egocentrism and moral realism, and thus achieves an interiorization of rules. A new morality follows upon that of pure duty.
>
> (Piaget 1965: 403–4)

But along with criticism there arise for the young person at least dim notions of cooperation and even justice and "In a word, cooperation on the moral plane brings about transformations exactly parallel to those of which we have just been recalling the existence in the intellectual domain."

From such immensely suggestive beginnings, Kohlberg took off. But now we see emerging a theory of development that goes well beyond early childhood, and indeed comes to include six stages. The first two levels correspond to the pre-conventional levels of Piaget's notice of egocentrism, not, to be sure, where the child is still simply thinking and believing her own thoughts, but rather when the authority of the adult wholly prevails. Progress is made when this gives way—still within the pre-conventional area—to a slightly modified form of rule-following such that one sees the value of rules

47

which serve one's own needs, but also the recognition that others have their needs too. Thus an element of fairness is already apparent.

In stage 4 one is into conventional morality, which Kohlberg sometimes describes as the "Nice girl/Nice boy" level. Now, though, there is some sense of loyalty and trust, with often a good feeling about living up to expectations. By stage 4—which Kohlberg later came to recognize as realistically about the fullest attainment to be expected (even so, for some pupils only) in the school years—there dawns the sense of following rules because of the necessity of preserving one's society. (Thus Socrates argues that for him to pay a bribe and escape from prison would be to tear down the Athenian morality which had been his whole social context throughout his life.) Now one has definite obligations for the good of the social order; in short, one has quite fully transcended an egocentric, individualistic perspective.

After a transitional stage, it is theoretically possible to go to a post-conventional level. In stage 5, there is a clear recognition that a society is grounded in a social contract (*à la* Hobbes, Rousseau, *et al.*). Humans have incontrovertible rights that overcall such rights and rules as pertain to smaller groups (family, neighborhood, clubs, local community, etc.)

Finally, there is the stage of the highest principles, wherein one comes to recognize the existence of an absolute: not an absolute *commandment*, like those of the Decalogue, but an absolute *principle*. Now justice assumes its rightful place as the supreme principle, that to which all other duties are subordinate. Now one may break laws with impunity if they are clearly seen to interfere with the imperatives of justice.

Of course Kohlberg did not believe that on either side of the developmental parallel, intellectual/moral, there was a guaranteed, even automatic progression. A person can remain at stage 1 all his life, and presumably a very great many never get beyond stage 2. But there is the possibility of progressing and this has to do with education, in and out of school. But the pedagogy of moral development is not at all hortatory, and on the part of the teacher is probably better accomplished by a kind of classroom management than more directly.

It is essential to see that, on this theory, *stages*, whether of the intellect or of the moral self, are distinct, discrete, and sequential. One does not leap from 3 to 5, for this would be like learning to walk before one can crawl. Nor is there much recognition of regression. But there is the recognition of a certain growing capacity to see the advantage of *one stage higher*. Thus, in a classroom discussion, if one is debating with a person who has a somewhat more comprehensive position than one's own, that the other's *is* higher may be recognized and it may later be, emulated. (Naturally Kohlberg didn't have to be told about human propensities for defensiveness, etc.) Thus it will be apparent that often the teacher's role is in recognizing where each of her pupils is located, regarding the stages, and there are fairly elaborate instructions for those who want to make a precise assessment of the stage at which someone has arrived, and then to set up the confrontation of, say, a stage 3 person with one who is one level beyond.

Kohlberg and his associates developed a number of so-called moral dilemmas which are useful not only for diagnosis, but for engendering discussion. The most often quoted of these dilemmas is that concerning a man named Heinz:

In Europe, a woman was near death from a special kind of cancer. There was one drug that the doctors thought might save her. It was a form of radium that a druggist in the same town had recently discovered. The drug was expensive to make, but the druggist was charging ten times what the drug cost him to make. He paid $200 for the radium and charged $2,000 for a small dose of the drug. The sick woman's husband, Heinz, went to everyone he knew to borrow the money, but he could only get together about $1,000, which is half of what it cost. He told the druggist that his wife was dying, and asked him to sell the drug cheaper or let him pay later. But the druggist said, "No, I discovered the drug and I'm going to make money from it." So Heinz gets desperate and considers breaking into the man's store to steal the drug for his wife.

1   Should Heinz steal the drug? Why or why not?
2   If Heinz doesn't love his wife, should he steal the drug for her? Why or why not?
3   Suppose the person who is dying is not his wife but a stranger. Should Heinz steal the drug for a stranger? Why or why not?
4   (If you favor stealing the drug for a friend:) Suppose it's a pet animal he loves. Should Heinz steal to save the pet animal? Why or why not?
5   Why should people do everything they can to save another's life, anyhow?
6   It is against the law for Heinz to steal. Does that make it morally wrong? Why or why not?
7   Why should people generally do everything they can to avoid breaking the law, anyhow?
7a How does this relate to Heinz's case?

(Cited from Hersh *et al*. 1980: 122–3)

A teacher in presenting such a dilemma will help students to focus upon the genuinely moral aspects of the tale, recognize the different possibilities for action, give some consideration to what is involved in each of the alternatives, and raise the question of whether there is some point of view superordinate to their own.

It perhaps needs to be reiterated that, just as in Piaget's scheme, there is here a very close tie between intellectual stage and moral stage. It is posited that it is simply impossible to be morally more advanced than the corresponding cognitive level. (Of course one could repeat by rote "a higher answer," but it would easily become apparent that this was not based upon a true understanding.)

As with Values Clarification, critics were not slow to respond to this elaborate and complex theory, raising questions about its nearly exclusive concentration upon the forming of a judgment (but does one always act in accordance with what one sees as right?); its enshrining of justice as obviously the highest of moral norms (but where, for instance, does this leave Christian benevolence or Buddhist "mindfulness"?); its suppositions about both the parallelism of the two kinds of development and the absolute sequentiality of the stages (though Kohlberg introduced at least one half-stage); its insistence that this is a universal hierarchy, without regard to cultural differences (except insofar as whole cultures may impose constraints upon advancement beyond a certain stage); its workability, pedagogically (for instance, the training of teachers to identify each of the stages is complex); its unduly heavy emphasis upon what has been called "quandary ethics"—that is, upon extraordinarily difficult and complex problems (Kohlberg later agreed); and (to make an early stop) upon the sample by which the theory was validated.

Carol Gilligan (1982) is the one most closely identified with the latter point, along with the emphasis upon justice as the supreme value. An associate of Kohlberg's, she was well acquainted with what had gone into the development of the theory, and what she pointed out is that it was tested upon all-male samples. (Some cross-cultural testing was done, however.) Her argument was that here was yet another instance of equating males with humanity, which might be permissible if the question had to do with tonsils, but was at best dubious with respect to at least the higher stages of moral development. She then ran some tests of her own, and reported that a considerable number of women disputed the claim of justice to the highest ranking, putting *caring* in its place. (This point will be returned to in a subsequent chapter.)[4]

Also, many critics of the Kohlberg program, and indeed of all programs that center upon the teaching of ways of making ever higher and better judgments, have insisted that there is only a loose connection between such learning and actual change of behavior. James Herndon makes the point in a sprightly anecdote: reporting his wife's day-long observation of a school, he writes:

She is appalled at the playground scene. It appears that the kids (kindergarten to sixth grade) are all running around yelling about *kill* and *murder* and *beat up* and about *stupid* and *MR* and *dumb-ass* and two kids are holding another kid while a third socks him in the belly (it happens to be Jay, our oldest, who is getting socked) and

50

two little white kids are refusing to let a bigger black kid play football
with them and so the black kid starts to beat them up and when the
playground woman comes over they all three give her a lot of shit
and run away and she can't catch them . . . another large group of
kids are playing dodge ball and throwing the ball hard and viciously
at one another's heads, and some of them are crying, and there is a
whole other population of kids who stand fearfully on the outskirts
of the grounds just trying to keep out of the way . . . .

Back in the classroom after lunch she observes the concerned
teachers trying to have some discussion with the kids about how to
treat other people, about violence, about calling names—suddenly,
says Fran, they are all these goddamn nice neat marvelous white
middle class children, even if occasionally black, talking about equal
rights and observing the rights of others and not giving way to vagrant
impulse and how war is bad and everyone is smart (even them
fucking MR's) and how in a democracy everyone must be responsible
for his or her own actions. They all know what to say! hollers Fran
to me. They have all the words! They discuss superbly. They are a
veritable UN of kids, schooled in the right phrase, diplomatic,
unctuous, tolerant, fair . . . the hypocritical little bastards!

(Herndon 1972: 51)

Kohlberg was a vigorous debater in all the controversies, but since his early
death in 1987 some of the esprit of his movement has, not surprisingly,
seemed to wane. However, in fairness it must be said that he himself seems
to have developed a number of doubts about the feasibility of the educational
aspects of his program, if not about the pure theory. We will return to this
point subsequently.

Next we turn briefly to the writings of the Oxford professor John Wilson.
Wilson's is a theory of moral education that begins with the individual,
though it fairly quickly takes on a social dimension. In an impressively large
series of articles and books, Wilson has tried to work out, not a program
strictly speaking, but a set of basic considerations through which the well
prepared teacher would help bring her students to genuine moral problems
in such a way as to be able to deal with them intelligently and sensitively.

His orientation is very strongly toward analytical philosophy; in his early
book *Reason and Morals* (1961) he goes so far as to announce his general
affiliation with positivism and spends some pages wondering why this kind
of philosophy has not proved more satisfying to the general, as opposed to
the tightly professional, audience which at that time was dominant in British,
American, and Scandinavian circles. What this orientation means, apart from
the avoidance of any consideration that departs far at all from rationality, is
that he wants to avoid as far as possible (in his professional capacity) any
commitment to particular moral beliefs, and to concentrate upon the

appropriate engagement in consideration of moral problems. (However, some of his critics have insisted that not far below the surface of his rational analysis lie some fairly transparent moral beliefs.) This is what he would have the classroom teacher do too, to ready the pupil for analysis.

It seems fair to say that his main contribution to the subject is the listing and description of what he has sometimes called "moral components" to which he attaches Greek abbreviations that are not obviously helpful mnemonic devices. There are four groupings of these components. We will here refer to them merely by numbers:

1 Our first need, if we are to approach moral problems intelligently, is a sense of being in touch with other people's feelings and interests and having them count "as of equal validity to one's own." This is something of a surprise in one so rationally oriented, for feelings do not often come under active consideration in many such works. (See Wilson *et al.* 1967; the other two authors, Norman Williams and Barry Sugarman, a psychologist and a sociologist, composed other sections of the book than are here under consideration.) In later developments of the theory, more attention is paid to having the *concept* of a person.

2 Also required is an "awareness or insight into one's own and other people's feelings: i.e., the ability to know what those feelings are and describe them correctly." (*Ibid.*) Similarly one needs to be aware of one's own feelings even at an unconscious level, and to be able to identify and name these feelings.

3 Yet one has to go beyond identifying with and being aware of others' feelings, for without a knowledge of what is likely to occur, if one acts on one's feelings in this or that way, one may easily bring about results wholly contrary to what one wishes. As an example he imagines someone who realizes that "negroes felt pain as much as white people did" and that this truly counts for him "in making moral choices; but, through sheer ignorance . . . he believes that (say) because negroes have less nerve-endings or thicker skulls they do not get hurt so easily" (p. 193).

4 Given these prerequisites, one needs to formulate "a set of rules or moral principles to which the individual commits himself, by the use of such universalizing words as 'good,' 'right,' etc., where these rules relate to other people's interests." (*Ibid.*) "Other people's interests" is a favorite phrase of Wilson's and indeed is part of the definition of what is required for the motivation of an act to be moral. These rules or principles he finds necessary in order to have a rational basis to guide action.

5 Something similar is required—that is, rational formulation of rules and principles . . . relating to one's own life and interests—for otherwise one may be inclined to act irrationally or in a mentally unhealthy way.

6 Finally, there is the ability to take action, "to live up to one's moral or

prudential principles." This implies, again, to act in the interest of others (p. 194).

The sensitive teacher, well schooled in these "moral components", should then be in a position to determine better the needs of her pupils individually, so that one might need special assistance in one category, another in another. In any case, put all the components together and one has a rational basis for moral decision and action.

Wilson is to be commended for not letting his "rules and principles" orientation and his emphasis upon rationality exclude the importance of empathy and a coming to terms with others' and one's own feelings from important consideration. However, it is not easy to see just how such a theory might be translated into preparing teachers to effect a program for moral instruction along the lines here advocated.

It is of some interest to note that whereas 19th century (and earlier) moral education put great emphasis upon avoiding the wiles of the "old deceiver Satan" and more generally of the ways of being immoral, recent theories have accented the positive. However, Nel Noddings, who, as we shall presently notice, has been the leading light in the promotion of *caring* as the attitude which in rights should dominate all schooling, has also come out in favor of explicit instruction on the reality of evil, or as we might say, in ascending order, the naughty, the bad, and the evil.

She notes that early in the century there appeared a book (White 1909) that extolled the virtues of various historical figures, with specific attention to the following traits: "obedience, honesty, fortitude, courage, heroism, contentment, ambition, temperance, courtesy, comradeship, amiability, kindness to animals, justice, habits, fidelity, determination, imagination, hopefulness, patriotism, and character—the last established by the practice of the preceeding 'principles of morality'." A section was devoted to each trait, with explicit suggestions for the inculcation thereof grade by grade (Noddings 1989: 237).

Yet, as Jung has been at such pains to show, there is a shadow side to each virtue or admirable trait. Thus:

> obedience/authoritarian acquiescence
> justice/rigid legalism
> patriotism/chauvinism
> hopefulness/Pollyana-ism

and so on. The large-scale historical figures in history all had their shadow sides, from Agamemnon to Napoleon and from Richard III to Mussolini, and in some cases the trouble is in finding anything *but* shadow, from Caligula right down to the late, unlamented dictator of Romania.

Noddings recommends that teachers pay attention in classroom discussion to the themes of "torture, cruelty, and misogyny in some depth" as they are exhibited in history and fiction alike. Many educators today are pointing out that we may have gone too far in promoting a moral relativism, all in the splendid cause of promoting the understanding of ethnic diversity and the tolerance of differences among the world's peoples in various ages. But the great hero Odysseus should be shown to be not only brave and clever and strong and perservering, but also cunning and bloodthirstily cruel. The endlessly charming and deep Hamlet, in engineering the revenge of his dead father, engineered also the death of his mother, his best friend, and himself. It is arguable that the more benign goals of Lincoln and Lenin could have been achieved without the ghastly killing of immense numbers of people. And so on. Nor are evil results simply the result of well-intentioned bungling. As Noddings says,

> When we acknowledge that pain, separation, and helplessness are the basic states of consciousness associated with evil and that moral evil consists in inducing, sustaining, or failing to relieve these conditions, we can no longer ignore that we do think on and intend evil when we perform such acts.
>
> (Noddings 1989: 229)

6

PROSOCIAL EDUCATION

It is evident that the school is and always has been a primary agency for socialization, but what are we to understand by this word? Immanuel Kant (who was a professor of pedagogy as well as of philosophy at Königsberg) taught that young children are by nature barbaric and thus in need of domestication. Then and now, parents normally accomplish most of what needs to be done in this respect, but the five-or six-year-old goes off to school (with excitement and no little trepidation) and has as a primary task learning how to behave appropriately in that new environment. The teacher doubtless acts, to a degree, *in loco parentis*, but with a more restricted group of duties: for instance, she does not cook meals, does not enforce bedtime rules, does not dress or supervise the dressing of the child in the morning. She is *teacher*, and the child has to learn what that particular being is, what sorts of things she does, how one addresses her, what sort of talk is appropriate, and when one must remain silent, and so on and on. The child is being socialized to the school and through the school to a larger society. Early along the child has learned what we Joneses do, but now what we, as members of this class, students in this particular school, participants in this neighborhood and sub-community, do; what is *our* proper, accustomed, regular, accepted, usual, right way of acting—even feeling and thinking. The child is thus inducted into the mores and folkways of his or her society.

The relation of the student (and teacher) to society is the particular domain of sociology, and the writings of Emile Durkheim have a virtually classical status within this field. To those who operate under the apprehension that generic man is a creature who *happens* to congregate in societies; or that first is the individual and then, derivatively, there is a congregation or society or culture of individuals; or that social morality is a kind of extension of the more basic individual morality, Durkheim responds that man is meaningless considered apart from society, that we are through-and-through social creatures, and that without society morality makes no sense: "Man is man . . . only because he lives in society" (Durkheim 1956: 70). One of his supports for this claim lies in the evidence that he gives for believing that suicide often is the direct result of separating oneself from the social institutions and groups that constitute one's most important support.

Sociology on this conception is a description not simply of the ways any given society operates but also, and in some ways more importantly, of the moral ideals that function within a given society. In turn these ideals did not, of course, simply arise out of nowhere (or as the result of an unexpected revelation from on high); instead, they "have grown up historically under the influence of specific social necessities" (Durkheim 1979: 12).

From all of this, it is an easy step to seeing a primary obligation of the school to be that of (again) socializing the child, which is to say, acquainting and familiarizing the child (and young adult, for that matter) with the prevailing social norms.

Suppose, however, that one could challenge Durkheim by asking of him the questions: "Are you saying, then, that each society necessarily must, and does, indoctrinate its pupil population (among others), and thus the extent to which one is educated is in direct proportion to how much a conformist one is to the status quo? Does this not then confirm the worst suspicions of those who say that schools are nothing but a tool of the state and society as it is, at any given time, constituted? And does this not then imply that sociology, which proclaims and urges the inevitability of this way of functioning, is a wholly conservative, even reactionary discipline, from the point of view of idealistic or reformist theory?" In short, is not Durkheim, who clearly *wants* education to have an important moral function, caught in a kind of social determinism, such that education cannot help being yet another of the societal forces which operate to perpetuate itself?

Durkheim, however, would not at all agree that this is what he says or advocates. The reason he can answer thus is by way of a distinction he makes between the kind of socialization that occurs with respect to prevalent practice in a society and that which occurs with respect to the norms and ideals of that society. The latter may of course be implicit, uncoded, and even difficult to specify. Thus a reformer—he especially cites Jesus and Socrates—may be so much out of favor with the power structure of his society as to be martyred, and yet appropriately claim to be in closer touch with these ideals than his critics.

Of course reformers have typically based their appeals on just such grounds, for instance that the society at present has lost touch with its historical mission, or has forgotten the precepts of its founding fathers, to which now they are being called back. Thus in the Anglo-American world appeal is sometimes made to John Locke and Thomas Jefferson, to Edmund Burke and Abraham Lincoln in support of even a radical change from present practices.

However, it is no less typical that, whether mentioned as such or not, genuinely new principles and ideals may be cited by such reformers, and it is not easy to see how these could be justified on Durkheim's principles, for they are by definition at odds with either the implicit or the explicit norms of their society. Thus it would appear that there remains an undeniably conservative element in the Durkheimian program.

No one knew better than Karl Marx the power of conservative and reactionary forces in schools and all other institutions. And there are not a few today, in and out of the ranks of sociologists, who argue the necessity of revolution. But for a less inflammatory reformer, we may invoke that progressive critic John Dewey.

For John Dewey, early moral education is quite simply a matter of providing children with the right kind of social environment. It has nothing to do with lessons "about virtues and duties"—at least, not in a democratic society.

> Direct instruction in morals has been effective only in social groups where it was a part of the authoritative control of the many by the few. Not the teaching as such but the reinforcement of it by the whole regimen of which it was an aspect made it effective. To attempt to get similar results from lessons about morals in a democratic society is to rely upon sentimental magic.
>
> (Dewey 1916: 411)

But neither is the question of what is a benign and effective social setting for learning morality a difficult or complex one. It is, he wrote in *The School and Society* as early as 1900, the "ideal home" where "we find the child learning through the social converse and constitution of the family." He continues:

> There are certain points of interest and value to him in the conversation carried on: statements are made, inquiries arise, topics are discussed, and the child continually learns. He states his experiences, his misconceptions are corrected. Again the child participates in the household occupations, and thereby gets habits of industry, order, and regard for the rights and ideas of others, and the fundamental habit of subordinating his activities to the general interest of the household. Participation in these household tasks becomes an opportunity for gaining knowledge. The ideal home would naturally have a workshop where the child could work out his constructive instincts. It would have a miniature laboratory in which his inquiries could be directed. The life of the child would extend out of doors to the garden, surrounding fields and forests. He would have his excursions, his walks and talks, in which the larger world out of doors would open to him.
>
> (Dewey 1900: 51–2)

It could almost be straight out of Pestalozzi! But if the reader says, "Yes, so much for the home, but what of the school?" Dewey immediately answers: "Now, if we organize and generalize all of this, we have the ideal school."

It must not be supposed that for Dewey this was armchair philosophy. In 1896 he had his elementary school at the University of Chicago; it was to become much the most famous and influential of "laboratory schools" in the United States, perhaps the world. In that school was to be born "progressive education," the kind of school meant to replace the traditional school of bolted down, uniform desks, bare walls, little or no room for "activity" but instead wholly designed for listening (quietly)—for passivity, and thus a laboratory for authoritarian, teacher-centered instruction. True to his own pragmatism, Dewey wanted a school in which children acted, played, worked, freely trying out and experimenting with *things*—and doing this in constant cooperation with peers. This was the child-centered school that was to be celebrated and excoriated for at least the rest of the century.

The "democratic way of life" was central to all of Dewey's philosophy. Human beings are taken to be naturally and properly engaged in interacting with their fellows in pursuit of a conjoint fulfilling life. Everything centers around that conception. Truth-telling and other forms of honesty *are* virtues because they are part of effective group activity. Dishonesty interferes with fruitful discussion. Healthy, unmanacled children will not be silent—far from it—but they will not long tolerate disruptive noise and behavior on the part of their fellows if they are engaged in work that is meaningful to them. Hurting others is yet again a disruption and a distraction from an ongoing project.

Knowledge itself has its value in directing activity toward desired ends. And since intelligent activity depends upon knowledge, morality for him is thoroughly cognitive. "In truth, the problem of moral education in the schools is one with the problem of securing knowledge—the knowledge connected with the system of impulses and habits" (1916: 413). By contrast:

> If a pupil learns things from books simply in connection with school lessons and for the sake of reciting what he has learned when called upon, then knowledge will have an effect upon *some* conduct— namely upon that of reproducing statements at the demand of others. There is nothing surprising that such "knowledge" should not have much influence in the life out of school.
>
> (Dewey 1916: 413)

Dewey has nothing against "character education" so long as it is realized that character is precisely the whole human being, in all "the offices of life," and by no means a selected group of virtues. Morals, for Dewey, have to do with—indeed, they *are* social relationships. What they "have to do" is help make those relationships productive.

His whole tone suggests his irritation with *moralistic* education. Such instruction is ineffectual but, worse yet, it is off-putting in that it withdraws attention from what is for Dewey the essential thing: getting on with communication. He had an abiding confidence that human beings can eventually solve any problem if only they keep open the channels of communication—and use them. He doesn't want to put morality into a separate category. Indeed, this is part of a larger, more general characterization: that he wants always to dissolve rigid distinctions, dichotomies, in favor of continuities. Or, to put it only slightly differently, he was consistently averse to rigid either/or's: means/ends, idealism/realism, body/mind, school/community—but also moral/non-moral values. One way he had of making the latter point is this: "All the aims and values which are desirable in education are themselves moral" (p. 417). Thus if learning to read is a basic end of education, as it so clearly is, then it is moral—but not in the making of edifying lessons available (say, ones drawn from the Bible or the Qur'an.) No, it is moral precisely in furthering the communication of meaning, which is always good, morally good. And if one wants to indulge the familiar dichotomy, then, for Dewey, any blockage to open exchange of ideas and feelings (another unnecessarily rigid dichotomy) is bad. Any place where "intercourse, communication, and cooperation" go on, any situation that extends "the perception of connections," is educational, morally educational. Or to use a still commoner Deweyan expression, anything that promotes "growth" is an instance of moral education.

Dewey has been roundly criticized for being so fascinated with various processes, activities, like thinking, problem-solving, communicating, growing, that critics have wondered, with a certain acerbity, what is the growth *toward*. His answer, that we grow toward a capacity, a disposition toward more growth, has been usually found more irritating than satisfying. Yet, to the question of what the various kinds of relatings, connectings, communications are thought to lead, he wrote, "The something for which a man must be good is the capacity to live as a social member so that what he gets from living with others balances with what he contributes." (The special quality of *balance* here is that communicating is a matter of alternately speaking and listening, writing and reading, giving and taking.) But then he says something more, something that perhaps can be granted recognition as an end (and not just another means). What a person "gets and gives as a human being, a being with desires, emotions, and ideas, is not external possession [much less eternal possession], but a widening and deepening of conscious life, a more intense, disciplined, and expanding realization of meanings." And then he adds,

> What he *materially* receives and gives is at most opportunities and
> means for the evolution of conscious life . . . . Discipline, culture,
> social efficiency, personal refinement, improvement of character are

but phases of the growth of capacity nobly to share in such a balanced experience.

(Dewey 1916: 417)

And then, thinking we may have lost the connection he makes of all this to education, he goes on: "And education is not a mere means to such a life. Education is such a life."

Another way he might have put this, in line with some of the distinctions we have explored above (see pp. 57–9) is in the form of the distinction he elsewhere makes between instrumental values and intrinsic values. Thus we don't just communicate for communication's sake (though talk can be pleasant and satisfying apart from any specific external accomplishments thereof). The "cash value" of such acts lies in (again) "a widening and deepening of conscious life—a .... realization of meanings." If it is asked, "What, in turn, is the good, the value of *that*?" there is no answer, surely no satisfying answer. Which is to say that unless one understands that that is a value in and for itself, nothing more can be said or understood.

But let us look a little more closely at Dewey's discontent with the means/ends and the instrumental/intrinsic distinctions. In a way, the first is easier to see, for only a moment's thought is necessary to understand that in education (particularly but not exclusively) the means one uses to reach one's ends are themselves going in some measure to determine the nature of those ends. One example might be afforded by a repetition of a passage from Dewey cited above: that that method of learning from books for recitation does indeed *teach* but what it turns out to teach is something not probably consciously aimed at, to reproduce "statements at the demand of others."

But the instrumental/intrinsic distinction comes out in quite different contexts when Dewey is wrestling with highly theoretical ethics and value theory. For instance, in one such place Dewey asks first, "What connection is there, if any, between an attitude that will be called prizing or holding dear and desiring, liking, interest, enjoying, etc.?" He follows this with another question: "Irrespective of which of the above-named attitudes is taken to be primary, is it by itself a *sufficient* condition for the existence of values?" (Lepley, 1949: 5). What he is getting at here is a criticism of a values theory which says, for instance, that any satisfaction of a desire is *ipso facto* an instance of value or worth. What he is leading up to is an assertion (argued for) that such satisfaction is not a sufficient condition, though it may well be a necessary condition, of intrinsic value. What else is required, in Dewey's scheme, is a considered *reflection* upon that instance of liking or desiring to see whether it holds up to conscious appraisal. Maybe it's a fly-by-night moment of enjoyment. Maybe it is one that will prove trivial or even contemptible when other values are taken into account—and thus be rejected from one's catalogue of valued things.

But there is another thing he wants to say, and that is that the instrumental and the end (or intrinsic) values penetrate each other. Therefore, they are (or can be considered) instances of the means/ends dichotomy, already seen to be not dichotomous, really. This is evident when we think of, say, having got an object we prize very highly, considered in and of itself, but which, since it was got by stealing, is tarnished by our own remorse.

But Dewey finds that it is not just that the intrinsic (experiential) quality of a value inevitably carries with it whatever led to its enjoyment, reinforcing or in some measure modifying that enjoyment; it is also the case that what is taken to be the very end of the transaction, the consummatory value, is itself most likely a means to further values. For instance, it is easy to imagine (or even remember), a time when hearing a fine performance of a beautiful piece of music, so invigorated one that right afterwards there was an influx of energy for doing some totally different work.

Of course this is not a new realization, for both Plato and Aristotle wrote of the kinds of things that are both good in themselves and means to further goods, and that was, understandably, considered to be the very highest kind of value. But for Dewey this is a further indication that any rigid separation of the instrumental and the intrinsic is falsified by reflected-upon experience.

It may be that though Dewey had recognized the intrinsic (but also, later, instrumental) value of "a widening and deepening of conscious life—a . . . realization of meanings" his concentrated study of art, especially painting and other visual arts, in preparation for writing his book, *Art as Experience* (1934), made him newly and more deeply conscious of consummatory experiences, that is, those that have a way of gathering up partial and contributory values into an experience so rich that we speak of it as "an experience," as in saying, "Now *that* was an experience!" Thus he writes in his one work on aesthetics:

> We are aware that thinking consists in ordering a variety of meanings so that they move to a conclusion that all support and in which all are summed up and conserved. What we perhaps are less cognizant of is that this organization of energies to move cumulatively to a terminal whole in which the values of all means and media are incorporated is the essence of fine art.
>
> (Dewey 1934: 172)

It is apparent then that, for Dewey, moral education was not something quite different from aesthetic education, nor for that matter different from civics or geography or history or English—or even from mathematics and science. We have seen him strongly oppose *direct* moral instruction as a means of indoctrination, a way of preserving the dichotomy between the powerful and the powerless.

Yet some would say that times have drastically changed. When he was writing *Democracy and Education* in New York City in 1915 only 5 percent

61

of American children reached high school and 50 percent dropped out by the fifth grade, at the age of about 10. Pretty obviously those who dropped out were altogether disproportionately those who were economically poor. The group who remained were, by present standards, relatively homogeneous in economic class and all that that in turn means about value orientation. Antisocial attitudes and behavior inside schools were relatively slight, and when there were fights, fists, not knives, were used. Today, many would say, we cannot afford to neglect direct moral instruction, though we still deplore indoctrination. Is there possibly a middle ground, such that the greatest emphasis is put upon school climate, the prevailing ethos of the school, but not at the neglect of more direct instruction?

Anthropologists have described whole cultures that differ importantly in their ethical orientation:

> Some cultures promote the development of primarily prosocial persons; others promote egocentric persons. The Hopi culture, for example, yields persons who are helpful, cooperative, noncompetitive, unaggressive, and concerned about the welfare, rights, and feelings of others. On the island of New Guinea, Margaret Mead (1935) found two tribes at opposite ends of the spectrum: The Arapesh, who were cooperative, generous, loving, and unaggressive; and the Mundugamor, who were aggressive, ruthless, and lacking in gentleness and cooperation.
>
> (Brown and Solomon 1983: 273)

The point that this passage is leading up to is that a school can be thought of as a subculture which can be influential upon individual attitudes and behavior in similar ways. There are known to be urban schools in England and the United States that are characterized by recurrent menace, aggressiveness, surly and defensive attitudes, outbreaks of violence—all this to a degree that a school comes to seem more like a prison than an educational institution, and even children who in happier settings would be eager and enthusiastic learners become defensive and guarded in their actions, so much on the watch for threats to their own security as to have insufficient energy for their lessons. Such schools are characteristically located in neighborhoods or larger sections of a city marked by similar ways of being. Obviously, the spread of drug trafficking in such schools has greatly exacerbated the already difficult situation.

But it may be argued that if communities and schools can deteriorate into such negative states, it ought to be possible consciously and deliberately to build a contrastive kind of ethos. Normally, of course, we think of an ethos as a condition that emerges so gradually that sight may be lost of that which it grew out of. Thus Western visitors to China have often been amazed to find how uniformly cooperative and receptive to learning whole schools are, with virtually no student behavior to the contrary, and this in turn is explained in terms of a thousand-year (or more) cultural attitude toward elders and teachers,[5] not at all something that was introduced by the Ministry of Education of the People's Republic. Yet an impressive array of theorists and practitioners today appear to agree that there are real possibilities for building a prosocial ethos, more especially in the earlier years of schooling. (Among those researchers who incline strongly in this direction are Jerome Bruner, Jerome Kagan, Uri Bronfenbrenner, John and Beatrice Whiting, Paul Mussen, Nancy Eisenberg-Berg, Robert Coles, and Irving Lazar.) One project along these lines that has had several years of apparent success is the Child Development Project of Danville, California. Beginning at the kindergarten level, the project has gradually expanded to include all the primary grades.

It was a deliberate decision of the project designers to begin the study under the most favorable conditions possible. Therefore a relatively affluent suburban community was selected as the initial site. In this community there was very little ethnic diversity, no poverty, parents who were willing, even eager, to cooperate, attending meetings at the school and extending aspects of the program into the home setting. Critics have not been slow to suggest that any success in such a program is hardly generalizable to the very different settings of many urban schools, and indeed recently the project has been extended to another community, Hayward, wherein there is far more ethnic and economic diversity, roughly half way between Danville and the ghetto schools of San Francisco, New York, London, and Manchester. In this new setting, the project directors are likely to encounter less parent cooperation, more tensions and, in the student body, far more children who have in their pre-school years been socialized in directions quite contrary to those fostered by this experimental endeavor.

Perhaps the single most important and pervasive feature of the program is what is now named Cooperative Learning (which of course includes school procedures that have been widely employed in less ambitiously pervasive ways). De-emphasizing competition, pupils are continually put into work and play groups wherein they are so strongly encouraged to work together in problem solving (a mathematics problem, interpreting or writing a poem, devising rules for a game, etc.) that there is little occasion for rewarding the high achievers and punishing the low. Some social psychologists, notably Elliot Aronson and his associates, have shown excellent results, especially in the way of progress in pupils who have been slow learners, when lessons have been planned such that all the pupils actively participate. Perhaps the best known instance of this is what Aronson calls jig-saw lessons, which is to say that the teacher works it out such that each child has a piece of information necessary to the forming of a whole answer (see Aronson 1978).

A second feature of the Child Development Project is a more general emphasis upon helping and sharing among children. Students do chores, both in school and (with worked-out arrangements with parents) at home. Pupils also help other pupils, sometimes older and younger students form "buddy" relationships, sometimes within a single room a good reader and one not so good pair off to read to each other. In general pupils are continually reminded that helping is part of what school is about.

A great point is made in this program about the importance of classroom or playground discipline being positive. Teachers are advised to downplay pressure upon pupils, proliferation of rules and externally imposed rewards and punishment. Instead, children are given a role in policy decisions and rule-setting.

There are strong efforts in this program to promote social understanding, especially in the development of empathic skills and more generally attempting to understand the points of view of others, including those from different cultures and different age groups.

The general thrust of the project is felt also in the choice of materials for study. A particular emphasis is placed upon a carefully selected group of poems and stories that help children become aware of shared societal values and of ways in which sharing and helping people in trouble can improve their lot.

A program like this of course requires exceptional commitment on the part of administration, faculty, and support staff, to say nothing of parents. The adult participants need special instruction and continuing encouragement, and schools must make an investment in the way of films, tapes, books, etc., well beyond the usual.

This particular program has now been in operation for long enough to have more than provisional data for evaluation, though research activities continue apace. According to one evaluator, "After five years, the research shows that children in CDP classrooms are more likely to be spontaneously helpful and cooperative, better able to understand conflict situations, and more likely to take everyone's needs into account in resolving them" (Kohn 1988: 5). It should be emphasized too that, in putting this much attention upon affective aspects of classroom learning, there is no diminution in emphasis upon purely cognitive goals, and again, provisional evaluations indicate that the achievement of CDP pupils compares quite favorably with that of comparison group children.

Of course prosocial attitudes and dispositions can be encouraged and taught in an indefinitely large number of ways and in various settings. Figure 2, though, is meant to summarize a variety of aspects of any concerted effort in this direction.

However attractive a teacher or other educator may find such a prosocial program, it is easy to imagine many of them saying, "But my school has *not* joined this movement, has not reconstituted itself so as to orchestrate the teaching of these values to children. Is there nothing short of a school-wide reform that can promote a powerful change in values education?" One answer comes from those programs described in Chapter 5 especially those that, like Values Clarifications, can be carried on to a lesser or greater extent

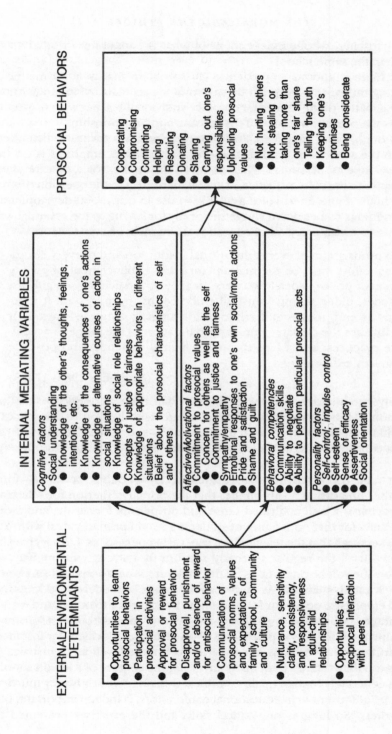

Figure 2. Hypothesized determinants of prosocial behavior

EXTERNAL/ENVIRONMENTAL DETERMINANTS

● Opportunities to learn prosocial behaviors
● Participation in prosocial activities
● Approval or reward for prosocial behavior
● Disapproval, punishment and/or absence of reward for antisocial behavior
● Communication of prosocial norms, values and expectations of family, school, community and culture
● Nurturance, sensitivity clarity, consistency, and responsiveness in adult-child relationships
● Opportunities for reciprocal interaction with peers

INTERNAL MEDIATING VARIABLES

Cognitive factors
● Social understanding
   ● Knowledge of the other's thoughts, feelings, intentions, etc.
   ● Knowledge of the consequences of one's actions
   ● Knowledge of alternative courses of action in social situations
   ● Knowledge of social role relationships
● Concepts of justice of fairness
● Knowledge of appropriate behaviors in different situations
● Belief about the prosocial characteristics of self and others

Affective/Motivational factors
● Commitment to prosocial values
   ● Concern for others as well as the self
   ● Commitment to justice and fairness
● Sympathy/empathy
● Emotional responses to one's own social/moral actions
● Pride and satisfaction
● Shame and guilt

Behavioral competencies
● Communication skills
● Ability to negotiate
● Ability to perform particular prosocial acts

Personality factors
● Self-control; impulse control
● Self-esteem
● Sense of efficacy
● Assertiveness
● Social orientation

PROSOCIAL BEHAVIORS

● Cooperating
● Compromising
● Comforting
● Helping
● Rescuing
● Donating
● Sharing
● Carrying out one's responsibilites
● Upholding prosocial values

● Not hurting others
● Not stealing or taking more than one's fair share
● Telling the truth
● Keeping one's promises
● Being considerate

by any teacher, wholly independent of what is happening in other class-rooms in the same school.

Yet there is another approach to this problem that is not a matter of adopting this or that program or system of values instruction at all, but is rather a matter of the reorientation of the individual teacher with respect to what is the primary purpose of the teacher/pupil relationship.

Although, as we have seen, Professor Nel Noddings advocates that attention in the schools be paid to real evil, her principal emphasis is on the positive aspects of ethics. Whereas for Gilligan the voice of care is an alternative to the voice of justice, at least with respect to the question of what is the highest and finest voice available to use in our moral development, Nel Noddings comes down altogether firmly for *caring* as the essential way of being to which every other educational aim must be subservient:

> The primary aim of every educational institution and of every educational effort must be the maintenance and enhancement of caring. Parents, police, social workers, teachers, preachers, neighbors, coaches, older siblings must all embrace this primary aim. It functions as end, means and criterion for judging suggested means. It establishes the climate, a first approximation to the range of acceptable practices, and a lens through which all practices and possible practices are examined.
>
> (Noddings 1984: 172–3)

Lest anyone should even suspect otherwise, she makes it perfectly clear that adoption of this stance does not at all mean an abdication of the school's "essential responsibility to train the intellect"—and indeed she herself has been a contributor to the theory and practice of mathematics education (p. 173).

But in the context of the school the teacher is—or rather should be—foremost the "one caring." This implies that the primary criterion for selection of a teacher is a well cultivated sense and propensity for caring, and more particularly for that population of students she will primarily deal with. Yet it is not enough that the teacher be a very caring person, as if to say that she goes about all the regular teacherly acts but in a strongly caring way. In addition she will be one who is on the lookout for occasions and situations in which care is manifest. As in the case of prosocial models, Noddings too would emphasize occasions for students to be of service to others and would encourage cooperation well above competition in classroom lessons and assignments. Emphasis is placed too upon dialogue, in which, for instance, the caring teacher exhibits her capacity to listen as well as to instruct. It means too that, oftener than many advocate, the content of a lesson should have a concretely human quality. "Critical thinking," which is very much in the limelight just now in educational conferences, is indeed important, but she writes, "So long as our critical skills and the exercises presented to develop them are confined to 'Ps' and 'Qs' and 'P implies Q' our schools will have the absurd appearance of a giant naked emperor" (p. 186). The emphasis must be upon human relations and opportunities for shared effort must be continually sought out. The teacher "is not eager to move her students into abstraction and objectivity if such a move results in detachment and loss of relation" (p. 182). Or again, "The one-caring really does not want her students to respect law and order for themselves, but for their contribution to the maintenance of caring" (p. 201).

This way of rethinking the dominant nature of the school has implications too, of course, for the student, the "cared for", as well as for the teacher and the administrators and counselors. As everyone knows, it is exceptionally hard to persevere in caring toward one who even over a stretch of time appears to remain indifferent or even hostile to this attitude on the part of another. But the pupil who responds warmly to the teacher's caring—as is surely natural to most children (and adults)—rewards and encourages such feelings and acts.

To reconceive the mission of the school in these terms is a large and difficult task, difficult in large measure because it runs so counter to most images of the school, except perhaps for the pre-school and kindergarten. So dominating is the idea of the school as a knowledge emporium which mounts a highly disciplined attack on sloppy and fuzzy thinking that any attempt to put care at the center of educational aims is bound to encounter opposition. Some will respond with embarrassment, for caring is something not often talked about outside of romantic relationships and perhaps between mother and small child. More antagonistically, some will portray such a novel emphasis as sentimental and soppy—a flight from rigor, discipline, and high intellectual standards. The very tendency to evaluate educational outcomes (and the schools that work thereto) by student marks, grades, and scores on tests is indicative of a fact already obvious, that schools are far from what a Noddings would have them be. To this claim, some teachers will protest that by and large their profession *is* one dedicated to service, that most teachers do in fact care for and about their charges, and that schools are generally warm, nurturing, and protective places, thus providing an environment in which close human attachments can readily form. And surely this is a fair and just response. Yet it remains true that to say, as Noddings in effect does, that caring is more important than the acquisition of knowledge and the development of ever higher cognitive skills is to imagine changes in teachers and schools that are vast. Noddings would respond that what she is advocating is far more likely than any of the usual curricular reforms to change the texture and structure of the whole society—and when one thinks of the abhorrent extent of alienation, cynicism, distrust, suspicion, irresponsibility, inconsiderateness, and violence abroad today, it may be that a turn toward caring might begin to make serious sense.

To get beyond more general solicitude or vague yearning, caring requires an understanding of the other, of what that person—for it is people we are focusing upon—needs and will best be helped by. Yet, this may be hard to manage if the other is rather different from oneself in personality, ethnicity, religious persuasion and so on.

Caring sometimes means *caring for* in the sense of protecting and nourishing. Furthermore, a person may be very altruistic but fall short of true caring by seeming unable to let him or herself be cared for in turn. This suggests that an element of power and control has crept in and marred the quality of caring. Then too, only a saint could exercise caring over a long period of time without some reciprocity, some return caring from the cared for, a point that Nel Noddings makes effectively in *Caring*.

7

THE POLITICAL
DIMENSION

For Aristotle the whole subject of Ethics was included within the larger frame of Politics, for man is, as he famously said, a social animal, and politics has to do with the social organizations of mankind. This is the way he begins his treatise, *Politics*:

> Every state is a community of some kind, and every community is established with a view to some good; for mankind always act in order to obtain that which they think good. But, if all communities aim at some good, the state or political community, which is the highest of all, and which embraces all the rest, aims at good in a greater degree than any other, and at the highest good.
>
> (1252a)

To be sure, Aristotle is not entirely consistent on the extent to which ethics is contained within politics, for he clearly believes that the highest form of activity for man is intellective contemplation, which is scarcely a political function, even though the well-run state could conceivably make it possible for its citizens to have time and occasion for such an exalted way of being—or, more likely, some few citizens who are so inclined and prepared.

In any case, Aristotle, like Plato before him, was intensely aware that the quality of life of every human is closely bound up with the type of government that is one's social habitat. Aristotle describes types of government as either good or bad; monarchy, aristocracy, and what he calls constitutional government are in the good category; tyranny, oligarchy (the oligarchs considered to be those who rule by virtue of their wealth), and democracy are the worst. With respect to the latter designation, it must be remembered that the Athenian democracy had in the 4th century fallen away from its previous glory and power and a good deal of cynicism prevailed about its being somehow responsible for the decline of Athens;[6] furthermore, democracy as it was then known was committed to the selection of governors by lot, thus denying any value to political acumen and administrative competence. He considered it to be a feature of the oligarchy to elect its

69

magistrates. Another of his principles is elegantly summarized by Bertrand Russell:

> Monarchy is better than aristocracy, aristocracy is better than polity [constitutional government]. But the corruption of the best is the worst; therefore tyranny is worse than oligarchy, and oligarchy than democracy. In this way Aristotle arrives at a qualified defence of democracy; for most actual governments are bad, and therefore, among actual governments, democracies tend to be best.
>
> (Russell 1945)

More than Aristotle, Plato (who had a similar judgment about the good and bad forms of government) found a closer correlation between the structure of the individual self and that of the state (remembering too that, for both, a state is a small city or large town, by modern standards), so that there is a tyrannical psyche as well as a democratic one, etc. But however that be, it is obvious that the form of government tends to have a considerable influence upon the quality of life of its citizens. This is best seen in the case of extreme examples. Hitler's Germany was such that hardly any German escaped the influence of the Führer. The model of an authoritarian personality, when it holds sway, is likely to be highly contagious. Not only was it the case that dictatorial power tended to be the ideal all the way down the line, through every aspect of the bureaucracy, businesses, schools and right into the home; but also there is that about the authoritarian personality such that it is exceedingly assertive if it holds power, exceedingly subservient to those who hold the power it lacks. It is not to be denied that this type of personality has its attractions for a portion of any given population, but for those who have experienced the non-authoritarian ways, tyranny is likely to be attractive only in cases of desperation, as when it becomes evident that a community or state can be saved only by the exercise of an unusual concentration of power.

The history of Russia from 1917 and of China from 1949, however, tells us something about the possibility of a state that, though founded on the noble principle of "From each according to ability, to each according to need," can itself become politically tyrannical to a degree unsurpassed by any state that is obviously organized so as to aggrandize the few.

The democratic way of politics (regardless of how it is skewed along the economic axis of capitalism/socialism) has a different relationship to public education than to any other form of government. The reason for this is not far to seek, for democracy alone has a built-in commitment to the encouragement of full participation of the populace in the decision-making processes of government, with leaders ever susceptible to correction and removal by well-guarded regulations and procedures.

From ancient times it has been recognized that the formal processes of education in some sense reflect the nature of the entire polity, but the reflection has often been cloudy, for sometimes even authoritarian states have been unable to control student and faculty dissidence, and altogether too often the schools of a democratic state have at the very least erred on the side of not educating its students *in* democracy. It is not to be forgotten, either, that students, especially university students, have in many places served as a liberalizing force inside of a democratic state, most notably, in recent history, in the case of the American involvement in the Vietnamese War.

Ideally, there exists the model of democratic ideals becoming operative in the processes of national and local government, in business and industry, including both labor unions and employers' groups, in schools, clubs and other associations, and in homes. On the larger scale, the hope is that internationally too, at the very least in organizations of states (along non-military lines) such as the European Community, democratic ideals may prevail. Hopes for a democratic world community have been notoriously difficult of achievement, but are far from abandonment.

But what does "democracy" mean at these several collective levels? Today to an extent unpredictable even a generation ago, democratic ideals of equality have been invoked on behalf of ethnic minorities and women in a bafflingly great variety of contexts. Businesses have become increasingly conscious of their own prejudices, in hiring and advancement, against women and minorities, and some progress can be cited. Lately, in English-speaking states, universities have become better aware of their own unwitting (?) domination by caucasian males, and have made some small progress in their employment and promotion policies. Many labor unions have seen their domination by a strong-arm leader or clique exposed and to some degree corrected. Very interestingly, churches within a number of denominations have been witnessing a challenge of centralized authority, on such issues as birth control, the freedom of clergymen to depart from established creeds in a number of ways, and increasingly now with respect to the ordination of women, members of ethnic minorities, and just recently of members of other minorities with respect to sexual preference.

It is a bitter irony that perhaps the greatest limitations ever effectively placed upon human thought and action have occurred in the 20th century, whereas the two preceding centuries went beyond all previous ones in establishing the human rights of freedom and equality. We cannot here trace this long history from its earliest announcements in ancient times through Hobbes, Locke, Rousseau, the spokesmen for the French Revolution, and Thomas Jefferson, but it is appropriate to stop for a while on the seminal work of John Stuart Mill, *On Liberty*, for however often it is read, cited, and discussed, its principles are so important that a frequent reminder of his argument cannot but be useful.

Early on he says:

The object of this Essay is to assert one very simple principle, as entitled to govern absolutely the dealings of society with the individual in the way of compulsion and control, whether the means used be physical force in the form of legal penalties, or the moral coercion of public opinion. That principle is, that the sole end for which mankind are warranted, individually or collectively, in interfering with the liberty of action of any of their members is self-protection. That the only purpose for which power can be rightfully exercised over any member of a civilized community, against his will, is to prevent harm to others. His own good, either physical or moral, is not a sufficient warrant. He cannot rightfully be compelled to do or forbear because it will be better for him to do so, because it will make him happier, because, in the opinions of others, to do so would be wise, or even right. These are good reasons for remonstrating with him, or reasoning with him, or persuading him or entreating him, but not for compelling him, or visiting him with any evil, in case he do otherwise.

(Mill 1859: Ch. I)

It is important to notice that for Mill the requisite freedom is even deeper than that of speech: it is freedom of consciousness, conscience, feeling and thought—on every conceivable subject. It is also freedom of action, singly or collectively. Furthermore, the constraints he deplores are not simply those of constituted authority, but those of neighbors and associates, the kind that are expressed by a frown or a curt word as well as by a fuller kind of reproach.

Mill knew as well as Thomas Jefferson did and better than most of us today that human liberty cannot be had and exercised in ignorance. Someone who is not exposed to opinions strongly in contrast with those that are the stock-in-trade of her own group is just as bound in her power to discover the truth as one who is expressly forbidden to say (or even think) the heretical thought. One must be helped to become acquainted with views, religious, economic, political, moral (etc.), that represent unorthodox stances. If one imagines that this requirement is taken care of by some authoritarian voice (priest, minister, pundit, mayor, teacher) saying piously, "Now let me tell you about what others may say on this matter," we must listen to Mill adding:

Nor is it enough that he should hear the arguments of adversaries from his own teachers, presented as they state them, and accompanied by what they offer as refutations. That is not the way to do justice to the arguments or bring them into real contact with his own mind. *He must be able to hear them from persons who actually believe them: who defend them in earnest, and do their very utmost for them*. He must know them in their most plausible form . . .

(1859: Ch. II)

The need for comprehensive knowledge as a condition of freedom prompts Mill to advocate, ahead of its time, compulsory education for all. But even here he is wary, lest this education itself be a subtle form of restraint. It would then be

a mere contrivance for moulding people to be exactly like one another: and as the mould in which it casts them is that which pleases the predominant power in the government, whether this be a monarch, a priesthood, an aristocracy, or the majority of the existing generation, in proportion as it is efficient and successful, it establishes a despotism over the mind . . .

(1859: Ch. V)

As a utilitarian Mill, himself a powerful social reformer, not least with respect to the widespread curtailment of opportunity for women, was aware that freedom finally comes down to the freedom to fulfill our own desires (always provided these do not infringe the liberty and other rights of others). He was aware too that we have duties to ourselves, for our own development, but he stopped short of allowing that these can be required of others, thus justifying legislation on the ground that it is necessary in order that people have the proper amount of self-respect. Indeed, his belief in the liberty of consciousness, taste, feeling and opinion is grounded in his commitment to the right and importance of the pursuit of happiness. One way in which people gain happiness is in the discovery of truth. But the discovery of truth prospers with freedom of inquiry and withers and dies under tyrannical censorship. As he says, "We can never be sure that the opinion we are endeavoring to stifle is a false opinion; and if we were sure, stifling it would be an evil still" (ch. II). One of the things he prizes most about the human mind is man's realization that "his errors are corrigible. He is capable of rectifying his mistakes, by discussion and experience" (ch. II). And this once again points to the school as a prime agency for furthering liberty and thus happiness, for where else is a child more likely to engage in the open discussion of controversial issues, and indeed to have direct instruction in how to conduct and participate in such discussion, and supporting or refuting an opinion by means of evidence and rational suasion?

Yet freedom is not, for Mill, so much something one is born with (except of course as a right to acquire) as it is something to learn. That is, if we are progressively freed by knowledge, more especially knowledge through an examination of diverse views, then a question can be raised as to when we have sufficient freedom to assert our entitlement to equality in decision-making.

Just as, in the home, the two-year-old has no clear voice in decisions about moving the place of residence, so his sister who is six is not consulted about teacher salaries. Of course people are quick to point out that the two-year-old and the six-year-old are not by any means forgotten in the decisions their elders make to some degree on their behalf. The new home should comfortably accommodate the youngest member of the family, and the pupil is fully entitled to the best teachers available.

Mill himself had doubts about recognizing either "primitive" peoples or children as yet ready for such participation. And of course even today there is disagreement about the age at which in a democracy young people may gain the right to vote. One telling point in favor of lowering that age from, say, 21 to 18 is that a person should not be asked to serve his country in the armed forces and yet denied the vote.

But how much exercise of freedom is justified in the classroom itself? Bertrand Russell, himself very strongly in the tradition of John Stuart Mill,[7] distinguished three theories of education in the modern world:

> Of these the first considers that the sole purpose of education is to provide opportunities of growth and to remove hampering influences. The second holds that the purpose of education is to give culture to the individual and to develop his capacities to the utmost. The third holds that education is to be considered rather in relation to the individual, and that its business is to train useful citizens.
>
> (Russell 1932: 2a)

Russell regarded the third kind, education for citizenship, to be much the worst of the three, since "citizens as conceived by governments are persons who admire the *status quo* and are prepared to exert themselves for its preservation" (p. 13). Since the *status quo* is (certainly *was* in the early 1930s, and doubtless he should say no less today) a disaster, he was obviously appalled by citizenship education. Just how bad he conceived it to be comes out plainly in the following passage, which is grounded in the belief that it is the state that determines the nature of education:

> Can it be wondered at that a world in which the forces of the state are devoted to producing in the young insanity, stupidity, readiness of homicide, economic injustice, and ruthlessness—can it be wondered at, I say, that such a world is not a happy one? Is a man to be condemned as immoral and subversive because he wishes to substitute for these elements in the moral education of the present day intelligence, sanity, kindliness, and a sense of justice?[8]
>
> (pp. 247–8)

His general position is "for the greatest possible freedom in education" (p. 32). Obviously the important word here is "possible." Thus he comes out for the teaching of hygiene, for honesty, and for the absence of coercion.

"Children who are forced to eat acquire a loathing for food, and children who are forced to learn acquire a loathing for knowledge" (p. 33). However, what he calls "apostles of freedom" themselves go astray, for instance in not recognizing the need for routine in the schoolroom, for "a life of uncertainty is nervously exhausting at all times, but especially in youth. The child derives a sense of security from knowing more or less what is going to happen day by day" (p. 39). But above all,

> complete freedom throughout childhood does not teach him to resist the solicitations of a momentary impulse: he does not acquire the capacity of concentrating upon one matter when he is interested in another .... The strengthening of the will demands, therefore, a somewhat subtle mixture of freedom and discipline ....
>
> (p. 40)

But above all for Russell the requisite freedom in school has to do with the freedom of pupils to talk as they like (including swearing and the use of "indecent" language), and the right to their own beliefs on any controversial subject.

> If they express opinions on religion or politics or morals, they may be met with argument, provided it is genuine argument, but not if it is really dogma: the adult may, and should, suggest considerations to them, but should not impose conclusions.
>
> (p. 63)

At one point in his life Russell and his then wife Dora ran their own school in which they tried to achieve a fine mixture of freedom and intellectual rigor. Naturally the school was lampooned, as in the apocryphal story of the clergyman who paid a call at the school to find that his knock was answered by a girl stark naked. "Good God!" said the cleric, whereupon the child said, "There is no god," and slammed the door.

Other reformers have taken the position that the democratic principles of freedom and equality can never obtain in schools that are themselves functions of societies otherwise disposed, which includes all the so-called democracies of the Western world. This position has been followed most prominently by those who argue for the Marxist doctrine that it is economics that drives politics, not the other way around. Many Marxists—though recently there have been exceptions—have taken the position that not only are "liberal reforms" ineffective, and very possibly counter-productive, but that the very virtues sponsored by programs for moral education in the home, religious institutions, or schools are likewise insipid or worse. Leon Trotsky, in *Their Morals and Ours* (1942) mounted an unrelenting attack on "conservative banalities of bourgeois morality." But even non-banal, working-class-based morals, according to this way of thinking, are

75

impossible of accomplishment short of a revolution to replace capitalism by communism. Lenin put it this way:

> In reality the school was wholly an instrument of class domination in the hands of the bourgeoisie .... We deny any kind of morality which is taken from the non-human and non-class conception, and we regard such morality as a fraud and a deception which blocks the minds of workers and peasants in the interests of landowners and capitalists. We say that our morality is entirely subservient to the interests of the class struggle of the proletariat.
>
> (Quoted in Pinkevitch 1929: 180)

One person who knows a lot about such domination is the Brazilian educator philosopher, Paulo Freire. He first came to general notice by his work describing how he taught adult workers in the north of his country to read and write—namely by helping them to see how literacy is a requisite skill in order to have some impact on the world, to have a hand in important decision-making. Thus the techniques of teaching in this account take a place very much subordinate to the social motivations of such an endeavor. Later he did similar work with Chilean peasants, with similar results: in learning to read, these people gained not only a sense of new-won power but a realization of how through language one creates a world.

Freire has made famous the distinction between two conceptions of education, genuine dialogue and what he has metaphorically called "the banking concept." In the latter "the students are the depositories and the teacher is the depositor. Instead of communicating, the teacher issues communiques and makes deposits which the students patiently receive, memorize, and repeat" (Freire 1971: 58).

In this way of proceeding the teacher is the one who knows, the student is ignorant and basically passive, receptive. What the teacher "puts into the bank" can later be withdrawn and used—with interest accrued!—by the students: so the promise goes, which is supposed to be motivational. Such a process "regards men as adaptable, manageable beings" (p. 60). It minimizes their creative power and increases their credulity, their dependence on authority. Not only is this ineffective pedagogy—consider how many underprivileged children fail to learn to read, or anyway read at all adequately—but it is above all a manifestation of power, the sway of the exploiters over the oppressed. Indeed, he says that this kind of education indoctrinates pupils to adapt to the existing oppression.

A far preferable kind of education, in the Freire scheme, is the one he calls "problem-solving" or "dialectical" education. Such education "bases itself on creativity and stimulates true reflection and action upon reality, thereby responding to the vocation of men as beings who are authentic only when engaged in inquiry and creative transformation" (p. 71).

Now, unlike some other radical reformers, Freire does not claim that only with an initial political transformation of society, most particularly a social-ization of the economy, can such education take place. On the contrary, he himself was using these ideas in countries dominated by authoritarian regimes—until he was deported. Teachers themselves thus can further the larger changes necessary to carry such reforms to their fullest extent. Or, as he puts it in another context, "While only a revolutionary society can carry out this education in systematic terms, the revolutionary leaders need not take full power before they can employ the method" (p. 74). There are partial methods too that can help, notably in a place like Brazil by Land Reform, a movement strongly led by a radical wing of the Catholic church, to break up the huge land holdings of the rich in order to make landowning widespread (see, for instance, Freire 1985).

Just as the prospective empowerment of the adult through a new-gained literacy is essential to this philosophy, so too the continuing empowerment through all of the other kinds of education that literacy makes possible is of course part of the program. More recently, followers of Paulo Freire, such as Donaldo Macedo and Henry Giroux, have put particular emphasis upon the empowerment of teachers so that they become vital contributors to curriculum making and pedagogical methods, rather than subservient per-petrators of the kind of pedagogy and curriculum which they see as perpetuating the dualism between the privileged and the oppressed, modeled by the duality of the active-knowing-teacher and passive-ignorant-pupil. Of course teachers' full and active participation in the processes of providing more adequate financial support for the schools is also strongly urged by these writers, as part of a larger movement to reduce the enormous inequalities among the professional classes, with law, medicine, and engin-eering on one side, education, social welfare, and nursing on the other.

Two other theorists, Samuel Bowles and Herbert Gintis, have become well known for their close relating of the whole enterprise of schooling with the dominant capitalist economy of America, Great Britain, and most of the nations of Western Europe and South America. Their hard-hitting and influential book, *Schooling in Capitalist America* (1976), though denying that school reform must wait for broader economic and political change, argues that educational changes organized from within the profession will be ineffectual unless they are concomitant with more sweeping modifica-tions of capitalism. Central to their position is the argument that liberal attempts to lessen inequality by such reforms as are indicated by the phrase "open classroom" typically founder and fail, even after initial support from beneficent foundations, government outlays, and school board endorse-ment, so that "the educational system mirrors the growing contradictions of the larger society, most dramatically in the disappointing results of reform efforts" (p. 5).

On this view, schools not only perpetuate (reproduce) the prevailing class structure, but they legitimate it by meritocratic professions. Thus it is often insisted that, in the school, everybody starts from scratch and then, by dint of the unequal natural distribution of innate ability and conscientiousness, students sort themselves out in an academic hierarchy, when in fact it turns out that with predictable regularity the students who receive praise and honors are the ones who come from privileged homes, and the drop-outs and persistent failures come from lower class backgrounds. School tracking or streaming (which despite seemingly serious efforts to equalize educational opportunity persist, often in disguised ways) further assures only middle class students of enriched opportunities for classes and higher levels of achievement that lead to university and thus preparation for the professions and management positions.

Furthermore, those democratic economies which feature "local control"—thought to be a way of keeping schools in close touch with their immediate community—differ considerably on the tax base from which schools are supported, and as a consequence schools from rich districts are indeed richly appointed with fine buildings, abundant materials and supplies, extensive electronic and other equipment, swimming pools, etc., which the poor districts cannot afford.

From the beginning, the pupils who come from homes containing books, with families that encourage visits to the public library and take their children, even at quite young ages, to the theater and concert hall, and give them music lessons, driving them to recreation centers, with extensive family travel during vacations, are precisely the sort of pupils teachers prefer, by virtue of the similarity between the values of those parents and the teachers themselves.

But Bowles and Gintis go further: they see schools not only as reproducing the extreme inequalities of any capitalist society, but also as *designed* so to do. This is the schools' principal function. Not only do they thus keep the poor poor and the comfortably well-off safe in their affluence, but they legitimate these differences and subtly disguise these functions.

Other social theorists, while agreeing with most of these descriptions of school structure and practice as reflecting the economic structure of the supportive society, take issue with this "functionalist" explanation (see Cohen and Rosenberg 1977).

The phenomena discussed here are of course by no means unique, except in specific detail, to the United States. Pierre Bourdieu has studied French universities and found there a heavy emphasis upon the inculcation of middle class values. Those students are favored from the beginning who have the preferred ways of speaking, dressing, exhibiting certain sorts of manners, even their gestures and postures. Students with deviant styles often fail, or count themselves out as probable failures, before examinations (Bourdieu and Passeron 1977).

Paul Willis (1977), argues that, in British schools, children coming from working class families are inclined to be antagonistic to the prevailing middle class culture of the schools, which in turn, of course, calls down on them disapproval from teachers and administrators—and once again the old order prevails.

Better known is Basil Bernstein's explanation for strikingly different levels of school achievement according to class origins: a fundamentally different way of using language prevails in the two groups. By and large, he says, working class families employ in the home a "restricted code," with strong emphasis upon concrete realities. Children from middle class homes, however, tend to employ an "elaborated code" that includes a far greater differentiation and far more attention to abstraction. Since the latter way of thinking, talking, and writing is also the one which dominates school language, it is not surprising that there is a sharp difference between the two groups in terms of academic success and going on to advanced education (see Bernstein 1974, 1973). J. C. B. Gordon (1981), among others, has, however, mounted an attack on the whole notion of some students having a verbal deficit.

Still others, though, look in different directions for a way to ameliorate social ills, arguing that the democratic governments of such nations as Denmark, France, the new Germany, Britain, Canada, Australia, and the United States, though always improvable, already provide the mechanisms for ever greater approximations to the ideals of a just society. What the schools can contribute to this advance, without waiting either on sweeping political changes or even basic changes in the school curriculum, is to mount a strong effort, right through the whole range of the school grades, in that subject not now in many places receiving much attention, namely Civics. For one thing, as has been noticed elsewhere, programs of instruction on the ethics of political behavior are much less likely to run afoul of skepticism or even antagonism than are programs having to do with personal ethics. Even parents who represent religious or ethnic minorities will often grant the importance of everybody's understanding civic rights and responsibilities, whereas they may be suspicious of instruction that runs counter to their own mores.

Programs in civics or government can, of course, be relatively factual and informative, thus more easily integrating with such school subjects as history, the natural sciences, grammar, and mathematics. Indeed, in some schools virtually the whole of what instruction is offered about current governmental structure and laws may come about in studying history, which often in effect *means* political history, so that the signing of Magna Carta, the rise of parliamentary power under Charles I or the signing of the Declaration of Independence and ratification of the federal constitution will be taught as being the origins of present day policy and practice.

This is somewhat less likely to be the case with respect to units of government beneath the national level, where also it is sometimes possible for students to have a more direct experience of local politics, the enactment of statutes, etc.

Still, the case is often made that it is the duty of a citizen in a democracy—and for those who will be citizens when they attain voting age—to participate in policy formation, modification, and repeal, which in turn requires knowledge of procedures. But it also requires knowledge of the characteristics of democratic and constitutional government. The following is extracted from a handbook of one statewide board of education in the United States. Similar language can be found in such documents prepared in other states and in Britain, Ireland, Canada, Australia, and other democratic nations:

Characteristics of constitutional democracy. By the use of a written constitution and the separation of powers, a constitutional democracy provides for the responsible use of power. This type of government assumes that the law can change to meet the needs of a changing society but that the basic structure and processes of government, tested by time, should be changed only after careful scrutiny. Change should occur only to enhance, not restrict, the fundamental purpose of freedom for all citizens under the law. Because this system of government is complex, the careful study of its processes rather than its form alone is essential for an accurate understanding of its worth. Constitutional government relies for its success on the participation of a large number of enlightened and mature citizens, responsible political leadership, a responsible opposition, and open processes that allow groups and individuals to exercise their influence and to state their views freely. Such a government is both limited and open. It is responsive to change but rests on stable social and political foundations. Constitutional government encourages and thrives on individual and group diversity, at the same time requiring self-restraint and adherence to the processes that allow diversity to thrive. The process of problem solving and decision making in a constitutional democracy differs from the process followed in totalitarian systems of government. Instead of the dictation of policy by a single authority or a self-chosen group of superiors, which is the practice of totalitarian regimes, constitutional democracy requires popular consent in election and decisions by a variety of persons in various branches and at various levels of government. In a constitutional democracy great value is placed on equal rights and fair procedures. Students should understand the processes, the principles of freedom and diversity, and the complexity that are hallmarks of constitutional government. Students should especially understand that, as in any other political system, constitutional government never attains its ideals perfectly. Due process of law, freedom of speech, protection of property rights, and rational

consent by open-minded voters in free elections are only approxi-
mated. The success of the constitutional system can be gauged only
by estimating carefully whether the system is moving away from or
toward the realization of its ideals.

(California State Department of Education 1988: 25–6)

Such documents as well as textbooks on government and civics will also
typically describe such basic elements of constitutional democracy as the
rule of law for settling disputes among citizens and between government
and citizens, without resort to violence; "due process of law," which provides
that anyone accused of violation of law must be informed of the charges, to
be given due notice of an occasion for a proper hearing, the right to counsel,
and trial by judge or jury, along with the need for the accused to be found
guilty beyond reasonable doubt if punishment is to be allotted; the right to
privacy and property, the right to oppose governmental edict in a lawful
manner, and such well known democratic rights as that of peaceful gathering, freedom of expression by word of mouth or in writing, and of electing
one's own form of religious affiliation.

Students are also taught about issues on which opinion is divided, such
as the platforms of opposing political parties, and on such controversial
subjects as the right to bear arms, and laws affecting sexuality, abortion, and,
with the invention of various mechanical and electronic means of sustaining
life, what is now often called the right to die.

Democratic governments all have policies advocating equality, but since
new inequalities are often discovered and publicized, students need to be
informed about differing judgments on the basis of distinctions such as those
between males and females, the rich and the poor, those who hold and those
who do not hold real property, and those at either extremes of the life-span.
Today there are increasing numbers of resolutions in favor of ethnic, racial,
and religious diversity, as themselves, beyond the tolerance legislated in the
name of equality, essential to healthy nationhood, but such ideals were
already put forth more than a hundred years ago by John Stuart Mill, among
others. Controversy continues about such issues as freedom from surveill-
ance by such means as wire taps and "bugging" devices, and for the
protection of criminals and alleged criminals from even fairly subtle types of
coercion. Controversy continues to rage too about capital punishment, the
degree of liberalism in granting parole, and eugenic measures against rapists.

In all such matters, and many more, students are widely urged to inform
themselves and by means of critical inquiry to arrive at reasonable positions,
which they will upon occasion give utterance to, and themselves defend
against challenges.

Increasingly, too, the point is made that it is not enough for citizens of a
democracy passively to enjoy constitutional rights and privileges, in addition
there is the obligation more actively to participate in civic matters, by

81

petition, joining in peaceful demonstrations and debates, and of course by voting—this at a time when, especially in the United States, often a shockingly low percentage of eligible voters cast a ballot even in elections considered important.

It will also be apparent that the purely informative elements of civic education quickly edge into rights and responsibilities, and thus into social ethics. As has been noted above, this in turn raises questions about democratic processes within schools and systems of schools. Heads, principals, and other school administrators are to be found who keep a very great amount of power in their own hands; in other instances, faculty members participate to a considerable degree in policy formation and application; in still others, but relatively few, students are given more than a nominal voice in such matters.

On one side it is argued that not only are students, practically by definition, immature, but also that they are but highly temporary members of the school's body politic. On the other, various democratic ideals can be evoked on behalf of student participation in government, to say nothing of the training students thus get in citizenship.

Late in his life, Lawrence Kohlberg, somewhat disillusioned with the prospects of moving students to the higher stages, conducted an experimental program in a high school, wherein students were given exceptional power in school governance. Kohlberg wrote:

> The aim of civic education is the development of a person with the structures of understanding and motivation to participate in society in the direction of making it a better or more just society. This requires experiences of active social participation as well as the learning of analytic understandings and moral discussion of legal and political issues.
>
> (Kohlberg 1980: 32)

He went on to propose that what the schools must do is to create "opportunities for social role-taking and participation" (p.32).

Thus Kohlberg moved away from hypothetical dilemmas presented for reasoned solutions, which he began to see as altogether too much derived from pure theory. Now he argued that "Valid teachers' decisions must be based on the assumption of the growing freedoms and dignity of the child" (pp. 38–9).

8

LIFELONG
DEVELOPMENT

The phrase "character education" has in many quarters given way to "moral development." Of course this is not just a terminological switch: the two expressions tend to have quite different emphases. There is especially no doubt about the importance that the word "development" has taken on in the psychological and mental health communities. We have had a brief look at theories of the early origins of ethical and other valuational sensitivities and awareness. Yet no matter how much importance we attribute to those beginnings, no one can seriously doubt that our characters, our convictions, our habitual practices continue to change right through the whole range of the formal schooling period. And beyond. Development, cradle to grave, is very much an "in" subject. Recently there has been a new spurt of interest in the characteristics of late and old age. The capacity to undergo (sometimes by deliberate undertaking) important changes is early evident and fades very late. By contrast, other animals tend to attain maturity quickly and then to stay much the same until they near death.

It is evident that the problems having to do with values vary according to a person's gender, social class, nationality, ethnicity, family affiliation, schooling, adult occupation, circle of friends and acquaintances, individual temperament (genetic and learned), and time of life. It is age, time, period, phase, stage of life that will here occupy us, though of course development along a time-line involves the other categories as well.

Even though developmentalism is *comme il faut* right now, the realization that human beings go through more or less well marked periods in their life-span must rank among the most primitive of human observations. The itinerant philosopher Jaques in *As You Like It* described the periods in a passage many a schoolchild has been required to memorize:

> All the world's a stage,
> And all the men and women merely players.
> They have their exits and their entrances,
> And one man in his time plays many parts,
> His Acts being seven ages. At first the infant,

Mewling and puking in the nurse's arms.
Then, the whining schoolboy, with his satchel
And shining morning face, creeping like snail
Unwillingly to school. And then the lover,
Sighing like furnace, with a woeful ballad
Made to his mistress' eyebrow. Then, a soldier,
Full of strange oaths, and bearded like the pard,
Jealous in honour, sudden, and quick in quarrel,
Seeking the bubble reputation
Even in the cannon's mouth. And then, the justice,
In fair round belly, with good capon lin'd,
With eyes severe and beard of formal cut,
Full of wise saws, and modern instances,
And so he plays his part. The sixth age shifts
Into the lean and slipper'd pantaloon,
With spectacles on nose and pouch on side,
His youthful hose well sav'd, a world too wide
For his shrunk shank, and his big manly voice,
Turning again toward childish treble, pipes
And whistles in his sound. Last scene of all,
That ends this strange eventful history,
Is second childishness and mere oblivion,
Sans teeth, sans eyes, sans taste, sans everything.

(II, vii)

Thus Elizabethan England, but the concept of the Ages of humankind is by no means a Western tradition alone. In India, the Laws of Manu, an ancient poetical work that deals with religion, law, custom, and politics, described the four orders (periods) of him(*sic*) who would aspire to the condition of the brahmin.:

1 *The student*. In the eighth year after conception, the teacher undertakes the instruction of the student in purification, conduct, sacrifice, and devotions. Living a life of abstention (from honey, meat, perfumes, women, sensual desire, anger, dance music, gambling, lying, idle disputes and hurting others, and by intense and prolonged study of the ancient scriptures, the Vedas and Upanishads), the student may remain as much as 36 years in this stage, but may leave it sooner if his learning is sufficient.

2 *The householder*. The man marries and establishes a household, fulfilling his duty of supporting those in the other three orders. He too will live a pure life, never following the ways of the world, and must strive toward perfect contentment, this disposition being considered the root of happiness.

3 *The forest-dweller*. Having seen his skin become wrinkled, his hair turn

white, and having become a grandfather, he departs for the forest, committing his wife to his sons or taking her along, where he will beg for his food and continue in ascetic ways, faithful in his devotions, making no effort to obtain pleasure, sleeping on the ground without shelter.

4 *The wandering ascetic*. Having "got rid of his body" and abandoned all attachment to worldly things, he wanders alone, indifferent to all but his meditation and taking delight in the true Self. "He who has in this manner gradually given up all attachments is freed from all the pairs (of opposites), reposes in Brahman alone." (Radhakrishnan and Moore, 1958: 177–84. The foregoing summary is a composite of quotation and paraphrase.)

Women, as in so many other respects, have historically been considered largely in terms of their child-bearing function, such that the onset and cessation of the menses have been thought to mark off the essential period. For males, in agricultural no less than in industrial societies, one's work life is bounded by early childhood play and retirement.

Sigmund Freud, as in so many other respects, pioneered a new way of considering life development, such that early childhood experience is a determinant of later sound mental health and all the deviations therefrom. As a psychologist he was not much interested in adult development, as if to say, if only we can survive and come to grips with the traumas of early childhood, working through our tendencies to become fixated, we are ready for love and work—and the ordinary miseries of life. His answers were very simple in fixing upon early childhood sexual development with particular reference to the mother and father as "sex objects." After one goes through (more or less *through*) the phases in which a child's mouth and then anus are the chief source of sexual gratification, the genital period is introduced by the dawning recognition of not only one's own genitalia but those (strikingly different) genitalia of father and mother. After early identification with the mother, the boy child moves to an identification with the similarly equipped father, who, however, becomes then a hated rival for the mother's affection; whereas the girl child remains identified with the mother even when her sexual desires move toward the father. One further crisis remains for the girl, or perhaps young woman—something the boy is spared—the change from phallic (clitoral) concentration to the vaginal. The boy's fear of castration, the girl's belief that she is castrated, are essential in this period. As all the world knows, weathering this Oedipal period was considered essential to later emotional health. For instance, weakness of identification with one's own-sex parents, Freud believed, made for what he regarded as a perversion, homosexuality. But more to the point of a broad spectrum of value considerations, Freud argued that the two genders differ with respect to the formation of the conscience, or in his terminology, the "super-ego"

85

(*Über-ich*). In this internalization of parental moral prohibitions, the father is assigned a particularly important role. Whereas usually, and to a degree, the boy is able to overcome his Oedipus complex by realizing that he does not have the power to overcome the father, nor yet to marry the mother,

> The girl remains in the Oedipus situation for an indefinite period, she only abandons it late in life, and then incompletely. The formation of the super-ego must suffer in these circumstances; it cannot attain the strength and independence which give it its cultural importance, and feminists are not pleased if one points to the way in which this factor affects the development of the average feminine character.
>
> (1933: 166)

(The point about feminists is a severe understatement!)

For all of Freud's insistence that the super-ego is nothing more than parental socialization, Philip Rieff has in his *Freud, the Mind of a Moralist* insisted that, so far from rising above morality in the ultra-scientific stance he so much admired, he remained well within the confines of most of the morality prevalent in his time and place. However, it may be added that recently Freud has been posthumously criticized—severely so—for what today is called "unethical treatment of human subjects," especially women.

Freud in late mid-life changed his theory of instincts. Although he retained eros, the instinct for pleasure which has sexual pleasure ever as its exemplar, he replaced the ego instinct (or, better, *drive*) with the death drive, that in all of us which moves us to be destructive and hurtful in the ultimate endeavor to return to an inorganic stasis. These basic drives color our lives, first to last, but for the most part Freud remains silent on the subject of the values which do or might or should prevail in our lives, content to say that the task of psychoanalysis is to remove the compulsiveness which limits our freedom to choose for ourselves how we wish to live.

Erik Erikson is a Freudian who has made a far more important contribution to developmental theory than did his master. But before entering upon the sketch of his exceptionally interesting position, let us address the question what is the relevance in a work on teaching and learning better access to important kinds of value of psychological description of how humans occupy different stages in their life-span? The question is the more apt since writers like Erikson are not much inclined to "draw morals" from their accounts, but to tell us "how it is," which is to say to describe the particular psychological problems, social and individual, that we humans face in growing up and growing old. Yet characteristic problems that we face in the maturing (and post-maturing) processes have a way of coloring and even in a sense dictating the sorts of values that surface during these several periods. Thus descriptions of, say (in Erikson's case), the "identity crisis" show how we are in a sense dictated to by these crises as to what is important.

And, in another sense, such descriptions suggest, if they do not specify, differences between a successful and a failed attempt to meet these problems. Above all, they show how interests change in emphasis—again something known to common sense, but now with expert help.

Naturally there is an initial problem about what "identity" means, and then how can there be a crisis with respect to one's identity? Erikson admits right at the beginning that "identity" is what Freud called an overdetermined concept: it means too much to permit of clarity—more especially the kind of clarity required if we are to provide tests that tell us where we are according to specifiable criteria. But here is one of Erikson's characterizations—it would be too much to say it is a definition: "a *subjective sense* of an *invigorating sameness and continuity*" (1968: 19). He goes on to cite William James's words in a letter to his wife:

> A man's character is discernible in the mental or moral attitude in which, when it came upon him, he felt himself most deeply and intensely active and alive. At such moments there is a voice inside which speaks and says: "*This* is the real me!"

Erikson says that for James (and himself) such experience always includes

> an element of active tension, of holding my own, as it were, and trusting outward things to perform their part so as to make it a full harmony, but without any *guaranty* that they will. Make it a guaranty . . . and the attitude immediately becomes to my consciousness stagnant and stingless. Take away the guaranty, and I feel . . . a sort of deep enthusiastic bliss, of bitter willingness to do and suffer anything . . . and which, although it is a mere mood or emotion to which I can give no form in words, authenticates itself to me as the deepest principle of all active and theoretic determination which I possess . . . .
>
> (p. 19)

Identity for Erikson is at once an individual and a cultural phenomenon. On the individual side, identity gets formed by

> a process taking place on all levels of mental functioning, by which the individual judges himself in the light of what he perceives to be the way in which others judge him in comparison to themselves and to a typology significant to them; while he judges their way of judging him in the light of how he perceives himself in comparison to them and to types that have become relevant to him.
>
> (pp. 22–3)

An ethical consideration comes into Erikson's account when he speaks of the responsibility of adults to provide forceful ideals to younger people at various stages of their crises. The overall end of the developmental process is a healthy personality, which Erikson describes, following Marie Jahoda's account, as one that "*actively masters* his environment, shows a certain *unity of personality*, and is able to *perceive* the world and himself *correctly* . . ." (p. 92). It must not go unnoticed that a word like *healthy* here is normative as well as descriptive: this is taken to be an optimal way of being.

With this much of an introduction we are ready to glance at the stages of development marked by the several characteristic crises which we humans undergo. Needless to say, any given crisis may be more or less traumatic for an individual. If some persons seem to float with amazing smoothness right through one or even conceivably all these crises, there are surely others of us who have a much harder time, and of course even fail, with resultant neurotic consequences.

Erikson names eight critical periods, each taking the form of an opposition between a favorable and an unfavorable way of being. The first, encountered in infancy, is summarized by the words Trust vs. Mistrust. The trust in question is directed both at others, the primary caretakers especially of course, and at oneself, that is, a sense of one's own trustworthiness.

The second stage is marked by the opposition Autonomy vs. Shame, Doubt. This is the stage in which the child moves from almost total dependence toward becoming his or her own person (which is of course not to deny that parents very early detect distinctive features in a newborn's personality). Taking his cue from Freudian "anality," Erikson generalizes to the whole matter of withholding and expelling, keeping and throwing away, which has to do with the development of a will—often willfulness. If shame and doubt imply an uncertainty in one's own power, autonomy implies a strength and confidence, a power of resolutely pursuing immediate goals.

The third crisis is that between Initiative and Guilt. (Now it is apparent that a guilt *culture* is more developed than a shame culture. Now the child begins to anticipate roles and is faced with the problem of "what kind of a person he may become" (p. 115). Although still strongly identified with the parents, the child now moves freely, has a considerable vocabulary, and can exercise imagination to conjure up possibilities. But it is also the time when conscience begins to figure prominently—hence the possibility, indeed the inevitability, of guilt. It is interesting to see that, on this scheme, excessive guilt feelings are considered to be inimical to a healthy initiative.

Stage four presents Industry vs. Inferiority. Now the child is in school and is presented with tasks to be accomplished, masteries to be achieved. But the school lessons and their tasks may appear to the child alien and irrelevant, or induce the suspicion that he is not up to this level of achievement. Erikson believes that there is a particular threat here to boys, in that by far the greatest number of primary level teachers are women, which fact may "lead to a conflict with the nonintellectual boy's masculine identification, as if knowledge were feminine, action masculine" (p. 125). But in the more fortunate instances the child learns how to organize his energy resources to accomplish increasingly complex tasks.

The stage of adolescence is, not surprisingly, seen as of especially great importance, as is clear from the naming of the opposite possibilities: Identity vs. Identity confusion. The adolescent typically looks fervently, almost desperately, for persons and ideas to have faith in. Now there is a conflict between the strongly assertive freedom of will and the danger of being forced into activities that would engender self-doubt and ridicule from others. Now the imagination about possibilities of what one might become is almost too fruitful, and thus confusing. The young boy or girl is faced with the necessity of considering what one wants to be in the concrete form of a vocation. The plaintive words of a young man in Arthur Miller's *Death of a Salesman* are cited: "I just can't take hold, Mom, I can't take hold of some kind of a life" (p. 131). The very need, requirement, to take hold is at once exhilarating and frightening.

Assuming, then, some degree of success in taking hold, of establishing a basic identity as to one's place in the world, the sixth crisis is named Intimacy vs. Isolation. Although during adolescence sexual intimacy will probably have been experimented with, now the problem is the larger one of having or failing to have "the capacity to develop a true and mutual psychosocial intimacy with another person, be it in friendship, in erotic encounters, or in joint inspiration" (p. 135). Promiscuity usually represents as much a failure to establish intimacy as do withdrawal and isolation. Interestingly, though, Erikson speaks here of an inner intimacy as well, that is, of being able to consult oneself beyond the stereotypes presented on all sides. Freud's answer to the question as to what a normal person ought to do well, "Love and work," is surprising for its simplicity, and yet it gets to the heart of the matter of this crisis, for now the developing person is at the stage of establishing (or failing to establish) his or her own family and embarking on a career.

Stage seven pits Generativity against Stagnation. What Erikson means by the healthier of these alternatives is the concern and capacity for guiding the next generation Whether with one's own children or with those of others, part of the process of maturing is that of "continuing the species, not just biologically but socially, culturally, intellectually, morally. What threatens such accomplishment though is a pervading *sense of stagnation*, boredom, and interpersonal impoverishment" (p. 138).

Finally there is the crisis of Integrity vs. Despair. Here *integrity* names, in part, the wisdom that has been traditionally and ideally associated with old age, but adds to it a sense of wholeness of the self. Only one who has found meaning and dignity in life can stave off the disgust with which many people, in their *declining* years, look out upon the world (which is not what it used to be, alas) and perhaps look back upon their own life with a pervading sense of its futility—perhaps because it must end in death. Worse yet is the possibility of despair, and a collapse into self-pitying whining. But the alternative is a certain nobility and loftiness of outlook. "If the simplest moral rule is not to do to another what you would not wish to have done to you, the ethical rule of adulthood is to do to others what will help them, even as it helps you, to grow" (Erikson 1980).

Our next consultant from the realm of depth psychology is C. G. Jung, but his complex theory is so thoroughly developmental that one must for present purposes be content with a severe condensation of his major points. For Jung, psychic development is *from* the unconscious *toward* personality, which he describes as "a well-rounded psychic whole that is capable of resistance and abounding in energy. . ." (*CW* 7, para. 286). The key terms in this passage require elucidation. To say, as Jung does, that the unconscious "covers all psychic contents or processes that we are not conscious of. . ." (*CW* 6, para. 837) may on the surface seem unhelpful, yet we can easily be conscious of our own consciousness, but can only infer from strange things that happen that the psyche is indefinitely larger than the field of our present awareness, including all manner of drives, complexes, tendencies, presently unrecallable memories, unrecognized aversions, wishes, desires, a wealth of emotions and proto-ideas that may at any time surface, along with an immense realm of collective dispositions that Jung believed to be inherited. Animals and very young children may have a great many conscious perceptions of their environment without any self-consciousness. The two-year-old child has the beginnings of this way of being in learning to say "I" or in learning the distinction between "I myself " and another. All psychic development, then, has its origins in the unconscious. Consciousness is attained by fits and starts as one begins to learn differentiations: not only between me and my mother, but between hot and cold, edible and non-edible, near and far, up and down, wet and dry, and an immense number of other opposites and lesser kinds of differences. (The propensity toward making differentiations and distinctions Jung calls by the name of *logos*.)

In the early years of growing up, we all have strong identifications with our primary caretakers, but also much concern with siblings, pets, and other frequenters of the home environment. The going-to-school represents a movement into a more objective environment, where we become taken up less with personal relations and more with acquiring skills in reading, writing, and arithmetic. Now too the personality of the teacher, a kind of public personage, supplements and in part replaces the influence of family personalities. Children early begin to assert themselves against parents, no doubt in part in order to acquire a degree of the independence that is absolutely necessary for more than rudimentary development.

But it is not primarily the school curriculum as such that is taught and learned. It is, more basically, certain orientations toward the world and certain ways of functioning therein. Every child has certain strengths and corresponding weaknesses in these regards; development consists in part of learning ways of functioning other than those that come most naturally.

Jung's best known differentiation of orientations or attitudes toward the world is between introversion and extroversion. We all upon occasion turn inward, notice our own desires, doubts, wonderings, images, ideas, and so on; but we also turn outward to the external world of people and things and perceive the variety and the samenesses there in their interactions. But, Jung said, we tend to favor one of these ways of being more than the other, and use that way habitually, and thus come to be classified as introverts or extroverts, of varying degree. It is important to note that neither of these is *per se* an aberration, but both are perfectly normal ways of being: this is worth noting because sometimes these labels have been used in such a way as to make extroversion healthy sociability, and introversion unhealthy, a shyness, fear of other people, and undue concern with oneself. Still, it is an important developmental task, one in which the teacher can assist, to help children develop their own weaker way of orienting, for each of us naturally inclines in one of these directions—and thus away from the other.

Then there are what Jung called the basic functions, which he named *thinking*, *feeling*, *sensing*, and *intuiting*. Again, we all use all of these functions, daily, probably hourly, but again have our preferences, the ones that we employ most comfortably and readily. Some children and adults run naturally to conceptualizing and relating concepts, which is called thinking. (Having such a tendency is no guarantee of being an especially good thinker, nor does it preclude excellence in other functions.) Feeling, for Jung, is quite different from having emotions or being emotional; instead, he uses this word to mean something like "a sense of values" or a capacity to regard things (inner or outer) from an evaluative point of view. Whereas the thinker may try to keep a value neutrality in making conceptions, the feeling person tries not to let logical categories and processes interfere with a more direct apprehension of the goodness and badness of the world. Sensation is not only all the uses of the sensory organs, but also a propensity for seeing the world in terms of the practical here and now, with emphasis upon workability and taking things one at a time. By contrast, intuition looks in a future direction, with a conception based therefore upon potentiality, and what contrasts with the stark given reality of the present.

It is now believed from a considerable body of research, with tests that try to reveal propensities in these regards, that the "types" are by no means uniformly distributed among humans, and that they do strongly influence the ways we conceive our studies, our work, our human relations, and our selves.

Each of these functions (as well as the orientations) can be regarded as a perspective upon the world. Therefore, no one enjoys a particularly privileged position. Thus to know anything at all adequately, Jung taught, one must regard it from the vantage point of each of these perspectives. But,

91

once again, we incline to favor what comes easiest for us. Thus development means growing in other regards as well.

Now, the prevailing metaphor in all this is that of moving from lopsidedness to roundedness, as—back to his definition of the personality that is the goal of development—a "well rounded psychic whole." We become more nearly rounded into a whole as we learn to function introvertedly as well as extrovertedly, feelingly as well as in thinking, intuitively as well as in the sensation mode.

Three other concepts merit brief mention in this scheme. There is the pairing logos/eros. Logos has already been parenthetically characterized as the force or tendency toward discrimination between opposites and lesser forms of otherness. As long as we fail to make such basic distinctions, we remain largely unconscious. But we can overdo such analytic procedures, which requires correction by the opposite way, which Jung called *eros*, the linking, relating, synthesizing tendency and process. Logos puts asunder and eros brings back together—not in the fused way of the unconscious, but at another level. In a way that has recently become controversial, Jung thought that generally speaking males are more inclined toward logos, females toward eros, though he hastened to say that here too the less immediately available way of function is susceptible to an indefinite amount of strengthening. And that again is part of development.

Next, and somewhat similarly, there is the basic bisexuality of each human being. In addition to our evident gender, we have, mainly in the unconscious, the tendencies and interests of the opposite. He gave the name of *anima* (Latin for "soul") to the male's feminine side; *animus* to females' masculine side. No one can go far in the development process without to some extent coming to terms with (i.e. making consciously available) the contra-sexual side of one's being. This too can be construed in terms of personality achievement.

Finally—though Jung would count this as advantageously early in adult development—there is the recognition and integration of the *shadow* side of ourselves, which is to say those unconscious tendencies toward negativism, mischievousness, and the whole range of ways of being that we (usually along with our whole culture) find obnoxious or disagreeable. "Nobody is perfect": the old maxim reminds us and Jung makes the point in terms of the unavoidability of having a shadow side to our being. But against this (though we cannot simply eradicate it altogether) we may through increased consciousness qualify and moderate our more dubious propensities.

In these several ways (and others not entered upon here), Jung describes the possible, but by no means necessary and inevitable, progress toward consciousness, toward personality. This is not to be conceived as an isolated, entirely lonely process, and we shall see in another context that it has its implications for morality, but as just one insistence that such progress is a social one there is his warning: "Respect for the personality of others . . . is absolutely indispensable if one would avoid arresting the development of the subject's personality" (*CW* 7, para. 459).

Jung's name for this attainment (of course never complete) is *individuation*, which he describes as "becoming a single, homogeneous being and, in so far as 'individuality' embraces our innermost, last, and incomparable uniqueness, it also implies becoming one's own self. 'Coming to selfhood' or 'self-realization'" (*CW* 7, para. 266). Or in a burst of eloquence he says of the personality that is the result of individuation that it is

> the supreme realization of the innate idiosyncrasy of a living being. It is an act of high courage flung in the face of life, the absolute affirmation of all that constitutes the individual, the most successful adaptation to the universal conditions of existence coupled with the greatest possible freedom for self-determination.
>
> (*CW* 17, para. 289)

But the great process of individuation is an adult task. Jung never tired of dividing life into two parts. In the first, our task is mainly that of adaptation, of establishing ourselves in the world, slaying all the menacing dragons that lurk on the outward scene, and with good fortune settling on our life work, a home, and family. At around the age of 35, Jung saw a mid-life crisis (a phrase that was to become popular after Jung's time), as a person more and more (typically) turns inward in order to ask not so much how to get on with the course of life thus begun, but most seriously to reflect upon the meaning thereof—though, needless to say, such reflections can unsettle the seeming stability of that established life. But this is the time for the deepest probing, the consultation with the inward Self which he took to be the guiding model of balance, well-roundedness and wholeness. Jung leaves us in no doubt about the second half of life's being much the more important one; indeed, the first half is quite simply preparation for the second, the foundation on which the superstructure is to be built. To shirk the first task is to provide but sandy foundations for further building. To shirk the second task is to fail to answer the challenge of constructing a distinctive life, one which somehow answers the call of one's own destiny, becoming as Pindar had said in ancient times that which we are.

In the middle of the 20th century both sociologists and psychologists—the latter now carving out a specific sub-field for themselves, Developmental Psychology—took up Jung's task with (or usually without) acknowledgement of Jung's pioneer work in this field. Almost suddenly it became popular to think in terms of life's stages. Thus the sociologist Robert J. Havighurst (1953) carved out these periods: 0–5, 6; 5, 6–12, 13; 12, 13–18; 18–35; 35–60; 60–.

Further fine-tuning was achieved by Daniel Levinson and his associates in *The Seasons of a Man's Life* (1978), where boyhood, adolescence, and all parts of women's lives were left out of consideration. Levinson was especially taken with the middle life crisis, but like Erikson he saw a number of crises (occurring in the transition periods between Early and Middle adulthood, and between Middle and Late, these three periods roughly corresponding to the ages 20–40, 40–60, and 60 onwards. Difficult as are the transitions from living at home to setting up a new abode, of finishing schooling and settling in a job, of conducting the rituals of courtship and preparing for marriage, the period of 39–42 was found to be even more tumultuous in the struggle a man has with self and the world. "Every genuine reappraisal must be agonizing," this study insists, "because it challenges the illusions and vested interests on which the existing structure is based" (p. 200). The word "structure" is central in this conception, for the challenge of any transition period is to create a new structure that will accommodate and give some unity to the period upon which one is entering.

Nevitt Sanford (1966) emphasized the possibilities for personality development at any stage of life whenever there occurs either some challenge from the environment (as, for instance, a new possibility for one's career) or an insight into one's own self (as in realizing that one had "dried up" on the aesthetic side). In this, as in the other theories, the human being is seen as self-reflecting, self-regulating, and, to a degree, self-determining. (The Greeks were exceedingly wary of *hubris*, the overestimation of one's power to determine one's fate.)

Another developmentalist, now again one who takes the whole range of human (male and female) life into its compass, is that of Jane Loevinger. What she sees developing is the ego—but she takes this concept in a broader sense than Freud or the "ego-psychologists" who came in his wake. She says:

> The fundamental characteristics of the ego are that it is a *process*, a *structure*, *social* in origin, functioning as a *whole*, and guided by *purpose* and *meaning* . . . . We acknowledge both *consciousness* and the possibility of freedom and the validity of the *dynamic unconscious*; so the ego is not the same as the whole personality. It is close to what the person thinks of as his self.
>
> (Loevinger 1976: 67)

Unlike many other theorists Loevinger does not—indeed, she refuses to—accompany her stages with ages, saying that she is concerned with what people of a certain stage have in common, whatever their age when they reach that stage. Obviously, though, the early stages occur in infancy and early childhood.

Pre-social stage. This could as well be designated as the pre-ego stage, for the newborn infant has yet to attain an ego by differentiation from the surroundings. The child who does not transcend this stage is called autistic.

Symbiotic stage. Even after objects are differentiated, the baby for a time is not clearly distinguished from the mother, a relationship that is distinctly symbiotic. (In being pre-lingual these two first stages, Loevinger points out, are especially hard to recapture in later memory.)

Impulsive stage. Part of the establishment of an ego is impulsive assertion and action, and the concomitant rejection ("No!") of directions from others. Impulses are mainly closely connected with physiological attributes, and judgments tend to be simple and peremptory. At this stage the child is exceptionally centered in the present.

Self-protective stage. Herein the child learns control of impulsiveness and especially learns to guard against punishment—thus against getting caught. It is a period in which blame is an important feeling and certain techniques are acquired for shifting responsibility to others—or of course to inanimate forces: "It broke."

Conformist stage. A momentous step is taken when the child starts to identify his own welfare with that of the group, usually his family for the small child and the peer group for an older child. Trust is the cement for the group to which one belongs. A strong rule consciousness arises, and consequent stereotypy.

Self-aware level. Here Loevinger inserts a transition period which she describes as modal for our society. It involves an increase "in self-awareness and the appreciation of multiple possibilities in situations" (p. 20).

Conscientious stage. Now the capacity to internalize rules becomes strong, and one comes to protect not only oneself but others of the inner group. There occur the beginnings of distinctions between kinds of value, say the aesthetic and the moral, or between the merely conventional and the genuinely (perhaps universally) moral. A person now "experiences in himself and observes in others a variety of cognitively shaded emotions." Motives come to count as well as acts and results (p. 21).

Individualistic level. Here is another transitional period in which not merely conformity but also the dictates of conscience begin to be seen as sometimes inimical to one's own achievements and the pursuit of lofty goals. "Moralism begins to be replaced by an awareness of inner conflict" (p. 22).

Autonomous stage. Now we reach a level to which many never arrive, involving "the capacity to acknowledge and to cope with inner conflict, conflicting duties, and the conflict between needs and duties" (p. 23). Recognition not only of one's own autonomy but the equal importance of other people's now enters awareness. This kind of person "expresses feelings vividly and convincingly, including sensual experiences, poignant sorrows, and existential humor, the humor intrinsic to the paradoxes of life" (p. 26).

Integrated stage. This is the culmination of the whole developmental process. Loevinger speaks of the difficulty of description at this point, partly because in being rarely attained it is little described. Interestingly she now defers to Abraham Maslow and his account of the "self-actualizing" person. Maslow, one of the psychologists who reacted to the overemphasis upon neurosis and other aberrations and spent a large part of his career trying to describe what human beings are *at best*—not necessarily persons of eminence and fame, but, whatever their station in public life, ones who are or were remarkable for their maturity, their largeness of selfhood or, as he liked to say, their achievement of self-actualization. Here is a schematic list of the characteristics of such persons.

1 More efficient perception of reality and more comfortable relations with it
2 Acceptance of self, others, nature
3 Spontaneity, simplicity, naturalness
4 Problem centering
5 The quality of detachment, need for privacy
6 Autonomy, independence of culture and environment, will, active agent
7 Continued freshness of appreciation
8 Mystic experiences, peak experiences
9 *Gemeinschaftsgefühl* (feeling for community)
10 Interpersonal relations—more profound and deep than with other adults
11 Democratic character structure
12 Discrimination between means and ends, good and evil
13 Philosophical, unhostile sense of humor
14 Creativeness as a personality style
15 Resistance to enculturation, transcendence of any particular culture
16 Firm foundation for a value system, based on a philosophical view of man, with unique idiosyncratic values built on it
17 Resolution of dichotomies

Still another important work in developmental stages is Robert Kegan's *The Evolving Self* (1982) (and others). Although he correlates his stages with those of Loevinger, there are important differences between the two theories, Kegan regarding the developmental process as the movement toward ever more comprehensive ways of making meaning, the process consisting in leaving the "balance" of one stage for a period of turmoil in transition to a new and higher balance. This work is very much worth consulting, but here we must content ourselves with simply listing his stages: Incorporative, Impulsive, Imperial, Interpersonal, Institutional, and Interindividual. Only at the last stage—he does not go to Loevinger's height of the Autonomous—does true intimacy become possible, for one has achieved a strong self, beyond institutional roles, to bring to a personal relationship.

Finally, one other statement of the culmination of development, this time from Carl Rogers who calls his culminating condition the "fully functioning person":

He is able to live fully in and with each and all of his feelings and reactions. He is making use of all his organic equipment to sense, as accurately as possible, the existential situation within and without. He is using all of the data his nervous system can thus supply, using it in awareness, but recognizing that his total organism may be, and often is, wiser than his awareness. He is able to permit his total organism to function in all its complexity in selecting, from the multitude of possibilities, that behavior which in this moment of time will be most generally and genuinely satisfying. He is able to trust his organism in this function, not because it is infallible, but because he can be fully open to the consequences of each of his actions and correct them if they prove to be less than satisfying.

He is able to experience all of his feelings, and is afraid of none of his feelings; he is his own sifter of evidence, but is open to evidence from all sources; he is completely engaged in the process of being and becoming himself, and thus discovers that he is soundly and realistically social; he lives completely in this moment, but learns that this is the soundest living for all time.

(Rogers 1969: 288)

What if the conscientious teacher (or other educator) asks, "How do we go about working toward these exalted ends?" None of these visionaries—and they present a remarkably congruent set of ideals—would be even tempted to speak of pedagogical techniques or methods that can be employed in this great context. Instead they would say that it is a matter less of what the teacher does than of what she *is*. Though every healer is wounded and every teacher more or less ignorant, we are advised to get on with our own development, not least in the interests of those we may influence. No one makes this point more forcibly than C. G. Jung:

No one can train the personality unless he has it himself. And it is not the child, but only the adult, who can achieve personality as the fruit of a full life directed to this end. The achievement of personality means nothing less than optimum development of the whole individual human being. It is impossible to foresee the endless variety of conditions that have to be fulfilled. A whole lifetime, in all its biological, social, and spiritual aspects, is needed. Personality is the supreme realization of the innate idiosyncrasy of a living being. It is an act of high courage flung in the face of life, the absolute affirmation of all that constitutes the individual, the most successful adaptation to the universal conditions of existence coupled with the greatest possible freedom for self-determination. To educate a man to *this* seems to me no light matter.

(CW 17, para. 289)

No teacher needs to be told that little in the way of important stages of lifelong development can be taught to youngsters, and the sooner any of us begins to see his or her life in a larger perspective the better. But especially important is it for the teacher herself, looking both backward and forward, to see some of the patterns of the unfolding of meaning in life: this cannot but help in subtle ways to influence the teacher's guidance of her charges.

9

THE RELEVANCE OF
PERSONALITY

If we go with the long-standing (though often neglected) tradition of human happiness as, in its fullest and most fruitful conception, long-term living well, living up to the best possibilities that human nature allows, living optimally right across the range of our potentiality, then it will behoove us to look more closely at what is meant by this range, by the manifold accommodations and built-in readinesses of the human organism—which is to say, the ensouled body, the spirited animal, or the embodied psyche.

One way of doing this is by developing a typology of the principal kinds of human values, which can then be consulted in the way of a checklist. How well are we doing? Which ones are we neglecting—to the detriment of our human economy? We have already glanced at two such value typologies. But now let us try another tack, which is that of examining some ways of conceiving how we function, attending both to differences and to similarities among human beings. Concern with differences will constitute a reminder that any theory we have of how we can be happy must apply to a wide spectrum of kinds of human beings.

There are, of course, a number of ways of considering this topic. Thus there is gender difference: was there ever a human culture that did not incorporate some deep-seated beliefs about what the appropriate life is for women and for men? Probably equally ancient is the consideration given to the different "stations" people occupy in their culture. For instance the eighth century BC epics, the *Iliad* and the *Odyssey*, tell us a great deal about the Homeric conception of a good life—and the bad—but their concern is almost entirely with the warrior class and more particularly with the leaders, the kings among warriors. Call the roll of the epic characters and it will be quickly apparent that it is a list of the kings and princes of Ithaca, Mycenae, Sparta, Pylos, Troy, and so on. No doubt our mental camera pans the battlefield and vaguely notices the ordinary foot soldiers, the archers, the arms-bearers and so on, but we focus in upon Achilles, Patroclos, Aias, Odysseus, Nestor, Hector, Paris, and others whose names are almost as famous today as they were way back then. (And to some extent on Helen, Penelope, and other noble women.) From the Homeric poetry we gradually build a composite sense of what it is to live well. For instance, there is beauty of face and body: thus Achilles was praised as tall and handsome. But of enormous importance is physical strength and guile in men. One isn't a leader at all without being the best of fighters in hand-to-hand combat. Thus part of what it is to lead the good life is having exceptional strength and agility, specifically that which has to do with throwing the spear, striking out and fending off with the sword and shield, clobbering with battle-ax, drawing a bead with the bow and arrow, and running. To win in battle is a great joy, both in thus living for another day, and for the ego in this fierce competition for honor and glory. But the soldiers are also shown to be sorrowful, for the losses of their friends and companions-in-arms, for losses in prestige, but also in their longing for home and the quieter joys of family feasts, hunting, story-telling around the fire, the company of wives, concubines, and children.

Doubtless it is somewhat the same with the common men, but this is the Age of Heroes, and it is the heroes we attend to, almost as if there were no such thing as happiness for the ordinary person—certainly no such thing as living well, which is to say on a grand scale—by the standards of the time.

Beyond the determining force of the social hierarchy, there is the matter of who tells the stories, who (later) writes the books. We know nothing of Homer—not even whether he is singular or plural, and someone suggested he was a woman!—but we know something of what Homer thought about a life so largely taken up with fighting, both for the fighters and for the women and children back home or behind the walls.

Nothing in the *Iliad* is more touching—and revealing of the universality of certain feelings, even though made more common by the prevalence of war—than these words Homer composed for a young wife:

> Dear husband, you died young and left me your widow alone in the palace. Our child is still tiny. The child you and I, crossed by fate, had together. I think he will never grow up ... For not in your bed did you die, holding my hand and speaking to me prudent words which forever, night and day, as I weep, might live in my memory.
>
> (Weil, 1983: 241)

We do not, much of the time, know how typical was the view of this or that writer. Yet it takes no great astuteness to guess that when Plato or Aristotle praised a life containing much time and leisure for the intensest intellectual deliberation, they were speaking for a tiny minority of the people of their societies—nor did they pretend otherwise.

But in a more complex age, such as that of Elizabethan England, the poet may help us to see people quite different from the kings, heroes, and intellectuals. Thus Falstaff takes for himself, a life-enjoying libertine, an unofficial view of honor that doubtless was shared by the rag-a-tag soldiers he led into battle: Shakespeare has the roistering Falstaff, now cast in the unlikely role of warrior on a battlefield where high patriotism and honor are everywhere the motives for courage, deliver a soliloquy. Prince Hal has just exited on his line, "Why, thou owest God a death."

> *Falstaff* 'Tis not due yet; I would be loath to pay him before his day. What need I be so forward with him that calls not on me? Well, 'tis no matter; honour pricks me on. Yea, but how if honour prick me off when I come on? How then? Can honour set to a leg? No. Or an arm? No. Or take away the grief of a wound? No. Honour hath no skill in surgery then? No. What is honour? A word. What is in that word honour? Air; a trim reckoning! Who hath it? He that died o' Wednesday. Doth he feel it? No. Doth he hear it? No. 'Tis insensible then? Yea, to the dead. But will [it] not live more with the living? No. Why? Detraction will not suffer it. Therefore, I'll none of it. Honour is a mere scutcheon: and so ends my catechism.
>
> *(Henry IV*, Part I, Act V, scene I)

And for this and other reasons, honor is no longer much esteemed in 20th century lists of virtues, at least in the post-industrial nations of the West. (See Berger, 1983.)

In other ages and places, we have literary accounts of the splendors of life possible to the courtier (and courtesan), the wily diplomat, the merchant of fabulous affluence, but also of the wondrous power and satisfaction of the prophet calling down warnings of dire fate upon the multitudes within sound of his voice.

Yet these powers and joys are set at naught by still other accounts, those describing the life and wisdom of Lao-Tse, Confucius, and Gautama Siddhartha, all of whom exemplified in their own way of living, we are given to think, the sage advice of their winged words, which may speak to our condition or *sometimes* speak to it—or to some of us more than others.

Just as one does not have to be a cultural relativist in order to recognize that one's culture (and subcultures) affect both the form and content of the moral life, so one need not be an individual relativist in order to recognize that temperament too affects ethical, aesthetic, and other value experiences and judgments. Temperament in turn is affected by, or has as some of its aspects, one's age, gender, and body type, and in turn these seem to have something by no means trivial to do with one's values.

Take age. At the very least, it is obvious that a child of three, an early teenager, a 30-year-old, one near retirement age, and again someone in the final stage of long life tend to have different interests, different matters of concern, different problems to focus upon, and all of these will influence values. Elsewhere we have glanced at such developmental theories as those of Erikson and Loevinger and remarked some of the differences of life's stages.

Most people, both scholars on the subject and those of us who speak only from "common sense," believe that there are interesting differences between men and women in the area of values. Few if any gender differences in this respect are such that one can legitimately speak of what all men and all women are like, but that females on the average tend one way and males another is very commonly accepted. For instance, one researcher of school and playground activity has noticed that boys spend a lot of time in their game activity arguing about rules, but rarely let such arguments, no matter how vehement, break up the game. Girls are said, on the other hand, not to argue nearly as much in that way, but when disputes arise the game will often be abandoned, presumably lest personal relationships be endangered (Janet Lever's 1976 study, cited in Gilligan 1982: 9–11). Many people believe that girls and women tend to be more interested in personal relationships than abstract matters, with boys and men often tending in the opposite direction. Males are frequently described as more inclined, females less inclined, toward aggression, directed either at others or at things. (For example, little boys seem to take particular glee, oftentimes, at knocking down a castle built of sand or blocks. Is this related to adult warfare?)

Perhaps a majority of those who accept such differences go on to attribute them at least in part, but perhaps as a whole, to social learning, whereas not a few, especially biologists, believe them to be innate, or at the very least believe that there are such innate propensities.

As to body type as a determinant of or influence upon values—that is much less widely accepted, but a fair number of people have gone along with William Sheldon (1954) and his classification of mesomorphs (large muscles), endomorphs (rounded physique), ectomorphs (slender, even wiry bodies), with corresponding differences in interests, dispositions, and behavioral tendencies. Still others believe that a typology of personalities obtains among humans, whether or not these correlate with physical build.

To many minds, there is something immediately suspect about taking personality or temperament seriously. It is not that there aren't idiosyncrasies among individuals—indeed, there are far too many of them—but they are surely not to be dignified by any claim to take them into account in a study of values. And yet no less a psychologist and philosopher than William James shocked the learned world when in 1907 he claimed in his important work, *Pragmatism*, that temperament must not be ignored as we strive to understand the differences in philosophies.

> The history of philosophy is to a great extent that of a certain clash of human temperaments. Undignified as such a treatment may seem to some of my colleagues, I shall have to take account of this clash and explain a good many of the divergences of philosophers by it. Of whatever temperament a professional philosopher is, he tries, when philosophizing, to sink the fact of his temperament. Temperament is no conventionally recognized reason, so he argues

impersonal reasons only for his conclusions. Yet his temperament really gives him a stronger bias than any of his more strictly objective premises. It loads the evidence for him one way or the other, making for a more sentimental or a more hard-hearted view of the universe, just as this fact or that principle would. He trusts his temperament. Of course I am talking here of positively marked men, men of radical idiosyncracy, who have set their stamp and likeness on philosophy and figure in its history. Plato, Locke, Hegel, Spencer are such temperamental thinkers. Most of us have, of course, no very definite intellectual temperament, we are a mixture of opposite ingredients, each one present very moderately . . . . But the one thing that has counted so far in philosophy is that a man should see things, see them straight in his own peculiar way, and be dissatisfied with any opposite way of seeing them.

(James 1907: 6–9)

James went on to say:

Now the particular differences of temperament that I have in mind in making these remarks is one that has counted in literature, art, government, and manners as well as in philosophy. In manners we find formalists and free-and-easy persons. In government, authoritarians and anarchists. In literature, purists or academicals, and realists. In art, classics and romantics . . . . In philosophy we have a very similar contrast expressed in a pair of terms, "rationalist" and "empiricist," "empiricist" meaning your lover of facts in all their crude variety, "rationalist" meaning your devotee to abstract and eternal principles.

(James 1907: 9)

Here James was leading up to his famous distinction between the tough- and tender-minded, which though it has passed into our language has got oddly distorted from its original meaning. In "The Sentiment of Rationality," where he put forward the amazing claim that we recognize a rational conclusion through a certain feeling, he went on to argue that:

Idealism will be chosen by a man of one emotional constitution, materialism by another . . . . To say then that the universe essentially is thought, is to say that I myself, potentially at least, am all. There is no radically alien corner, but an all-prevading intimacy . . . [Materialists] sicken at a life wholly constituted of intimacy. There is an overpowering desire at moments to escape personality, to revel in the action of forces that have no respect for our ego, to let the tides flow, even though they flow over us.

(James 1956: 89–90)

Now "temperament" is, all by itself, a somewhat vague word, which has the effect both of seeming innocuous in a serious argument and also relatively unhelpful in our pursuit of the reasons for human variability in value preferences, aversions, and indifference. What is needed is something rather more definite and specific, something in between the assertion that each person is absolutely unique and, what is little better, that there is a bewilderingly large group of classes or types of such personalities, even though, by taking into account a large number of qualities, it would be fairly easy to generate such. Doubtless the most ancient typology of temperaments or humors is the fourfold one of sanguine, choleric, phlegmatic, and melancholic, but this, interesting though it continues to be, suffers from being based on a hopelessly outdated physiology having to do with the four chief fluids of the body. Even so, one can certainly recognize these as good descriptors of one's acquaintances, even though others may seem to fall outside these prevailing moods.

Any attempt to get along with only two types is doomed to failure. James's own "tough-minded" and "tender-minded" classification is not at all bad in describing philosophies, but it does not tell us much in other respects. Wilhelm Ostwald's "classical" and "romantic" is similarly limited.

However, the personality typology of C. G. Jung, in having a considerable amount of "face validity" or plausibility, and in remaining manageable in the number of categories it provides, without serious oversimplification, and in being applicable to whole personalities, and not just limited aspects thereof escapes this limitation.

As we have seen, Jung begins by distinguishing attitudes from functions. An attitude, for Jung, is "a readiness of the psyche to act or react in a certain way" (CW 6, para. 687). In the present instance what one is considered to act or react to is: objects. The process of internalizing the objects of experience is in this system called introverting. The opposite attitude affirms the importance of the object as something that properly belongs outside, in the environment, which is called extroverting. Every person frequently introverts and extroverts, but, it is said, we differ with respect to our easier, more favored attitude, which gives us the two basic types: introvert and extrovert. (It is now often forgotten that this classification began with Jung, so common has it become, but other users of the terminology usually assign somewhat different meanings to the key words than did their coiner.) For Jung, the sociability of the extrovert and the more withdrawn tendency of the introvert are by-products of the way each regards the objects and relations of the outside world: directly, head-on for the one; indirectly, by way of one's own internal monitor, for the other. In a crude simplification, the extrovert sees the tree while the introvert observes himself seeing the tree.

As we have seen earlier, in Jung's account of psychic functions, the sensation type likes things that are concrete, eschewing abstraction and the imaginative. He rather dotes on details, for instance being able to show how something (an engine, an inventory, a stew) is put together, what it consists in. He tends to have an eye for detail, and enjoys citing facts and figures. He is impatient with the intuitive's "Cloud 9" ideas and quickly wants to get the discussion down to earth.

Contrariwise, the intuitive quickly grows impatient with whatever happens to be the case and rushes on to consideration of how it might be otherwise. As in Ezra Pound's title, his motto is *Make it New*, for he has little tolerance of routine, repetition, and tried and true practicality. With Whitehead he will think that it is more important that a proposition be interesting than that it be true.

It is easy enough to conclude, as we once again turn more specifically to implications for values, that the thinker especially prizes ideas and their orderly arrangement, and the capacity to deal with intellectual matters; the feeler prizes sensitivity and sensibility, and niceties of value judgment; the senser prizes practicality, usefulness, and good, solid reality; and the intuiter prizes change, difference, even the "far out" and whatever offers an alternative to accepted ways.

Jung called the axis on which thinking and feeling are located that of judgment, whereas he called "perceptual" the axis along which the other two functions are placed. This immediately suggests that both the sensation and intuitive types, "opposite" as they are in so many ways, share a tendency to content themselves with the way things are or might be, apart from making any final judgment upon their worth; whereas the opposite judging types continually appraise objects, the one in terms of criteria for the true, the other in terms of criteria (not necessarily made explicit, much less systematized) for the good. This way of putting it suggests very strongly that the whole subject of ethics would tend to be dismissed or ruled out as uninteresting by the two kinds of perceptual personalities. As Jung puts it in one place:

> Just as the world of appearances can never become a moral problem
> for the man who merely senses it, the world of inner images is never
> a moral problem for the intuitive. For both of them it is an aesthetic
> problem, a matter of perception, a "sensation."
>
> (*CW* 6, para. 658)

But, using the word "moral" in a broader sense, nearly in the way "ethical" is used in this work, he writes of the sensation type that "His whole aim is concrete enjoyment and his morality is oriented accordingly. Indeed, true enjoyment has its own unselfishness and willingness to make sacrifices" (*CW* 6, para. 606). He goes on to add that such a one is by no means always "just sensual or gross," for he is more likely to be highly discriminating and refined in his choice among objects found to yield pleasure.

If the intuitive too is likely to be somewhat dismissive of most cut-and-dried moralizing, nevertheless, as Jung writes, he too "has his own characteristic morality, which consists in a loyalty to his vision and involuntary submission to its authority" (*CW* 6, para. 613).

Finally, no one can be without ethical preferences. In some ways, the most important fact about any of us is what we regard as of most worth, of the highest importance—which is to say, of the greatest value. If in the case of the intuitive (taken in this, as in all our generalizations about these types, to mean the one who is very strongly characterizable in these terms) his "Consideration for the welfare of others is weak . . . He has equally little regard for their convictions and ways of life, and on this account he is often put down as an immoralist and unscrupulous adventurer" (*CW* 6, para 613), it is still the case that he tends to have enormous respect for creativity, for freshness of insight and outlook. The thinking type too, as is notably the case with those psychological and philosophical theorists about morality and ethics, may be far more interested in working out a tight and yet comprehensive account of how best to define the terms within this type of discourse, and to detail the criteria for a sound judgment, than in joining a good cause in behalf of the social welfare.

Thinking in such cases is useful in getting a fix upon the meanings of this classification, but must soon be given over for a realization that these are to a degree caricatures. Although virtually all real human beings are, on the whole, classifiable in one of these types, to a lesser or greater degree, we have also some capacity to deal with the world in terms of the other functions. The thinker whose next best developed function is sensation will turn out to be a quite different human being from she who combines thinking with intuition. Or again, the intuitive type who, purely with respect to her best developed function, is not all that much taken up with human welfare, may have for her second function feeling, which is the prime valuing function. In other words, this typology (like others) should not be used reductively, simplistically, to put people into tight boxes. Besides, Jung and others would argue that there is a meta-ethical position which says, in effect: whatever your type, your obligation as a human being is to develop your weaker attitudes and functions, to become more rounded, more comprehensive in your capabilities. We cannot, then, be excused for not having some important human virtue simply by virtue of our personality. If we say, "Since I am, as a sensation type, not much interested in possible better governments than the one we presently have . . . ," we need to be answered that this very acquiescence in our propensities is an abrogation of our developmental drives. Put still otherwise, each of the possible types constitutes a perspective on the world, including of course the world of values. Although the personality that is ours represents both the propensities and the limitations on how we comport ourselves in the world, personality is not a fixed state, but instead is modifiable, expandable. We reflective and reflexive beings can look at the personality we have (and are) with an eye to its change: in terms of the theory just given exposition, this would mean the extension of the perspectives open to us—which also means the expansion of our value repertory.

The teacher especially will think in such ways, not alone of herself, but also of her pupils, for it is obvious that such growth is high among educational goals.

10

HAPPINESS AND LIVING WELL

Aristotle begins his great work, *The Nichomachean Ethics*, in this way:

> Every art and every inquiry, and similarly every action and pursuit, is
> thought to aim at some good; and for this reason the good has been
> rightly declared to be that at which all things aim.
>
> (1094a)

He then goes on to distinguish those ends which we desire and aim at as
means to still other aims from those—or, better still, that single one—which
"we desire for its own sake (everything else being desired for the sake of
this). . . ."

After warning his reader that this very complex and difficult subject matter
does not admit of the precision that is possible in simpler affairs or in a field
like mathematics, which is prearranged, as it were, to provide exceptionally
definite and precise answers, he goes on to note that common sense has
something to say about our difficult subject of what humans want most.
Verbally, he says, "there is very general agreement; for both the general run
of men and people of superior refinement say that it is happiness, and
identify living well and doing well with being happy. . ." (1095a). However,
though all kinds of people agree on the name of this single end of life, they
disagree as to what happiness consists in. Common people "think it is some
plain and obvious thing, like pleasure, wealth, or honour . . . ." Furthermore, not being careful thinkers, they change their minds about it from time
to time, such that they think health is what brings happiness when they are
ill and wealth when they are poor. Obviously Aristotle thinks of himself as
one of those of "superior refinement," and perhaps assumes that we his
readers are equally fortunate—otherwise what would we be doing reading
him at all? In any case, he then sets out on his task, which will turn out to
be a long and difficult one, to provide a much better answer than is provided
by "some plain and obvious thing." What this is we can for the present put
off thinking about in order to explore a little that word *happiness*.

A popular dance band leader used to begin his act by rather smarmily
crooning into his microphone a question to the dancers: "Is *everybody*

happy?" This invariably brought cheers and applause from the audience, which presumably meant not only that he had asked the right question, but that the answer was Yes. Perhaps the answer to the question of what "being happy" in that way means is simply this: feeling a convivial glow of anticipation appropriate to an evening of dancing and other festivities. About a particularly pleasant time of relaxed enjoyment, of sociability among kindred persons, one might enthusiastically report that it had been a very happy occasion and that a good time was had by all. Now, a Cinderella-type ball, a Junior Prom, a party culminating the school year, or the like might indeed be both anticipated and remembered by some young people as the happiest time of the whole season. Especially if (not surprisingly) there should be an element of romance involved, such an occasion might well seem—and has often been so portrayed in novels and films—to be the very pinnacle of satisfaction. And yet it is doubtful that the happiness experienced in just such ways would be thought by many to be that good "at which all things aim." Even the most romantic and sociable of people would hesitate to cite such events—or even a whole string of them—as the aim of life.

"Well, ño," they might say in a sober moment, "that is not a life aim, but I still think of certain times like those as among the happiest moments of my life." There might well be those for whom life has been all downhill within a short time of such joyful occasions. Others, asked to think of their very happiest times, might well mention their wedding day (possibly a consequence of some such party as mentioned above) or the birth of a child, the attainment of a long aspired-to position, the gaining of some public honor or the achievement of a creative work as the pinnacle of happiness in a life reflected upon from some vantage point.

Advertisers for a time fastened upon a little formula, "Happiness is . . . :" a stuffed penguin, a bowl of cereal, a new shirt. And it is just pedantry that would make one say, "Well, that's not so much how to define happiness as something that might make a person of the appropriate age very pleased for a time." Let us then willingly grant that there are particularly happy moments but not that a good life is made up of these. At the very least, these paradigm cases may serve as touchstones for at least certain kinds of happiness so that we say, "If only I could recapture in the present what I experienced then, I would be gratified— even grateful."

But in addition to happy events, we also speak of happy friendships, happy marriages, and of the happiness brought by one's work or avocation. Thus one might say, "One of my happiest discoveries was that of gardening. It has brought me a great deal of joy ever since."

Furthermore, certain periods of a life may be singled out as particularly happy, as when it is said, "My childhood, up to the time I went away to school, was a particularly happy period." This might be followed by: "My years in boarding school were singularly unhappy—sheer misery." Or one could have equally strong feelings about one's army experience or a time of protracted illness.

Sometimes happiness is not ascribed to a single individual alone; thus there are happy friendships and marriages, where it is thought to be a shared happiness. A family may be described as happy, and also other groups, a club, working associates and collaborators, even a particular school class.

Elizabeth Telfer, who has written a fine little book called *Happiness* (1980), has distinguished several common ways of being "happy" and experiencing "happiness," each different from the others. To begin with, there is "a happy temperament or disposition." That is to say, happiness is not necessarily associated with an event or a longer period of time and may be independent of any particular occasion or external cause or reason. In short, a person may be of the kind who has a distinct propensity toward happiness. This may possibly strike a dour person, like the Duke in Browning's "My Last Duchess", as having "a heart too soon made glad." For such a one, anything at all can be the occasion for an exclamation of joy: a breath of air, a dandelion, a cherry on top of a scoop of ice cream, a pun, a glint of sunshine on the way. But perhaps most people, themselves of somewhat soberer bent, find this readiness for being pleased contagious and the person so happily endowed one to be envied as well as praised.

Then there is a "happy mood or frame of mind: feeling happy. . . ." Whether common or uncommon, then, there is a certain feeling, from the most momentary to one that is called a mood by virtue of being pervasive of the whole of a person and over a period of time. One might say, "I awoke feeling that God's in his heaven and all's right with the world. Wherever I turned things were just fine." In such a state, one is altogether likely to be predisposed to finding all kinds of things praiseworthy. Next there is the use of "happy" to be synonymous with the experience of joy or pleasantness. This is not just the disposition to feel in a certain way, but the actual occasion of happiness, something that "makes me happy." Finally, there is "happiness in life," a matter to which we will presently turn.

Occasionally there are to be encountered some persons who seem averse to happiness, who, that is, are either so inured to the unpleasant, or so suspicious or fearful of pleasure, that they seem virtually to fend off anything that promises satisfaction. There is the little joke: "She is one who enjoys poor health." Even short of neurotic masochism some people seem threatened by happiness and devise ways to explain away or forestall the occasion that conduces that way. "Oh, yes," they say of the blazing sunset, "but it will soon fade," or they will otherwise contemplate the fragility of life's gratification, or again, find the shadow lurking just to the side of the bright moment. "O rose, thou art sick," said Blake (though he himself was not of a negative cast of disposition). Or there's Winnie the Pooh's friend Eeyore.

Optimism is clearly a disposition toward happiness, not merely for the satisfaction that is taken in contemplating a happy outcome to the present state of affairs, but also because favorable expectations have a way of being a "self-fulfilling prophecy." In *Candide* Voltaire mounted a famous satire against the philosophy of Leibniz, summarized by the expression "All's for the best in this best of all possible worlds." Innocent Candide, the embodiment of this attitude, confronting a series of dreadful disasters, instantly bounces back from earthquake or plague with a cheerful reaffirmation of his conviction that even this was somehow good. But if Voltaire's is a corrective to an unjustified optimism, there is surely more to be envied in the life of an optimist than in that of a pessimist, even though there is doubtless some gratification to be taken in things having turned out to be just as bad as one had predicted. The manic-depressive personality may be regarded as one that alternates between the cheerfully optimistic and the sullenly pessimistic. Interestingly, though, there has been discovered an important positive correlation between this type of personality (short of its psychotic extent) and creativity. There is a long list of great artists whose depressed states have apparently turned out to be somehow stages of preparation for the subsequent manic-creative periods. Unfortunately, though, depression is no guarantee of a subsequent happier state, so that many depressives can realistically look forward to nothing better than a "non-depression" as the alternative to their worst-feared times, and these are just as predictive of prevailing unhappiness as cheerfulness and optimism are of the opposite.

Generally speaking, we naturally associate the state of happiness with the realization of hopes or more generally the achievement of goals we had set ourselves. "I've wanted this [object, recognition, promotion, etc.] for a long time, and now finally I've got it! Hurrah!" Still, we can be gratified by eventualities we did not particularly seek or even realize we wanted. Then, too, there is the all-too-familiar experience of the mountain peak, laboriously climbed toward, which is shrouded in fog, the hoped-for view obscured. The notorious pessimist, Arthur Schopenhauer, characteristically put it this way: either we get what we want or we fail. If we fail, we are frustrated; if we reach our goal, we learn that that is not what we wanted after all. People differ as to the frequency of that latter realization, but no one fails to experience it upon occasion: " I always thought that if ever I got to be. . . . I should have reached the summit of happiness, but now that I've done it, it somehow seems not all that great: my life is much as it was before." Still, we are goal-setting animals and the person who gives up prematurely of having hopes for the future, things she wants to accomplish, ways she wants to become, earns our disapproval. Of course it isn't necessary that the goal be extremely exalted—Prime Minister, President, chief executive officer, world-class athlete or artist, millionaire, famous doctor, lawyer, astronaut, or engineer—but we rarely fail to have some ambitions and encourage others to have such, too, for we know that part of what it is to be happy lies in achieving goals we have, more or less deliberately and consciously, set ourselves.

But at some point we also begin to realize that part of this kind of success is a matter of luck. As long ago as the ancient Greeks the two worst undeserved fates were thought to be, to be born ugly and to be born into slavery. Of course in Greek, Hebrew, and other ancient thought, such unhappy conditions were often regarded as divine punishment and therefore, to some extent at least, merited, if only by the neglect in ritual and sacrifice of some god or other. The famous disputes Job had with his friends had to do with their supposition that the disasters that happened to this famously upright man must necessarily have been by way of punishment from on high—for anything to the contrary seemed to them to deny the omnipotence and beneficence of God. But Job himself and many another have maintained that there is unmerited unhappiness, just as there is happiness that one can take no credit for: sheer good fortune, the smiling demigod. As athletes sometimes say about a victory in which they played poorly: "It wasn't pretty, but we'll take it anyway."

Whether as a result of luck or as a matter of just deserts, it takes no argument to show that a life marked by major disasters is hardly a candidate for a happy one. Sometimes people will claim that their lives have been happy—up to now—largely because of their having averted such large-scale misfortunes, but such a life can also be a singularly lacklustre one, with little in the way of either achievement or pleasure. Shall we say, then, that it is only the individual person who can judge whether her life deserves the characterization of "happy"? Certainly in most ways each of us is in the most privileged position to make a judgment on that score, if for no other reason than that nobody else is at all likely to know as much about what that life is and has been like, what has been undergone, what experienced, what pains and pleasures realized.

Still, it is not hard to imagine wanting to dispute somebody's claim to be quite pleased with her life, on either of at least two grounds. First we may strongly suspect, and have evidence to support our suspicion, that a certain person in saying, "I am very pleased with my life—I count it happy," is exaggerating the pleasant qualities. For instance, she may quite recently have come onto a smooth patch which, perhaps, makes her forgetful of how many hardships have preceded this time. Or again we may decide that the claimant has asked so little of her life that getting what she wanted still didn't amount to much in comparison with persons whose similar claim we would tend to agree with. Imagine a teacher deciding that the school year just past has been a successful one on the ground that half the students learned the times tables up to 3. Unless the pupils are very young, we might legitimately say that the teacher had set her sights so low as to make success practically guaranteed. So too with happiness.

One of the continuing points made in this work is that value realization is not simply a matter of getting what you have specified as desirable; often it is far more a learning to want more than has been one's wont. Given two students neither of whom can sing "Mary had a little lamb", they still may differ importantly if just one of them wants to learn. The assumption that there is experienced value in learning to sing a simple song—especially as it may pave the way to singing better songs and even aid in the appreciation of others' singing—is surely not hard to support. Although it is possible to learn to sing (and to achieve other skills) without specifically desiring so to do, who can doubt that the desire is altogether likely to expedite the achievement?

However, it may be objected that as one increases one's wants, one thereby increases the possibility of frustration, and this cannot be denied. But of course it is not just a matter of increasing wants, no matter what they are. For starters, they should much preferably be realistically grounded. But beyond that, they should be such that there is good reason to believe that they may yield satisfactions that are not just trivial. Generally, what teachers hope for their pupils to learn, by way of gaining access to new or deeper values, are goals based upon at least their own experience and very likely the testimony of others. Although it may turn out that a young person, having given a certain kind of value a reasonable try, may decide against building that kind of value into his own repertory, at least that exclusion has not been made, in such an instance, by default.

Happiness in life, then, appears to be a comprehensive intrinsic value (that also often serves as instrumental to other intrinsic values). Typically, in our own instances, it is possible to give a responsible assessment and answer to such a question as "Would you count your life, taken as a whole, as a more than ordinarily happy one?" But the answer would be corroborated if others who knew the person well said that they agreed, this serving to correct any exaggeration or any paucity of goals and wants in the subject.

But now it is time to ask a question that has been debated for at least 2,500 years: is happiness the same as pleasure, so that, for instance, what we are claiming in calling a life happy is that it has had a substantial margin of pleasures over pains? It surely is the case that many people, looking for a way to make their lives happier, think first of increasing the amount of pleasure in it, and this seems justified. And in turn, if we are looking at some patterns of values in people's lives, we would probably not be tempted to count as happy those that seem unusually low on the side of experienced pleasures. But there is a real question as to whether pleasures derived from quite different activities (and passivities) are commensurable. Some have thought they are.

Most famously, Jeremy Bentham in the early 19th century worked out what he called a "hedonic calculus" on the assumption that it is theoretically possible to assign to any given experience a certain number of units (called "hedons") of pleasure. Without going into detail, it can be acknowledged that the calculus is fairly complex, so that, for instance pleasures are quantified not only by intensity (which might conceivably be measured by some sort of neurological gauge), but also by their relative absence of compensating pains (simultaneous with or subsequent to the pleasure), duration, and so on. John Stuart Mill a generation later tried to save this theory from the indignant criticisms of those who labelled it "piggish philosophy" (since a piggish life might, under favorable circumstances, pile up an impressive number of pleasure units) by asserting that some pleasures are simply qualitatively better than others. Critics were not slow, in turn, to point out that this change in the theory requires introducing other criteria than pleasure itself into the reckoning, in order to justify the belief that Socrates would be right in preferring his life of contemplative dialogue to one of swinish wallowing. Mill's answer was, though, that you can tell which kind of life is better by asking a person who knows both sides. The pig is of course disqualified, but even a relatively ascetic philosopher knows something about the competitor's values. It is not clear, though, what Mill would do with the undoubted cases of persons who have sampled the intellectual values but found them wanting in comparison with a heavy emphasis upon sensuality.

On the whole it seems more sensible simply not to put all that much weight upon pleasures, making them synonymous with values. Surely there are a number of experiences which have been sought and attained to the gratification of some person which have, on a reasonable account, required a considerable deprivation of pleasures. But of course that in turn depends upon what counts as a pleasure. If the term is so widened as to take in all forms of gratification, including for instance the suffering of martyrs and the sacrifice of all manner of creature comforts in the interest of creating a masterpiece, the pleasure theory wins out. But it seems far closer to common usage to say, for instance, that though this or that person's life has been relatively short on pleasures for instance, those associated with warmth, food, drink, sexuality, security, affection, and commendation—it still may be rightly called a happy one because of the notable achievements (involving of course satisfaction therein) that the person reached. One can think of famous artists, scientists, philosophers, and other creative types, who have had lives marked both by great achievements and by an abundance of mundane pleasures, and these would have to be counted as happier still than the agonized spirits such as Beethoven, Newton, Nietzsche, and Van Gogh, but it is hard not to believe that the latter company also had lives that they were so pleased with by virtue of what they were able to create that they merit classification with the happy.

This emphasis upon achievement brings us, then, back to Aristotle and his belief that all people aim at *eudaimonia*, which though almost always translated as "happiness" meant something rather different from what most people have meant by this word. Such expressions as "living well," "possessed of true well-being," "truly fortunate and well-off" have been thought better to translate *eudaimonia* than "happiness." Aristotle believed that you could tell what people meant by "the best end of living" by seeing what in fact they pursue, how they live (when they are given the choice). Thus there are those who seek pleasure and others (he thought) who seek honor. But there are still others who have a more comprehensive conception of what they should seek. For Aristotle and many a later thinker, this has a lot to do with human potentiality. Put it this way, to begin with: one may complain about the present state of one's life, even though it is marked with many pleasures and a sense of accomplishment, when what is missing is that one is not living up to one's own mark, but falling short. Not only falling short but also missing out in large measure regarding certain capacities that one realizes are there, but largely lying fallow. Drawing up a kind of reckoning of one's life until now, then, one could say, in this and that respect, I fare pretty well, but I have not yet gone beyond the bare beginnings of realizing myself in this other way. Of course we all have potentialities that we are quite happy *not* to have realized: it is the others, the ones we honor but alas neglect, that make up the negative part of our own score sheet.

Many thinkers have said that these have especially to do with the distinctively human characteristics. The Greeks more than any other ancient people—and more than most modern ones—especially celebrated the functions of thinking, reasoning, being intellective—all ways of being that are possible only to the human being. It would be strange—indeed, pathetic—to find near the end of life that one had not much realized one's most noteworthy *human* possibilities. To be sure, some critics have thought that Socrates, Plato, Aristotle, and their descendants exaggerated the importance of the intellect, but then the task becomes how to give a more balanced picture of what our distinctive and admirable potentialities are. And not necessarily utterly distinctive, either, for why should we be at such exquisite pains to make ourselves so different from our cousins, the animals? Since Darwin it has been harder and harder for us to regard the human creature as completely apart from the whole world of fauna. Nietzsche said that man is the animal with red cheeks, yet we know that a dog may evince something rather like shame and embarrassment on occasion. Ernst Cassirer called man "the symbolic animal," yet there are chimpanzees who have learned to say (that is, symbolize by means of gestures, oral sounds, and the manipulation of counters) something like "Judith, bring milk." (And see Vicki Hearne, 1987, for a more subtle and searching account of animal language.) Like geese we humans have courtship rituals. And so on and on. We are differentiated from other animals primarily by our great capacity to look before and after, and inward as well as out. We reflect on where and what we have been as a set of clues to our present condition, which in turn bodes something for our future life—and death. For each child the realization that one must some day die is hard and reluctant to come by, and can by effort be kept out of mind, yet its genuine realization colors our life and not altogether darkly, for some of our accomplishments are dependent upon our consciousness of mortality.

What it is to live well differs according to a great many conditions, the time of our life, our gender, our innate and acquired personality characteristics, the culture into which we are born (or sometimes move into), our economic status, our most intimate associates, and much else. Our sudden decisions to effect a radical change in our manner of being-in-the-world may on later reflection appear as futile as Till Eulenspiegel's decision to escape the mire underfoot by lifting himself by his own pigtail. And yet we are different from the simpler animals in being able to change important aspects of our lives as a result of carefully considered decisions. If no one can succeed in simply willing to be happy or to live a blessed existence, at least the realization of some of the chief deficiencies of our life can gradually guide us if we will—toward changes, toward better realizations of our too neglected and most promising possibilities.

It is imaginable (if only just barely) that some saintly character might be found who always did his duty, never failed of fulfilling a moral obligation, was just, fair, kind, tolerant, caring—and indeed had all the celebrated moral virtues, but yet by no means had a good life. (Let us imagine we have some notion of what that means.) Now, if this were due entirely to circumstances beyond the saint's ability to alter, such as being seriously and painfully crippled or living under a tyrannical dictatorship, our appropriate response would be one of pity and sympathy. If, however, this person seemed to have been so wholly caught up in being morally good and doing the right thing that he or she had given no thought at all to the value of living well, we might try to persuade this unfortunate one to take a larger view and to see whether it might be possible to combine a devotion to duty (etc.) with living well. (No doubt there would be some conflicts, as when our ex-saint wanted to attend a concert but was torn by the realization that the time and money could be spent helping the hungry and homeless.)

Presumably by far the greater number of teachers and other educators would agree that there are value considerations beyond those we have identified as moral. If, as seems wholly obvious, we see people around us who give every evidence of living lives that are poor, mean, nasty, brutish, and short, and others who seem to be living lives that are remarkably full, interesting, stimulating, with varied types of fulfillment and satisfaction, then surely we would agree that education should be directed at increasing the likelihood that pupils will live more like the latter than the former. Naturally, no education can guarantee success, more especially on this grand scale, for, as has always been recognized, there is a large element of chance and luck in life.

Part II

THE AESTHETIC

11

THE AESTHETIC KIND
OF VALUE

Education begins with poetry, is strengthened
through proper conduct and consummated
through music.

(Confucius)

"Aesthetic" is an adjective of wide application. Most evidently, there are
aesthetic objects like pieces of music, paintings, statues, poems, plays, films,
fountains, a view from on high of the curve of a bay, a snowy peak rising into
the clouds, the pink clouds of a sunrise, a handsome face, a commanding
building that we look at, not merely use. The list is virtually endless. Even
objects we may call ugly or stark, or frightening in their vastness, may be
aesthetic objects. The British philosopher G. E. Moore, trying to think of
something that is just good-in-itself, came up with the notion of a planet too
far away for any earthling to travel to, and yet which was even more beautiful
than the most splendid scenery accessible to view: now compare this with
another such distant planet that was simply a garbage heap. The one would
be infinitely preferable to the other, a thing of beauty, good in and of itself.

And yet aesthetic objects seem *especially* to have their value in experience,
whether in imagination or in external presence to our senses. For one thing,
it is easy to think of objects that go unnoticed for their aesthetic qualities
and yet are part of a familiar environment. Think, for instance, of sitting
down to dinner with a companion, from the first so engaged in a stimulating
conversation that only after half an hour one says, "Funny thing, I only
noticed just now that this china we're eating from is exquisite." A plate is a
useful object and we are not very apt to notice usefulness except when it
fails us—the instrument that breaks, the container that leaks, the tire that
goes flat. Yet many things that are functional are also quite susceptible to
rewarding our aesthetic attention: a pen, a clock, a pewter mug, a camel-hair
coat, the engine of a train, a rug on the floor. Yet any of them may go
unnoticed in being used and perhaps semi-consciously appreciated for their
functionality. (This is not to say, however, that function is something
necessarily apart from aesthetic appeal, for if the teapot we admired for its

119

looks turns out to pour dribblingly, even its looks are somehow marred for us—unless we assign it a purely decorative place on the shelf.) One remembers a school of architecture (that *eminently* useful art) that insists upon form's following function.

Our particular interests usually determine what we attend to. The moving man trying to get a large painting through a door is not likely to pay any attention to the colors and composition of the painting itself, and the engineer at the radio station may be so concerned to adjust the sound being transmitted that he notices not at all what recording is being played.

Thus there is such a thing as an aesthetic attitude, a mental preparation by which we focus our attention in a special way. As the lights go down in a theater we tune out to a degree from the people around us and direct our attention to the stage—but, more than that, get ourselves set to see that particular kind of process that is called a play or a film, thus entering a kind of make-believe world.

Of course the adoption of an attitude is not always so deliberate as that. We may glance at the skies for a sign of possible rain and then be caught by the very sight of the skittering clouds and forget about the weather. We weren't walking in order to catch a sight of a flower, but the early spring daffodil almost forced itself upon our attention and we look at it, not probably with the eye of the botanist, but with the eye of the beholder for beholding's sake. (Which is not to say that the beauty is *in* that eye.)

These are the simple, everyday kinds of instances of "taking an aesthetic attitude." But we also have a lot to learn about directing and sustaining that attitude. For instance, we may go into the art gallery, with a determination to look appreciatively at the paintings, but find that in this case we simply do not know how—perhaps because of something unusual in our experience, such as the fact that all the paintings are of straight lines. We may turn away in disappointment or even contempt and our aesthetic attitude vanishes. We turn on our classical music station but hear atonal music for which our ear is not ready and once again our attitude changes. Or we find ourselves in a theater where a Japanese Noh play is being performed. The audience shows every sign of being enchanted, but we feel wholly left out in the cold, not being able to make head or tail of it.

The pupil confesses that she found an assigned poem boring and the teacher says, "Did you notice the strange rhythms?" No, they had not been noticed, but now that there is something unusual to attend to, just possibly the aesthetic attitude can be sustained right through all four stanzas. This does not, of course, guarantee delight and esteem, but at least one is doing what the reader must do, if the experience is to have any chance of succeeding.

Besides aesthetic objects and aesthetic attitude, there is the possible aesthetic experience itself. There is an indefinitely large number of ways in which we prize experiences, events, but the aesthetic way is one—and one which is not easy to describe. Some have described it mainly negatively, as in saying, with Kant, that it is disinterested—that is, that it is not useful toward any end outside the experience itself. But this seems neither a necessary nor sufficient condition for aesthetic experience of value, and besides it is not very descriptive of the experience as felt.

Yet it is not hard to point to an example. One kind of case is that in which one's mood pleasantly covers practically everything one looks at and hears, as expressed in the old musical comedy song, "O, what a beautiful morning"; then whatever one looks at seems to glow in a particularly wondrous way. But this is excessively subjective for our purposes, so let's turn to a different kind of experience say, one in which we close a novel we have just finished and have the sense that we have been guided in our imagination by one who writes vividly, even melodically, with a keen eye for the succeeding scenes in which well drawn characters act out some parts of their lives within a unified plot that consummates for us a sense of having extended our awareness of the human condition. Now we may say, not what a beautiful morning, but what a beautiful book. Or think instead of the last time one was caught up and enraptured by a song. Or, having driven around a bend in the road, presented with the sight of a mountain lake that makes one catch one's breath.

These are the kinds of experiences that we label as aesthetic. John Dewey put it this way: whereas all of our conscious lives are a stream of experience, from time to time we have occasion to say, "Now *that* was an experience." (See Dewey 1934: 35 and chapter III generally.) What seems pointed to is above all a vividness that characterizes the felt experience itself, permeating the whole of it, marking it off from the experiential flow more generally and diffusely. Typically, some of the vividness will have to do with sights and sounds, the sensory elements, now taken not as mere signals of something else (as a traffic light is) but as something there to be attended to for itself and enjoyed. Further, the experience will in such a case have a distinctive and compelling form—temporal, spatial, or both—but especially important, psychologically. That is, the experience will have a peculiar coherence in its structure. It will at once invite and reward the aesthetic attentiveness we have already noticed. (For an elaboration of this point, see Jarrett 1957: chapter 7.)

If this will do, at least for the present, to pick out and very briefly characterize a *kind* of experience, we have found yet another use of the adjective *aesthetic*, so that it modifies the names of objects, a certain kind of attitude, and a distinctive sort of experience.

Like perhaps all categories of experience, this one shades into other kinds, rather than having sharp edges. Sometimes we would be hard put to say whether a given experience was primarily or only secondarily aesthetic, the other component being intellectual, moral, sensual, or even self-satisfaction. Or again we may argue as to which qualities, if any, are absolutely essential to the aesthetic. Take the case of the sensory element. The poet Edna St Vincent Millay wrote a poem that begins:

Euclid alone has looked on beauty bare.

But, we might ask, can beauty ever be bare of the qualities of the senses? Is not geometry too bare, in being so exceedingly rational, to be called beautiful or even aesthetic? "Elegance" is an adjective that seems to belong to the realm of the aesthetic, and it is dearly loved by mathematicians, who will scorn a proof that is awkward and contains superfluous elements—even though it truly does *prove* its theorem. Alfred North Whitehead, having announced that "What education has to impart is an intimate sense for the power of ideas, for the beauty of ideas, and for the structure of ideas," gets around to discussing the second of these three:

> the most austere of all mental qualities; I mean the sense for style. It is an aesthetic sense, based on admiration for the direct attainment of a foreseen end, simply and without waste. Style in art, style in literature, style in science, style in logic, style in practical execution have fundamentally the same aesthetic qualities, namely, attainment and restraint.
>
> (Whitehead 1932: 19)

This *style* Whitehead praises (and exhibits) seems ever so much like what has here been called "elegance." A little later he calls it "the ultimate morality of the mind" where his accent falls upon *mind*. And as he says, it applies to logic, science, and practical matters no less than to the fine arts. Yet though it is not feasible to deny to elegance of style an aesthetic quality, surely for what we normally want to call an aesthetic experience style by itself (if such can be imagined) is a little too austere. We want some other feelings present too; for instance, we may express our reservations about a violinist who plays with consummate elegance but is somewhat lacking on the emotional side. Similarly one may be a consummate draughtsman, but too cold for comfort—or a more commodious delight. It seems then that a variety of kinds of experience may have some aesthetic component. Sinking into a hot tub on a chilly day is participation in a fairly vivid sensual experience, but we may hesitate to call it an instance of a genuine aesthetic experience for lacking other qualities, such as form.

Perhaps an absolutely *aesthetic* experience (with nothing non-aesthetic involved) is just as much of a will-o'-the-wisp as a purely intellective experience, as "doing science" is sometimes said to be when it is described as "value-free." But as Polanyi and many another recent authors have pointed out, the scientist who did not have a strong interest in how his investigations turn out and who was free of a feeling of satisfaction in having made a discovery would be such a scientist as was never found on sea or land. Yet where there is interest and feeling, there is value.

Purity aside, there can be no doubt that there are experiences marked by a strong and (once we know it for what it is) an undeniable aesthetic quality. Now if, as is surely the case, some people's lives are richer in regard to that strand of experience called *aesthetic* than others, the question naturally arises as to how this good way of being can be increased and heightened in you or me, him or her—or whole classrooms and schools of persons.

At least one thing is clear: aesthetic education must start early, the earlier the better. Educational theorists from Plato to John Dewey have emphasized the importance of song, dance, and story-telling in early childhood. In the 18th century, Rousseau, appalled by the spectacle of the stiltedness and artificiality in Parisian society, wanted to take his Emile into the country, where a great deal of his life would be out-of-doors and where there would be no pressure to rush into reading and abstraction. (The healthy child is by nature merry, he said over and over: let him alone and his merriment, natural curiosity, and goodness will prevail.)

If by and large adults work, children play, and in playing develop many of the capacities that will ease them into adolescence and adulthood.

> The little child spends many hours and much energy in vocal *play*. It is far more agreeable to carry on this play with others . . . but the little child indulges in language play even when he is alone . . . . Internal speech, fragmentary or continuous, becomes the habitual accompaniment of his active behaviour and the occupation of his idle hours.
>
> (De Laguna 1927: 307)

There are such games as cards, checkers and other board games, and the games of bodily movement from hide-and-seek onward, but perhaps even more important are the games of the imagination: the "Let's pretend" and "What if . . . " games wherein the very rules and limits of the game are as much up for suggestion and negotiation as the plot and characters. Children *naturally* play in such ways, but they also *learn* to play, and some learn—in this way as in all others—better than others, perhaps for having better teachers. As all but the chronically inattentive parents know, children like the regularities of ritual and often insist upon faithful repetition, as in their favorite stories; but no less do they like, or come to like, innovation. The impending visit to the dentist may arouse some anxiety that is in part "handled" through playing the game "Going to the Dentist!" (Feminist mothers will insist that the little girl be assigned the role of dentist and doctor as often as that of nurse or hygienist.) But if such are "realistic" games, others are and should be "fantastic," perhaps at first modeled on the tales they've heard of talking dogs, cats, and tigers, but gradually edging into space travel and Never-never Land adventure. The "props" needed for such games are easy to come by, from the pan cupboard as easily as the toy closet. Gradually, the imagination soars higher and higher and the child becomes more and more daring in playing new roles; but at the same time, children learn something about how even in fantasy there are certain conventions of consistency: if you've been able to fly by wagging your arms, you continue to be able to do this unless some deterrent intervenes. Many interpersonal skills and constraints emerge: there are the crises to be faced, such as with the poor loser who wants to pick up his marbles and go home, or the one who wants all the best parts and doesn't let the other have a turn. But more to the point of the present context, the imagination exercised in play is continuous with the directed imagination of free drawing, spontaneous choreography, and story-telling—either from books or in invention. Ludicrous situations inevitably develop and get recognized in laughter. Aesthetic empathy is employed and advanced in both the kinesthetic and emotional ways.

Bruno Bettelheim, who in his book *Love is Not Enough* made it clear that his approach to education is not a "soft" one, is still an important influence in his insistence upon the great educational significance of fairy tales and of play.

> From a child's play we can gain understanding of how he sees and construes the world—what he would like it to be, what his concerns and problems are. Through his play he expresses what he would be hard pressed to put into words . . . . Even when he engages in play partly to fill empty moments, what he chooses to play at is motivated by inner processes, desires, problems, anxieties.
>
> (Bettelheim 1987: 36)

The entire essay is very well worth reading.

"Man is only free when he plays," said Schiller, thinking even more of the adult than the child—free because play by definition is a freely chosen activity and one pursued for the satisfactions taken in the very processes, rather than dictated by external ends.

Though sometimes solitary, play is often a social activity. But dreaming—unless it be the shared day-dreaming that may be part of imaginative play—is a wholly introverted process. The child encouraged to attend to her dreams gets thereby acquainted with a purely spontaneous part of her psyche that can easily tie in with play, story, or just dream-swapping conversation. Dreams may be recognized as being gifts, something that happens to one, rather than made-up stories or spectacles. And yet they are one's own and thus represent a creative capacity that everyone wants to acknowledge as by no means the least of his powers, and sources of achievement.

In early childhood education, teachers commonly encourage children to draw freely and expressively, but how many do so musically? And yet children are no less imaginative in the construction of little tunes than they are in their little pictures. Furthermore the two can be combined. Robert Walker has done cross-cultural studies that show that children "provide drawings that faithfully represent, in visual metaphors, auditory movement in the basic parameters of sound: frequency, wave shape, amplitude, and duration." There is even surprising consistency in these respects increasing with age (Walker 1988: 218).

Just as with adults, child art activity is part invention, part performance, part appreciation. There are tunes that just get made up, the tunes of "Mary had a little lamb" and "Twinkle, twinkle, little star" there to be learned and sung. Dance may be purely improvisational or it may be mime, as of the ponderous elephant gallumphing along. Wonderful nursery rhymes are to be had by the bushelful, but rhyming afresh is an art within the compass of even quite a young child who may discover with merriment that his own name, "Fred", has a distinct similarity to "sled" and "bread." With crayons the child may work within the outlines provided by a copy book, but at times will want to start with only a blank sheet of paper. But the child likes too to see the drawings and paintings reproduced in a book, a source of wonder.

What, then, should be the place of the arts in schooling? Let us follow for a bit the lead of the late Sir Herbert Read who gave a radical answer to this question: "Art should be the basis of education." He meant just that (Read 1961: 1). He hastens to explain what he admits is, so starkly stated, something of a paradox, and this means giving his conception of the two key terms "education" and "art":

> The purpose of education [in a democracy] can then only be to develop, at the same time as the uniqueness, the social consciousness or reciprocity of the individual.
>
> (p. 5)

To him this means a continual concern with a

> psychological "orientation" for which the education of the aesthetic sensibility is of fundamental importance. It is a form of education of which only rudimentary traces are found in the education systems of the past . . . . It must be understood from the beginning that what I have in mind is not merely "art education" as such, which should more properly be called visual or plastic education: the theory to be put forward embraces all modes of self-expression, literary and poetic (verbal) no less than musical or aural, and forms an integral approach to reality which should be called *aesthetic* education—the education of those senses upon which consciousness, and ultimately the intelligence and judgment of the human individual, are based.
>
> (p. 7)

Finally he makes the point that "Education is the fostering of growth"—as John Dewey never tired of saying and describing—and that growth, except in its purely physical meaning:

is only made apparent in expression—audible or visible signs and symbols. Education may therefore be defined as the cultivation of modes of expression—it is teaching children and adults how to make sounds, images, movements, tools and utensils. A man who can make such things well is a well-educated man. If he can make good sounds, he is a good speaker, a good musician, a good poet; if he can make good images, he is a good painter or sculptor; if good movement, a good dancer or labourer; if good tools or utensils, a good craftsman. All faculties, of thought, logic, memory, sensibility and intellect, are involved in such processes, and no aspect of education is excluded in such processes . . . . The aim of education is therefore the creation of artists—of people efficient in the various modes of expression.

(p. 11)

To those who think that this involves a total neglect of science, it should be explained that earlier Sir Herbert has said that in his view there is no opposition between science and art, the former being the explanation, the latter the representation of the same reality.

Underlying his whole conception of his belief that aesthetic education, so far from being a frill, is indeed the very basis of education is C. G. Jung's classification of the fundamental psychic functions of mankind: sensation, intuition, feeling, and thinking. To the development of each of these functions aesthetic education contributes. All these functions are essential, but in some ways the one most basic is the one named "sensation", which is chiefly a matter of the senses.

Education of the senses is of course nothing new, either in theory or in practice. Pestalozzi gained his fame—to mention just one example from history—by his insistence upon the importance of taking children out of doors, there to help them see and hear—yes, and smell, taste, and feel. No teacher, when confronted with the question of whether education and training of our senses is important can but insist that it is; but how much of this conviction carries through into actual instruction? Sensing—that is, noticing and attending to the sensory qualities around one, developing a sensitivity to their nuances, their relations and combinations—is something the average teacher perhaps feels untrained to teach and perhaps is herself ill-equipped by personal experience of that kind as well. But registering this color and shade, this sound and echo, as Read tells us, is not yet enough without some expression thereof on the part of the perceiver.

Early on, Aristotle was cited in behalf of how we all by nature want to *know*. He went on to say: "An indication of this is the delight we take in our senses; for even apart from their usefulness, they are loved for themselves . . ." (*Metaphysics*, A, 980a). One teacher who specializes in natureawareness education (Cornell 1979) offers five tenets (not rules) for good nature-guiding with children:

1   "Teach less, and share more." By sharing, he means describing his own
    feelings in the presence of, say, a hemlock tree about how he wonders
    that such a tree manages to find nutrients in rocky soil and fierce winter
    winds, and how he "respects" the tree for its hardiness.
2   "Be receptive." This means a sensitive tuning into the spontaneity which
    so often the out-of-doors brings out in children, and responding to their
    verbal and bodily expressions of feeling.
3   "Focus the child's attention without delay." Here he has in mind setting
    a tone of curiosity and watchfulness at the outset of the expedition.
4   "Look and experience first; talk later." This is a warning against covering
    up the observations with too much conversation. Instead, he says look
    at an oak tree from different perspectives, feel and smell its leaves, sit
    for a bit in its shade.
5   "A sense of joy should permeate the experience." The teacher's enthusi-
    asm is likely to be contagious, and joy comes in many varieties.

Generally speaking, sensory education is thought to have to do with the
"higher" senses of eye and ear, but there is no a priori reason why taste and
smell should not be educated too, or for that matter the sense of touch,
which sometimes yields that kind of valued experience called sensual.

It is apparently by common consent that education for the heightening
of sensual value is omitted from the school curriculum. There are at least
two reasons for this. (1) Access to this kind of value is something that one
acquires "naturally," and so far from requiring special attention, lest its
satisfactions be neglected, the problem is rather to keep it within reasonable
bounds, lest it almost completely eclipse other—presumably higher—
values. Hence sex education, when it is included in the curriculum at all,
concerns itself with information about the reproductive organs and physiology along with cautionary instruction about unwanted pregnancy and
sexually transmitted diseases. The improvement of the quality of the sex life,
if the question should arise—it certainly arises in students' minds tacitly—
can be disposed of by mention of Alex Comfort's *The Joy of Sex* (and its
sequels) and Masters and Johnson's *The Human Sexual Response*. (2)
Guardians of the public morality would not in any case permit such instruction in the schools. One might be tempted to mention a third reason, namely
that by and large teachers have no special knowledge in this area, but then
teachers are often asked to teach subjects that have not been included in
their training school curriculum. However, one need not go so far as
Bertrand Russell in saying, "It is the custom to leave sex education in the
hands of persons exceptionally ignorant, bigoted, and narrow-minded."
That he was writing in this way in 1932 becomes apparent when he goes on
to say:

The children of the well-to-do are left, during their first years, very
largely in the hands of nurses who are usually celibate and almost

always prudish. When later they come under the care of more educated women, these women are still as a rule celibate, and it is expected that they should be of impeccable moral character. This means that as a rule they are timid, sentimental, and afraid of reality. It means also that their opinions on sex are vehement, but uninformed. Schoolmasters, while not necessarily celibate, are expected to have a high moral tone, viz. to decide practical questions by traditional prejudice rather than by scientific psychology. Most of them would think the psychology of infantile sex a nasty subject, concerning which it is well to be ignorant. Of the harmful consequences of their ignorance they remain blissfully unaware.

(Russell 1932: 118–19)

However, the first of these can certainly be contested, at least in so far as it assumes that all people acquire and enjoy a fully satisfactory sensual life, which in fact must be confined to those who have been remarkably fortunate in their home upbringing and in their choice of intimates.

However, it should not be supposed that the sensual is coterminous with the sexual, even though it was for Freud. Though usage differs, it is feasible to distinguish the sensuous, having to do with taking delight in any of the senses either directly or through imagery, including that induced by works of art; whereas the sensual has to do with delight in the tactile sense, including that arising from the touching of such surfaces in addition to skin as those of velvet, silk, marble—but since it is not just soft and smooth textures that are pleasant, there must be added Rupert Brooke's "the rough male kiss of blankets." So conceived, the tactile sense is added to the others as amenable to sharpening, widening, and deepening.

But if the training of sensory acuteness (and its appreciation) is an important school task, and it is, what of the calling up of images—another capacity that differs widely, the satisfaction therein highly correlating with the development of this arcane skill? Aristotle said, "It is impossible even to think without a mental picture" (*On Memory and Recollection*, 450a), but that claim is now discounted.

In recent years an unprecedented amount of attention has been paid to imagining and imagination. Imagination goes beyond the ability to image in applying to the whole range of possibility, including fantasy, of course, as well as of "actuality." A mathematician may imagine (with or without imaging) a different way of proving a theorem, an engineer a still better solution to his problem of connecting freeways, a child a slight change in the self-concocted rules of a game in order to make it more interesting. But here our concentration is upon imaging.

David Hume identified images with ideas, and other philosophers in the empirical tradition often describe mental image as a faint copy of the original perception: having seen the waterfall, I will later remember it, having (as we say) a mental picture of it. Indeed, I carry this picture around "in my head" for a certain amount of time, and yet when I return to the original scene I'm surprised at how much more vivid the sight is than my puny image. True, but physiologists and psychologists describe a wide range of variation in the way people use and experience images. Some few people have images of the kind called *eidetic* that are quite remarkably detailed and vivid. These are *not* well described as "faded perceptions." And of course not all images *are* memories of things seen (heard, felt, etc.) but are original concoctions. They may be a putting together of elements not found in nature, as in hippogryphs and mermaids or rock candy mountains, or they may be faces—or any sort of object at all—that are original. Everybody knows these from dreams, for, in addition to the dream characters whom we recognize and name, there are those who make their first appearance in the dream world itself.

But we don't wait for sleep for our imaging to work, but with full consciousness put ourselves into the imaging frame of mind and—up they come. Or perhaps sometimes we draw a blank. Do we then know ways of priming the pump?

Rudolph Arnheim is a world-beater among psychologists in the field of *Visual Thinking*, the title of a major work in which he discusses the range of abstraction in images from highly concrete to abstract representations of freedom, causal relations, etc., as in the paintings of Paul Klee (Arnheim 1969).

Gareth Matthews, one of the philosophers now interested in children's philosophizing and good ways of cultivating this in schools, has discussed how children's stories can be philosophically significant. He says, "Typically, a philosophically sensitive story presents a thought experiment that exposes something problematic about a concept, an hypothesis, or an attitude." For instance, in Babbitt's *Tuck Everlasting* the characters, especially children, are seen and heard (imagistically, of course) discussing attitudes toward death.

Robin Barrow rightly says that when we speak of someone's being imaginative we mean first that that person has a capacity for calling up unusual scenes, plots, etc., but also ones that are in some way effective, interesting; otherwise we dismiss them as bizarre.

The analytical psychologist Rosemary Gordon has shown an educational value of good imaging that goes beyond its intrinsic delightfulness. Children, she says, with poor control over the production of images are more susceptible to manipulation by stereotypes than those who have learned to be creative in their imagery.

These authors are represented in a valuable book edited by Kieran Egan and Dan Nadaner, *Imagination and Education* (1988).

Perhaps teachers help children (and post-children) learn to image and imagine better mainly by the examples they themselves noticeably afford— once again: teaching by modeling—but they may also set up imaginative stimulations for sensory imaging and the imaginative extension of possibility in their assignments. In history this can be done by trying to imagine what would probably have happened if . . . Caesar had not crossed the Rubicon, or as in James Thurber's funny representation of the consequences of Ulysses S. Grant's having been drunk at Appomatox. (He surrendered his sword to General Lee.) Imaging can be taught in *every* subject—certainly in mathematics, as *Flatlanders* demonstrates.

No one needs to be told that artists, in all media, are as good as they are—if they are—in great measure by virtue of their imagination. We are the beneficiaries of their imaginative gifts. But there is a vast difference between those who grow dependent upon others (like artists) to do the imagining for them, and those who develop their own imaginative potentialities through the examples set by the great imagers and imaginers.

12

THE TRUTH VALUE
IN ART

Some dialogues:

Eight year-old girl to her small brother (pointing to his drawing): What's
that?

Boy: The moon.

She: No, no, a moon's not got all those squiggles, it's perfectly round.

Critical visitor to an artist's studio: Is that supposed to be a horse?

Artist: No, it's supposed to be a picture of a horse.

Another critical visitor: I never saw a lake like that.

Artist: No, but you will, madam.

Poem: The sky is as blue as an orange.

Reader: That's absurd.

Who knows when spectators of drawings first began to compliment or scold
an artist for the success or failure of the likeness his work bore to "the real
thing"? We do hear of an ancient contest between the Greek painters Zeuxis
and Parrhasios. It was Zeuxis' boast that he could paint grapes which birds
would peck at, so Parrhasios invited his rival to his studio and asked him to
draw back a curtain which covered his new picture. When Zeuxis tried to do
this, he found the curtain was itself painted. Parrhasios was considered the
victor: where Zeuxis could fool birds, Parrhasios could fool men, even
another painter.[9]

In his famous *The Lives of the Painters, Sculptors, and Architects*, Vasari
says of Leonardo's "Mona Lisa" that the smile "seemed rather divine than
human, and was considered marvelous, an exact copy of Nature" (Vasari
1550: II, 164).

Certainly those who commission a portrait of a member of a family will
very likely be critical if it does not seem "a speaking likeness"—or a slight
flattery—of "the original."

Still, Plato had a certain contempt for imitative (mimetic) artists, but then

131

he started with a low opinion of physical nature itself, in comparison with the Ideal, so that at best a painting was a copy of a copy. But Aristotle believed that

> The instinct of imitation is implanted in man from childhood, one difference between him and other animals being that he is the most imitative of creatures; and through imitation he acquires his earliest learning. And, indeed, every one feels a natural pleasure in things imitated . . . .

For him this follows from its being part of the human condition to want to know, and one powerful way of knowing is from imitation (*Poetics*, III, 4).

The myth of Pygmalion tells of a statue that was so marvelously lifelike that its creator fell in love with it and was granted the boon of its being brought to life.

However, the incomparable Gombrich raises the question of whether a work of art, in being found to be like that which it sets out to represent, is therefore true—or true just to the extent that it is an exact likeness. He proposes to doubt this on the ground that, as logicians and epistemologists are wont to claim, only a propositional statement can be true *or* false. But more importantly, he offers many examples of how artists, and those who displayed their art in various times in history, have often seemed indifferent about the accuracy of the representation. For instance, Hartmann Schedel in the late 15th century created a woodcut of a city which was put into a chronicle—the very same picture representing Damascus, Ferrara, Milan, and Mantuca—as if to say that it was a city, in any case, and you are free to imagine that it is one or another.

But Gombrich plows deeper than this, pointing out that persons who set out to copy something, as well as those who try to identify a drawing, try to establish a "schema" and then go on from there. That is, they have some general ideal of how such-and-such a thing looks and this stereotype will very often prevail even if the artist is in the presence of a model. Thus a skillful Chinese painter painting Derwent Water in the Lake District of England comes up with a painting—very beautiful—that has an unmistakable look about it of Chinese trees and mountains—and even Chinese cows.

> All art originates in the human mind, in our reactions to the world rather than in the visible world itself, and it is precisely because all art is 'conceptual' that all representations are recognizable by their style. Without some starting point, some initial schema, we could never get hold of the flux of experience. Without categories, we could not sort our impressions. Paradoxically, it has turned out that it matters relatively little what these first categories are. We can always adjust them according to the need.
>
> (Gombrich 1962: 76)

Although a craftsman may be a skillful forger, of banknotes or the work of a famous painter, when it comes to an original portrait, landscape, still life, or face, "it is 'correct' like the useful map . . . . not a faithful record of a visual experience but the faithful construction of a relational model" (p. 78).

Doubtless some painters felt that the invention of the camera somewhat relieved them of any felt necessity for producing a close likeness in two dimensions of some aspect of the three-dimensional world, though professional photographers in turn will hasten to point out that they too do not typically aim at, nor would be satisfied with, such a likeness. To be sure, we like to have pictures of loved ones or of loved scenes in nature, both for the reminder that they afford of what the face or landscape is (or was) like and simply for having captured and thus given some permanence to a certain expression, or a certain slant of light on an object that pleases somewhat as the original sight would or did, but then we like photographs of sights we have never ourselves seen, for their beauty or for something unusual and interesting in the subject, and with the cameras now available, about which the advertisements say that one need only "point and shoot," little in the way of artistry is required. But the photographers who get their pictures displayed in galleries are often praised in terms identical with those used about drawings and paintings: the composition, the color, the expressiveness, etc.

Some painters and the occasional photographer have gone so far as to disown the imitative or (more broadly) the representational aspects of their arts altogether, saying in effect that such a feature may be present or absent in any given work, but that its presence is a matter of indifference. If, in thinking of wholly non-representational paintings or sculptures, we assume that this is an aspect of "modern art," we can quickly be reminded that in archaic times too there was art that was both purely decorative and art that was apparently intended to be expressive of feeling without its being anything recognizable as this or that kind of object; for instance, the so-called "geometric" style of Greek vase painting.

Then there is abstract art, which, as the name implies, draws from the real world certain features, yet stopping short of any entire representation of this or that object. The abstract and non-figurative kinds of art are often thought by the layman to be easy to do—as if it were a matter of simply splashing on blobs of pigment; such naiveté often irritates the serious artist both because she may have spent many hours trying to decide what precisely the next line should be and because of the assumption that art works are to be graded in terms of the difficulty or ease of putting marks on a surface. No doubt we are astonished by the skill and patience of those who construct an intricate ship inside a bottle or those who did the delicate filigree high on the side of a temple, but surely this kind of appreciation is at some distance from what we want to mean by the aesthetic kind.

In any case, the supposition that representation is essential to good art is severely challenged by the instance of music, wherein, though there are sometimes to be heard sounds we identify as a bird song or a train whistle, these are but incidental aspects of the music, which for much the most part is far from an attempt to represent the visible or aural world. (The "representation" of emotions and feelings is something else again, and will be dealt with presently.) Some have felt that music is the prototypical art for the very reason that it has such a high degree of autonomy. Walter Pater famously said that all arts aspire to the condition of music, which is surely at best no more than a half truth, but it may succeed in focusing our attention upon music as especially notable for allowing no distinction between form and content. Music is a singularly pure art, too, in that its very tones—not to mention its scales, harmony, and timbre—are nowhere to be found outside music itself. But in relation to our question of the extent to which a work of art is to be praised for a correct and truthful representation of something other than itself, music gives us a clear answer.

Yet it is literature that has oftenest been praised for its alleged truth—but also blamed for what is branded false. Obviously, literary artists use the same linguistic medium as do scientists, lawyers, reporters and all the rest of us. For this reason, we may be more alerted to questions of veracity in plays, novels, and short stories than in sonatas and landscapes. To be sure, a work of prose fiction may include factual statements, like the announcement that it was in 1914 that the Great War began. But as that example suggests, such statements' truth are scarcely the reasons we seek out a novel to read or why we praise it, if we do. In short, this kind of truth, at least, is quite incidental to the quality of the work, though we might be suspicious of an author who commonly made errors in this way.

At this point one may want to short-cut the whole exposition by saying, "But it is not truth that we are especially interested in when we seek out works of art, but beauty," and many a practicing artist and critic will say yea to that utterance. Some psychologists will say something like "Art belongs to the affective, not the cognitive realm." And many philosophers have differentiated the essence of the two.

But before we dismiss knowledge and truth as wholly irrelevant to the artistic enterprise, we need to pause to ask whether perhaps there are other *kinds* of truth than the factual and theoretical. As we have already noticed, artists do not seem much interested at all in simply "reproducing" something that is already there. Was it Whistler who said, "One of the damned things is enough?"

But artists often want to "say" something striking about a distinctive object, event, relation, or person. Claiming that artists are not interested in classes or groups of things, but only in singular concrete realities, is not quite right as a generalization, but it is still worth saying, simply because the artist is characteristically largely concerned with creating something *new* and, at least in some important (to him) respect, something that is unique. The story-maker may base his plot on something that really did happen, or may start a tale she has heard, but what matters most is what gets *done* with the givens. Henry James told of having picked up at a dinner party a story of the burning of a house and what he wrote was *The Spoils of Poynton*, but as he explains, having got "the germ of a story" from his companion, he tuned out from the details of her story, taking on the creation of the novel for himself. It is what happens to the germ as it gets nourished in its culture that matters. The painter often works by looking at a meadow, a mountain, a bowl of apples, or a live model, but he sees in these objects something the rest of us do not and cannot see, and expresses this perception—the perception itself richly growing during the process—in lines and masses of color on a surface. A scrap of a tune may pop into a composer's head, or be picked up from a passing hurdy gurdy, but this is more like an inspiration than like something presenting itself to be copied.

Furthermore if the scientist is at pains to keep himself out of his product, the artist is very much concerned to put himself in. This does not mean that he is not looking or listening very hard to what is out there, but only that what is inside is, right from the beginning and clear to the end, transforming the raw material—both in the sense of the medium itself in which he works *and* the initial experience that starts the process rolling.

The art historian may tell us the name (and, as it were, the address, the pedigree) of the model for "Young Girl at an Open Half-door" but we care very little for what "liberties" Rembrandt took with his subject: we may well love the outcome and rest content there. Again, except as social historians we are not much interested in the costume, the hair-do, or the commonness of such half-doors in 17th century Amsterdam, and yet are fascinated with her posture, her hands, her sidelong glance—is someone interesting passing on the street just then? We may also be just as interested, or more interested, in the intricate play of light and darkness, the way the open door frames the girl and the near symmetrical left/right composition—the deviation from symmetry receiving a special accent.

Looking at the painting, we may well not be concerned with "what we may learn" thereby or able to report what, afterwards, we think we know that we did not know before, and yet say that somehow it *speaks* to us, *says* something to us. Perhaps we think that it adds a tiny but important element to our knowledge of—shall we say "human nature" or "young women"?

Different is the case of any one of Cézanne's numerous "Pines and Rocks." Here perhaps we are most concerned with (and again, in a fashion exceedingly hard to detail) learning something about the dynamic interaction of the painted trees and boulders. It is certainly not anything that would be useful to an engineer, concerned with inanimate stress and strain. Yet we may come away from looking for a time at the picture feeling that we now better understand how the living trees can relate to the inorganic objects—against the sky.

135

If Cézanne can teach us something about spatial organization, Beethoven can teach us something about the temporal dimensions of experience. Yet if we are challenged to say what that *is*, we are likely only to be able to say something quite banal—or pretentious, and then we think, "But that's not right, either." Yet we know that the music arouses in us certain feelings and that these feelings change in ways that changes in tempo, tonal progression, loudness/softness, timbre, and rhythm somehow present. It would be absurd to say that this makes Beethoven a psychologist—but we become convinced from his music that he knew a great deal about psychic phenomena.

Or yet again, suppose we read Emily Dickinson's (1862) stanza:

> There's a certain slant of light,
> On winter afternoons,
> That oppresses, like the weight
> Of cathedral tunes.

Just this much and we may be amazed at how she relates, in a way that carries conviction, a sight and a sound—and does so in yet another medium, words, which is at once auditory and visual. Tunes, she says, can be heavy and a "slant of light" can oppress. It sounds right! We are likely to agree and yet notice that this has not occurred to us before. But of course the poem goes on:

> Heavenly hurt, it gives us;
> We can find no scar,
> But internal difference
> Where the meanings are.

> None may teach it anything,
> 'Tis the seal, despair,–
> An imperial affliction
> Sent us of the air.

> When it comes, the landscape listens,
> Shadows hold their breath;
> When it goes, 'tis like the distance
> On the look of death.

The poem can be analyzed, but, short of that, we may notice quickly just a few things. First, there is her observation that the slant of light or the cathedral tunes can hurt us, not of course in the way that sticks and stones do, but internally—"Where the meanings are." This is where works of art operate and what they operate with: meanings—inside.

Yet this too alters the world outside: "the landscape listens." And indeed who does not know that look of things that says those earless objects are listening? And even lungless shadows can hold their breath, waiting in suspense. *Weighing* in suspense. Finally, though, such events—the slant of light, say—can also affect us by disappearing, giving us that ultimately distanced experience, "the look of death."

If something in us *agrees*, says yes to this little poem, are we not agreeing that this rings true to our experience? Or perhaps it is more like being given a new experience, with reverberations of some had before, but now with a deeper meaning offered—and accepted as authentic.

All of this is meant to suggest that those kinds of values we give such names as *truth* to, the value of knowledge, insight, and understanding, are by no means foreign to aesthetic experience, to the works we regard with that special attitude called "aesthetic." It seems less important to try to decide whether this is an essential feature of art works, though we may surely agree that it is more conspicuous in some cases than in others—even when we are confining ourselves to works that we like and admire, or whether such value is secondary to whatever we want to mean by "beauty." Whatever we may mean, it does seem that in those works of art we love and esteem there is something that is more than amusement, more even than delight, something that expands our consciousness, extends the range of our comprehension, enlarges our understanding.

The theory of art as essentially imitative implies that a primary value of art lies in its affording knowledge—most obviously of what someone or something looks like. But this sounds more like the very unartistic photographs of "wanted" criminals hung up in post offices. Still, as we have seen, a more generous view of the mimetic function does tell us something about the artist's job and goal. Though the artist is characteristically responding to and in some way representing the world as it is, she is also representing it in its historical dimension and projecting into the possible future. (Aristotle said that whereas history tells us what did in fact happen, the poet tells us what would happen, if . . . .)

Northrop Frye says somewhere that Shakespeare's *Macbeth* tells us what it would be like to gain a kingdom and lose our own soul. Beethoven tells us in his last quartets something about how it feels to confront fate. And Michelangelo tells us how it might feel to be Adam brought to life by the touch of God's finger.

It seems that the greatest art is equally describable by the words "beautiful" and "true," though the truth it affords is of a very different kind from any that can be called informational, factual, or literal.

13

ART AS
COMMUNICATION,
EXPRESSION AND
EMBODIMENT

Someone sits down at the piano, playing this and that, improvising, and suddenly notices a little tune that has emerged, mysteriously, from the jumble of notes and chords. He stops and makes some marks on a score sheet, and goes back to play the tune again and then begins to weave some variations on it. There are false starts and stops, but some things that seemed worth saving are in turn inscribed on paper. After a while he grows tired and nothing seems to be happening, so he turns to other matters, but later in the day returns to what has been recorded and begins to work it over, modifying, extending . . . .

Another person is out on a solitary hike in the mountains. Something catches her eye: a little stream splashes up and around a cobblestone. She pulls from her backpack a sketch book, finds a stump to sit on and begins to sketch with a soft pencil. But it doesn't go well, she's not catching the particular play of light that first captivated her attention. She flips the sheet over and begins anew. This time it goes better and she begins to fill in the background with the quaking aspens that come almost down to the water. Now she has enough to take home and start to work from her easel.

On her way to school one spring morning, Julie finds herself walking, one, two, three, and—skip; one, two, three, and—skip. At first she hardly notices what she is doing, but then she does and smiles and starts saying, "Thud, Thud, Perklicky" to go with the movement of her feet and it occurs to her that that could be a kind of refrain as in a nursery rhyme. And she makes a mental note to try, maybe during recess, to see if she can make up a little poem to go with her refrain.

There is no end to the ways that creation can take place. Sometimes it must be *willed*, as when one has the assignment to write a story or just to do something with this blob of clay. But often enough, as in the little episodes recounted above, it just happens out of the blue. Sometimes the act fails: one loses interest, or it just doesn't come off and gets forgotten. But sometimes the activity issues in a product, however modest—say, a bit of doggerel for a Valentine. Something gets made. This is a difference between art and play. Play just ends, the activity stops, when the clock dictates, the players lose interest or get interrupted, and that's that. A creative act, though, tries to move toward the fashioning of some sort of object. (Improvisation in dance or music may be thought an in-between state.) And once that something is made, be it as temporary as a sand castle, it can be experienced by another—though of course it may be destroyed or hidden away by its maker. When the other looks or listens, she smiles, frowns, says, "How nice!" or can find only a noncommittal "Interesting" to utter. But what got made has served as a medium of communication, perhaps one a little more provocative than "Good morning, how are you?"

When somebody makes something and another person pays attention to it, registers it, responds to it, what is being communicated? An idea? A thought? An insight? A feeling? An attitude?

All of the above? Perhaps. And something else as well.

About that kind of making that is called *art*, one very common answer (from those who have thought about the matter in more than a casual way) has been feeling or emotion. (For the present these may be taken as interchangeable.) One artist and reflecter upon art who said so was Leo Tolstoy. After stating and rejecting a number of definitions by others, Tolstoy wrote his own definition:

> To evoke in oneself a feeling one has once experienced and having evoked it in oneself then by means of movements, lines, colors, sounds, or forms expressed in words, so to transmit that feeling that others experience the same feeling—this is the activity of art.
>
> Art is a human activity consisting in this, that one man consciously by means of certain external signs, hands on to others feelings he has lived through, and that others are infected by these feelings and also experience them.

So art is not a manifestation of the idea of beauty, not a way of letting off excess energy, not the production of pleasing objects, not a pleasure, not this nor that, but, he continues:

> it is a means of union among men [*sic*] joining them together in the same feelings, and indispensable for the life and progress toward well being of individuals and of humanity.
>
> (Tolstoy 1896: chapter V)

There are at least two aspects of this position which mark it off from others: the emphasis upon feelings and upon their communication. Thus, it is not to be called art at all if feelings are not centrally involved (but only, for instance, intellective matters or information), and it is not yet art if the feelings are just experienced, or experienced and then simply expressed in some form or other. No, one has to transmit or hand this on to others. Indeed, it is worth noticing that there is an intermediate step wherein one evokes within oneself a feeling previously experienced and then finds a way of externalizing it in some medium in order to communicate it. It is interesting that he even insists that this a *conscious* intention.

Something rather similar to this account had been arrived at almost exactly a hundred years earlier by Wordsworth in the 'Observations' prefixed to *Lyrical Ballads*. Although he spoke specifically of the origin of poetry, it is likely that he would have agreed that creativity is much the same in the other arts as well:

> Poetry is the spontaneous overflow of powerful feelings: it takes its origin from emotion recollected in tranquility: the emotion is contemplated till, by a species of reaction, the tranquility gradually disappears, and an emotion, kindred to that which was before the subject of contemplation, is gradually produced, and does itself actually exist in the mind. In this mood successful composition generally begins, and in a mood similar to this it is carried on . . . .

Both of these great artists are saying that (at least characteristically) an earlier emotional experience is remembered and then, at a later, quieter time, this original experience serves as the basis for a creative act. Both were thus fully aware that it is rare indeed that art is produced in the fine fervor of an act of love or in the midst of battle, or immediately after a harrowing accident. This is not to deny that there may be a sense of divine, semi-divine, or more mundane inspiration, and there surely are on record accounts of some significant piece of art being brought off in an excited rush, but this must be unusual.

But what Tolstoy adds to Wordsworth's account is his own particular emphasis upon the intent to communicate, and, in the successful instance, the fact of this communication (of feeling) actually taking place. We will examine in another context (that of the relations between the moral and the aesthetic) how Tolstoy believed that very often the feelings that art works communicate ought *not* to be communicated from the point of view of Christian egalitarianism, but presently the concern is purely with the aesthetic and in this realm Tolstoy's basic principle is simply this: "The stronger the infection the better is the art, as art." This is to imply that what the artist is after is the maximization of the communication, or, to continue his metaphor, the spreading to others of the infection with his own feeling. He goes on to list three conditions on which the degree of infectiousness depends.

First, there is what he calls the *individuality* of the feeling transmitted. His rule is: "The more individual the feeling transmitted, the more strongly does it act on the recipient . . . ." Presumably this means that the distinctiveness and specificity of the feeling affect its intensity; thus, not just some kind of generalized sorrow, but that very special sorrow that Anna Karenina felt before her suicide, is what makes for the intensity of feeling the reader experiences in reading this novel. But Tolstoy rather confusingly adds that the intensity also depends on the individuality "of the state of soul" of the recipient. That the attitude and readiness of the reader (or other art consumer) affects the quality of the experience had is beyond doubt, but Tolstoy does not offer us here any help as to what "individuality" has to do with the matter. In any case, he specifically does identify intensity of feeling with pleasure, so that the more individuality of feeling in this transaction, the more the pleasure in the recipient.

The second condition on which the degree of infectiousness depends is what he calls "clearness of expression." How exactly this differs from individuality remains itself unclear, but what Tolstoy is after here is that, by means of the feeling the creative artist "puts into" his work, the reader (viewer, hearer) is enabled to "mingle in consciousness" with the artist by coming to have the sense that here now is a feeling "he has long known and felt and for which he has only now found expression."

The third and last determinant of the degree of infectiousness achieved is the sincerity of the artist. Apparently, only if we recipients are convinced by the work that its creator has indeed experienced, in his own being, this particular and clear feeling is the answering experience going to be strong. Putting it the other way around, if the artist seems to us to be only playing a role, only pretending to have a given feeling, our defenses will be aroused, we will fight off any infection and will be coldly distanced, even repelled by the work.

But an artist is sincere in this way only if he is "impelled by an inner need to express his feeling." This is a point made over and over again by artists. For instance, if the tyro asks the veteran, "How do I know whether I am really an artist?" the answer comes, "If you have to ask that question, you are not an artist, for the artist is precisely the one who can do no other, who will dig ditches, sell his mother into slavery, or jeopardize his immortal soul if that is what is necessary to get on with his art."

Tolstoy is not going quite that far, but he is insisting that the communication of feeling depends upon the artist's truly having the particular feeling, expressing it in its full individuality with clarity, and in such a way as to leave us, the recipients, in no doubt about the sincerity of him whose feelings are presented through this medium. To fail in any of these respects is to produce not art but a counterfeit of art and thus to fail in arousing pleasure, in conveying to us the original experience and in arousing in us the sense that here at last is an expression of a feeling we have already known and felt.

Into a brief space Tolstoy packs so much that it is finally hard, perhaps impossible, to tell precisely what he means, even though the general drift is clear. The points that stand out are these:

1   The essential "content" of an art work is feeling.
2   If the work is to be genuine, it must express an experienced feeling of the artist.

3 In the successful instance, the one who is on the receiving end of the artistic transaction must be "infected" by the same feeling the artist has had and has succeeded in "putting into" his work.
4 Yet this infection apparently will happen only if the recipient has on her own already experienced his feeling.
5 In the ideal case there is a mingling of consciousness between artist and recipient.
6 All the same, the artist must be impelled toward expression not simply by the desire to infect others, but also by the desire to be infected by his own work so that he "writes, sings, or plays" also for himself.
7 And when these conditions are present, and an infection takes place in both artist and recipient, the result is pleasure in both parties.

Other theories have insisted on a decision being made between the primacy of either expression or communication. For instance Eugene Véron, writing two decades before Tolstoy's *What is Art?*, has little to say about communication, so much is he taken up with the act of expression, though he also recognizes another kind of art, which he finds to be of little interest to "modern artists," which he classes "decorative" and which is designed to gratify the senses by its harmony and grace and "has nothing in view beyond the peculiar delight caused by the sight of beautiful objects" (Véron 1960: 57–8).

Others (we are not here concerned to run through a catalogue of theorists) have put particular emphasis upon both the artist's desire to get across to others (as against "expressing himself") and upon the judgment of the quality of the work's depending on its success as a communicative object.

But there is no need to decide whether communication or expression is primary in art. Both have their importance—and other kinds of motivation can act as well, so let us take another tack, recognizing that within what may be loosely designated as the world of art and artists (along with those who experience and enjoy such works) there are many components and many differences of emphasis, depending on personality, schools of art, the medium of the artist, the place and time of the artist, etc.

Given that art may be considered as both a kind of activity and a kind of product, as in a work of art or artifact, let us go on to notice that since we speak of any sort of skill (from parachuting to digging wells) as an art, we need for present purposes to concentrate upon the *aesthetic* arts, by which we mean those arts that tend to produce objects whose main and distinctive value lies in inviting and rewarding aesthetic attention and attitude. We will here concentrate upon a fairly traditional conception of the "fine arts" even though we are conscious of risking a charge of elitism by so doing. (Later, concession will be made to various forms of craft and "popular arts" to supplement our present emphasis.) With this in mind, we may look at several aspects of the arts (taken as music, dance, literature, enacted drama [plays and films], sculpture, drawing and painting, and architecture), by means of several ways of seeing art as:

1 expression of feeling,
2 communication of feeling,
3 evocation of feeling, and
4 craft.

Let us work backward through this list. By art as craft is intended an emphasis upon the artist's characteristic fascination with a certain *medium* and with the possibility of exploiting characteristics of that medium by way of activities of *forming*. Imagine, for instance, the sculptor's arriving at his studio to find that a block of marble has been delivered. We may think of his walking around and around it, admiring it, stroking it, turning it this way and that to see it in various lights, attending to its peculiar hue, its distinctive texture, its veins, possible flaws . . . . He may soon begin to test its responsiveness to his chisels and other tools. With a loving and delighted eye (we imagine), he sees this block as a concentration of possibilities—which will be realized by forming. Form may be thought of as something to be "imposed" on the material or even something found as it were sleeping within, the latter point being whimsically made by the old saw that all the sculptor has to do is eliminate the superfluities.

Very different is that sculptor who has begun thinking in terms of a work that will be cast in bronze or another metal, so that a mold will be the immediate object-to-be-made; or again, the artist must ask if the primary material should be wood or a highly malleable substance like clay.

What, for the composer, is the material corresponding to the sculptor's shapeable physical stuff? One answer would be: tones and silences. But this is still very abstract. For instance, if this person is seen to sit down at his piano, he will already have made a fairly severe selection among possible tones, namely those denominated by the keyboard, which sets limits both of low and high and of the intervals between any two keys. (The violin, for instance, has more possibilities of tone between C and C sharp.)

But there is also the timbre of the piano, which is to say that it necessarily selects a different group of overtones for any given note. Then there is the percussive quality of the sound, so that the "same" note played on piano, flute, oboe, cello, and kettledrum is very different. Still another selection may be made by the composer in terms of key, which is to say of a dominant scale within which he will work.

The experienced painter will be intensely aware of the differences between water color, oil, and acrylic and also between such surfaces as paper, canvas, and wood, and his knowledge of these several potentialities and limitations will greatly influence his work. As in all arts, he will be conscious of the difference size makes and of the probable location of the finished work.

The verbal artist works with a material extremely different from that of her fellow artists, perhaps relatively deficient in immediate sensory quality (the sound of a spoken word as against one sung, or a blob of color), but the fact that words are more or less definable gives the poet or fictionalist an utterly distinctive medium in which to create. But will her words be foregrounded, as in the case of much lyrical poetry, or backgrounded, as in the usual novel wherein any individual word or phrase is not intended to be sounded out and doted upon? And as the musician will think from early on in terms of song, a sonata for solo instrument, a quartet, a symphony, an opera or whatever, so the writer will think of the possibilities of this or that genre: short story, play, novel, ballad, lyric or—most unlikely—epic.

The choreographer works with movements of human bodies, but also with music and physical setting, and all of that again brings to mind both real possibilities and limitations, for even the greatest dancer cannot transcend the law of gravity, however much a Fonteyn may seem almost suspended in space.

More than the others, the architect must think in terms of function—the ways of conducing to human dwelling and sheltering—in short, for what a given building is intended and how it will sustain and promote the activities central to those purposes. But again there are physical materials, the concrete and wood and brick, the girders and supports, the inner divisions (hallways, rooms, etc.) and the several facades, but also and very importantly the relation of the building to its ground, to other structures and natural objects, like the contour of the earth, the trees, openness to sky, and so on. Practicality is finally inseparable from the architect's visions, and yet he too is a craftsman, fascinated with how to realize a selection of the multifold potentialities that lie in his materials and possible forms.

The artist-as-craftsman (craftsperson?), then, is one who has a direct and immediate relationship to the very stuff in which she works, be it as palpable as clay or the pigments in tubes or as impalpable as words before they are written or sounded. And in this role or aspect of her work, she is concerned to call upon her mastery of ways of forming these materials to come up with an object that is—beautiful? Well, she may even find that word limiting; for instance, she may insist that she is after something downright ugly, or that she is far more concerned with finding what, as she may possibly put it, this stuff wants to become, what of interest can be done with it, how it may be helped to realize its inward nature.

In this way of thinking attention is neither upon what the artist "wants to say" or upon the possible or actual audience, but rather upon the confrontation between the human artificer and his chosen medium.

Very different is that way of thinking of the artist's task that is suggested by the phrase "art as evocation of feeling." Here, pretty obviously, the audience—if, as is not uncommon, that word with its built-in directedness toward hearing can be used for the other kinds of artistic medium as well—is right at the center of attention. If I'm going to evoke something in another, I must have some relatively good notion of what that other person is like, is likely to respond to.

One kind of example of this perspective is mood music, say the kind an airline might use to calm passengers' pre-flight nervousness (or, similarly, a dentist), or, by contrast, music that enhances suspense or forebodes disaster. So accustomed are most of us to the combination of visual images and music, as on television or film, that the music is very close to being subliminal. But if one happens to hear the music—say, walking into a room, before seeing the picture—one may become highly conscious of what the music is "doing," of how much it contributes to the feelings the actors and plot are calling out. But then, the very kind of soap opera or sitcom or mystery/detective or spy thriller that is here suggested may itself be primarily classifiable as evocation. That is, what the producer may be looking for, to fill this particular "slot" of time, is precisely something almost certain to excite, get the viewer involved, developing sympathy and antipathy to this or that character, feeling suspense, anticipation, and then experiencing the resolution of the problem and the consequent satisfactions. Such desired effects may be quite determinable in advance of a selection of the actual program. Thus the program director might say, "What I want is a series that will do (to our kind of audience) the following: . . ." Then the script will be written accordingly—very likely by a committee.

An even more clear-cut example is advertising art, for what above all is here asked for is something that will impel these people to buy this product: it's hard to think of anything more purely evocative than that.

In this context there is no need to invoke Tolstoy's prized sincerity of the artist. Scriptwriter, commercial artist, background music composer, the director and actors and other performers may, for all anybody cares, be wholly cynical with respect to the production and its audience. Just as the actor extolling the delights (and nutritious value) of a brand of corn flakes may himself boast—but not on camera—that he would not be caught dead ingesting even a mouthful of this product, so the actors in some sitcom may later make fun of the sentimentality of the script and of the people they imagine shedding tears in front of their television sets.

Yet this is not to say that all evocation is necessarily shoddy, insincere, or trumped up. For instance, the designer of a chapel may with complete sincerity and dedication want to succeed in calling out attitudes of devotionality in the communicants who are expected to visit the room. Music for films can be illustrated in the case of a production of *King Lear* with the composer a great devotee of Shakespeare and thus ever so much wanting to enhance the mood of this or that part of the play. Or the person painting a poster that is designed to enlist support for a cause may be wholly convinced of the worthiness thereof and will rejoice over reports that her work has been effective in the desired way: joining the army, voting for the right candidate, giving money to the Salvation Army, or supporting the teachers' union. But the very fact that one *can* evoke a feeling of sentiment without its being one's own has tended to prompt some hesitation in assigning this a respectable role in the process of art production.

Of course much the same can be said of art-as-communication. One can surely communicate or transmit what is not one's own. But it is perhaps commoner to think of communication as sharing: I have seen this sight, experienced these emotions, encountered this character, developed this insight, dreamed this dream—and now I want to pass it along to you, or even to as many yous as possible. Here too the audience is very much present-to-mind, sometimes (though by no means always) in the sense of their needs. "This is something that they want—or ought to want—and will profit from." But there is the artist's need, too, implicit in this perspective, the need to share, to spread the word, to get across to others—specifically *not* to keep it for oneself alone, to shut it off, to be secretive and possessive, retentive, but to spread the word.

Now, of course, the prospective audience may be selective or universal. It may be as selective as one special person. Stephen Spender once suggested that an artist always has somebody in mind that he is writing for, so that the poem (say) may somehow be especially beamed at just that person, but also at kindred spirits anywhere else. There have been times when lovers (as in *As You Like It*) pinned sonnets to a tree for the fair shepherdess to find and in turn to write one of her own to convey back like sentiments by the same means. In turn the letters of a Rilke or Lawrence or Van Gogh may come to be considered art works of their own and published as such, even though each one was originally written and sent to a single person.

But at the other extreme, anything written is potentially communicable to any literate person, now existent or in the illimitable future. Similarly any painting can be for anyone with eyes to see, music for all those who can hear and attend to notes and rhythms. It seems amazing, when we think of it, that Homer was in some sense writing for us, even though it would have been wholly impossible for him to imagine such an audience as we are or even to fantasize people reading (in translation) words written down millennia earlier. Still, we readers may have a sense not only that this story of Odysseus makes sense to us, but that it very particularly speaks to our condition and thus (almost) was intended for us.

Sometimes of course communication is accomplished not with just one person at a time but in groups, and this makes its own kind of difference. Not only is it quite different to read a play and to see it performed; it is also different to see the play (say, in rehearsal) where one is alone in the audience, and to see it as part of an audience of 400 people. So too with music and dance. Actors and other performers speak of the special chemistry of a given audience, and will in turn respond to the sounds that come back to them from this live audience. (Again there is the difference of acting "for" a camera or microphone and for live viewers directly.) At least subliminally one responds to the slight sounds and movements of other people in one's audience and this changes the experience of the performance.

Some people seem to feel more strongly than others that artistic creativity is best thought of as a transaction, from creator to recipient by way of the intervening art work. Conversely some recipients are especially aware of feeling communicated to by the work, sometimes going so far as to sense being "spoken to" by the artist in a way more intense than that of those who speak directly to them. Sometimes there will even be a sense of dialogue, such that one "answers" the artist, perhaps even correcting, modifying, extending what is found in the created product or saying to it yea or nay. Especially common is wanting, in the case of a favored work, to extend its audience by recommending it to one's friends, and if there is agreement that this is indeed a special communication one may gain thereby a heightened sense of communication.

Naturally, as with all communication, the recipient is an interpreter, and artists are known to differ importantly in the burden they put upon the reader, viewer, or listener in the way of filling out and understanding what is *in* the work in something like an objective way. Lawrence Sterne's *Tristram Shandy* is an example of a work that goes an unusually long way toward involving the reader as a "collaborator" in the novel as an experience. Perhaps all abstract art is noteworthy in this respect in some (but not radical) contrast to highly representational art or quite explicit art. So-called symbolic art, in various media, is another example of the kinds of work that require an unusual amount of interpretation. Now, this way of thinking takes some emphasis away from strict communication (where, metaphorically, the work of art may be an envelope carrying a message along a shoot from dispatcher/artist to receiver).

And finally there is the person who, at an extreme, regards the act of creation as purely a matter between the artificer and his or her material, such that once that-which-is-there-to-be-expressed *is* expressed, the act is finished the product has been issued, and if someone comes along and notices it, that is fine but quite unnecessary. In this emphasis upon expression (as distinct from communication, evocation, or craft), the relationship that is primary is that between something in the creator and the act of expressing in some medium to form a product that claims to be the expression of that antecedent state—a psychological state if you like. Form is still present; the primary question is not that of some ready-made form like a rhyme scheme or what is taken to be the standard form of a rondo, but rather upon forming what theretofore was a kind of jumble, something inchoate. Expression in this way of thinking is not simply transferring the words that already exist in the mind into sounded or written words (or the equivalent of this in the other arts), but finding out the "right words in the right order" that bring order out of near chaos.

Expression in this way of conceiving is not exemplified by the baby's yell when stuck with a diaper pin: that is simple ejaculation. Instead, it is the transformation of a pain or pleasure, impression or notion, perhaps a finding of a similarity where none had seemed to exist, into something that bespeaks and makes sensibly available an inner state that had not yet jelled.

Still another contrast is between what a social scientist might mean when she says that she has collected all her data and done her analyses and now there is left only the "writing it up." This strongly suggests that the latter act is something very like a transcription of what is pretty much already accomplished—to use a quaintly old-fashioned expression—already written on the soul but not yet made public.

Expression (as here fancied) is not needed when a mere literal utterance will suffice. Except for the pathologically tongue-tied, a straightforward announcement about the present state of the weather suffices in place of an expression, just as in turn it calls, on the part of the hearer, for no special interpretation. We set out to interpret what we find complex or indirect or convoluted, and we seek to express something for which the ready formulas of ordinary speech do not suffice. Fourteen lines of repeating "I love you" do not make a love sonnet, but the poet asks instead,

> How do I love thee? Let me count the ways.

But "count" will turn out to be something very different from a mere enumeration.

Similarly an ordinary map will not express what a city means to me, but if I have the talent and skill and sensitive psyche of a Pissaro, I may be able impressionistically to express something of Paris on my canvas. If I start with a kind of inner image of "the afternoon of a faun," I may be able to find the musical sounds and the dance that say what I come to mean in the course of my expressive act itself.

One of the best known theorists of expression as utterly central to the process of art is R. G. Collingwood, who wrote that expression begins when someone

> is conscious of having an emotion, but not conscious of what this emotion is. All he is conscious of is a perturbation or excitement which he feels is going on within him, but of whose nature he is ignorant . . . . From this helpless and oppressed condition he extricates himself by doing something which we call expressing himself . . . . His mind is somehow lightened and eased.

> It follows from this that the expression of emotion, simply as expression, is not addressed to any particular audience. It is addressed primarily to the speaker himself, and secondarily to any one who can understand.

> (Collingwood 1938: 109–10)

(This position is similar to ones held by Benedetto Croce, John Dewey, and Suzanne Langer, among others.)

But of course "expression" is used in other ways as well. For instance, we say of a person that she expressed her feelings, not in words, but by means of tone of voice and gestures. We can express confidence, among other ways, by simply saying, "I am confident that . . . ." (although the tone of voice may give the case away). A person's face may express surprise because such is a natural way of looking when one is surprised. Eyes may be called expressive when they seem unusual in their capacity to convey feelings to others.

Then, too, the expression "in" a work of art may not be so much that of the creator as of portrayed characters. What Iago expresses is certainly not what Shakespeare wants to say for himself, and there is no reason to believe that the expressive face of Rouault's "The Old King" is expressing the emotions of the painter—except as they are *imagined* by the artist.[10]

Still, if we are to believe that a work of art is never a purely objective representation, never one in which the artist keeps him or herself entirely out of the work, but always something wherein is recorded the artist's attempt to understand, fill out, and come to terms with what began as a confusing feeling, then "expression" in the rather special sense described above will necessarily be part and parcel of the creative art. If he or she cares to do so, it will tell the expresser, and us appreciators as well, something about that artist.

It is not at all necessary, and perhaps not very important, to try to decide whether art is *really* expression or communication or evocation or craft. It is surely all these, even before we have said much at all about what it is an expression *of*. We may notice too that artists differ in emphasis among these intentionalities and motivations—perhaps in part because of the nature of their own particular skill: for instance, some artists of consummate craft seem not to have a great deal to say. But one way of thinking about the very greatest artists in the various kinds of art is with respect to their high attainments in all their different ways (and doubtless others too). So too of our development as appreciators of art: which similarly calls for some versatility across these ways art is conceived *as*. Is this not teachable?

This account of some aspects of the creative act, its intentions and motivations, has proceeded without direct reference to value, yet it is surely clear that art works, modest or great, offer occasions of experienced values. Even amateur artists (both original creators and performers) have often testified to the peculiar intensity of satisfaction that attends a successful instance of this kind. And, indeed, in an age in which aesthetic education has proceeded well beyond its present modest limits, virtually all people will have access not alone as recipients but also as makers of art.

14

APPRECIATION

It is to be remembered that Tolstoy said not only that the artist expresses his own feelings, but also that we who read or otherwise experience his work will, at least sometimes, realize that this work has done for us what we had hitherto been unable to do for ourselves, to express the feelings attendant upon some experience that *we* have previously had. Then we say, "Yes, that's the way it was; that catches the very quality of the experience." If, for instance, Stendhal or Charlotte Brontë describes how one of the novel's characters felt in the process of falling in love, we readers may be astonished at the similarity with what we now recall. Of course the names and places and times were all completely different, but that only increases the wonder that it should be so very much like what we felt on that particular occasion (or perhaps more than once). Somehow we hadn't put it together for ourselves but now someone has done it for us. The youngster, however, who has not yet had this particular and distinctive experience can, let us say, read the words and even know their meanings, but will not quite see why such a fuss is being made over it. It doesn't answer to anything he has yet known and not surprisingly will seem blown way out of proportion. He has even heard before about grown-ups (or older siblings) "falling in love" but has not experienced it, so the writer, no matter how talented, will not be able to "express for him" as would have happened if the passage had been about how it feels to have your dog run away or die or for that matter how it felt when you had a sudden rush of love—for your mother.

Similarly it is well known that, up to a certain age, a child seems quite unable to believe that she is going herself to die. She can repeat the words, "Everybody must die some day," and realize intellectually that this must be the case, and yet such an event seems so remote, so altogether improbable, that it doesn't ring true as a genuine possibility. Thus Tolstoy's great story "The Death of Ivan Ilyitch" is not yet within her emotional compass. The parent or teacher will of course realize this and wait for a more appropriate time to recommend that story.

Of course we human beings do not literally have to duplicate the experiences characters in fiction have in order to empathize quite a lot with them.

150

None of us has had the hair-raising experience of seeing a Trojan warrior in helmet and armor bearing down on us with spear drawn back ready to plunge it into our entrails. But we have been frightened in ways that are enough like that to share quite a bit of the feeling. For instance, we have had nightmares from which we woke sweating and trembling when we had been menaced, threatened, and nearly killed by some creature or other. And on a very dark night, as children, we in our imaginations have conjured up the approach to our bedroom door of some completely unwelcome stranger.

Or yet again, if we as young readers seem not quite able to fathom the emotion conveyed or aroused in a particular scene, say that of the knocking on the gate in *Macbeth*, the teacher may need to reset the scene for us: "Don't forget that the soldiers had all been drunk, and that Macbeth and Lady Macbeth had done their grisly work, and now inside that very castle, when all is quiet and seemingly peaceful and calm, the king lies dead, covered with blood." With this much of a prompt, the messenger pounding on the gate demanding to be let in may take on its eerie quality of a mixture between bawdy humor and horror—as De Quincey described so vividly in his famous essay on the subject, which in turn serves as a reminder that critics too have their role, not merely as judges and recommenders but as (we hope) unusually sensitive perceivers of an art work and thus able to aid us, with our less developed sensibilities, to penetrate through to the heart of the vicarious experience that the art work may afford. Of course not all aspects of experiencing art are vicarious: the perceptions of the sounds, colors, lines, masses are every bit as direct and immediate as they would be if we were walking out of doors and listening to and looking at a bright-plumaged bird singing away at the top of a maple tree. But it is different when there is a dramatic element in the art work, as there is not only in live and filmed plays, prose fiction, and narrative poetry, but also in opera, ballet, and much representative painting and sculpture—even architecture and instrumental music. Thus a Praxiteles statue is seen with quite different eyes (and feelings) when one knows that the characters are Apollo and Hermes and knows something of *their* story. Schubert's "The Erl King" is heard differently and more weakly when one doesn't know the story (and can't understand the German words), and something as frequently repeated as the *Nutcracker Suite* is at some point brand new and puzzling to each young person.

Some of all this can be usefully got at through the concept of distance—or, as it was originally called (1913) by Edward Bullough, "psychical distance." The kernel of the idea is already known to common sense, namely that we are not likely to feel as strongly about something when it is far away as when it is near. We read about the sinking of a ship off the coast of Goa in the Indian Ocean and we cluck our tongue and shake our heads but in a moment have put it from our minds, whereas an event only a tenth as serious in our own bailiwick will strike deep and be hard to forget, even if we want to. But it is only slightly less familiar to use "distance" metaphorically, so that we say of someone, "I am no longer close to him," or "I feel now quite distanced from the whole thing," and again we are registering a diminution in sympathy or other feeling because of a psychical, not a spatial (or even temporal), separation.

Every teacher knows the problem of how to reduce the distance between a pupil and an object recommended for appreciation. Sometimes the problem *is* temporal and spatial. How, the young person (tacitly?) wonders, can it be interesting to read of something *that* long ago and *that* far away. But the poem written on the board may have been written earlier this year by somebody a mile away and seem every bit as distant from the child's comprehension as if it were a Sappho lyric, or a story by Lady Murasaki. So the teacher looks—sometimes almost desperately—for a way of lowering the distance—arousing interest—in short, of relating the poem to something closer to the child's own experience. (John Dewey again: problems are only truly engaging—thus arousing concern for their solution—if they are *problematic* to the pupil, not just to the teacher.)

All of this applies fully as much whether we're thinking about how to interest the child in the multiplication table as in the poem or the picture or a trip to Canterbury Cathedral: reducing the psychical distance in order that the experience be more than perfunctory and so that learning can take place. But in so far as the problem is an aesthetic one, it is not less important that the object of possible concern have enough distance as that it have too much. This again is something commonsensically recognized by such expressions as "Later on I'll probably laugh at it, but right now . . . " and "I'm afraid I'm too close to the whole thing really to appreciate it." In short, if the thing to be aesthetically experienced and enjoyed is so closely bound up with our everyday interests and values, our appreciation of it will not be aesthetic. This is easily illustrated.

Suppose the poem is Hopkins's "Glory be to God for dappled things." A pupil raises his hand and says, "In my family we don't believe in God." Later in the poem a Jewish and a Buddhist student have trouble with "the Holy Ghost." For them the poem is somehow untrue, not representative of reality, and gets rejected on that ground, and the teacher has the not-easy job of explaining—or may decide not to fight this battle now, but to leave it for a teacher at an upper level—how in dealing with art we set aside both belief and disbelief and just go along with the poem for whatever it has to give us. This, by the way, the child has already long ago learned to do when the story is about hippogryphs or dragons or Martian visitors, but it is not always so easy with religious, moral, and political matters. There is something "as if" about art so that we do not (properly) hold it to strict accounting, as for instance when Keats makes a mistake and has "stout Cortez" instead of stout Balboa looking on the Pacific with a "wild surmise." We may smile at the slip, but it does not really get in the way of the beauty of the poem. Neither do we have to share Donne's or Hopkins's Christianity, or brand of Christianity, nor Hardy's God who goes his "unweeting way" no matter what's going on on earth, nor Nietzsche's announcement that God is dead. And yet, most interestingly, this does not finally get in the way of the tale or poem or painting or even sonata as having (as we've already noticed) something about it that we want to call "true."

But now notice a difficulty that comes about from an opposite angle. Suppose a child says again about "Glory be to God for dappled things" something like "Oh good, I love poems about God." The teacher frowns, for it's no better to like the poem because it's about God than to dislike it for the same reason. After all, there are a great many very bad poems about God, and the learning of aesthetic appreciation requires discrimination, not just liking everything that comes along, or even everything that fits my preconceived beliefs. Image one of those little plaster casts of the Virgin Mary that are on sale in the vicinity of big churches on Easter Sunday: as a reminder of one's religious duties it may do very well, but as an aesthetic object it won't do at all.

There are other kinds of "underdistancing." Tools or other everyday useful objects may have their attractiveness entirely swallowed up in their being so frequently employed as to become all but invisible. After we're accustomed to it, it's hard really to look at our hairbrush or key chain or the kitchen clock. Even the silverware and crystal we admire very much may from frequent use virtually disappear from view, but then so may the painting on the wall, even though now it's not a matter of usefulness interfering with aesthetic enjoyment.

Or, for just one more example, take "calendar art." July may display a picture of a seashore, ever so much like the place where we especially enjoy taking a summer holiday. Immediately the sight of it conjures up in our imagination this or that pleasant experience we have had there: the picture has done its job of jogging our memory for a sentimental pleasure. Not that there is anything delinquent about that, but it is not exactly what we mean by aesthetic appreciation. It is very much a part of what we are; we have trouble in getting enough distance on it to notice its formal qualities of composition, color, and harmony. With such a picture, the teacher may decide to hang it upside down, which, though it will rouse a laugh, may gradually make its point that from that vantage point we are enabled, maybe for the first time, to look at the picture as something more than a stimulus of a sentimental memory.

From this we can easily see that the teacher is often confronted with something less than optimal distance for students' appreciation and will be set to thinking of ways of increasing or decreasing distance in order to focus attention upon something she herself sees as potentially every bit as much a source of aesthetic enjoyment for her charges as for herself.

But the very word *appreciation* can stand some attention. Doubtless the artist dotes on being appreciated, but she may be more discriminating than the rest of us who will take any old kind of appreciation that comes our way. In short, the artist wants to be appreciated for the right reasons. Whistler, for instance, presumably did not want his most famous portrait to be enjoyed by hosts of people who would say, "Oh, it reminds me ever so much of my own mom." Given the title "Study in Black and Gray," we might look at it differently.

Appreciation is not just a synonym for "taking pleasure in." Still, pleasure or enjoyment has something to do with it, for we would hardly say, "I appreciate that music very much but find it terribly boring"—or rather we might say it to raise a laugh. A far better definition of appreciation is: "cherished understanding," Harry Broudy's expression. I can enjoy something without understanding it, as when I simply bathe in a musical performance as I would lying on the strand and letting the warm/cool sea water lap over me. I can understand, as in being highly cognizant of the precise structure of a musical composition, and yet not enjoy. (Someone cruelly and no doubt inaccurately said, "A musicologist is one who knows all about music but doesn't like the sound of it.") But if I have some discriminating understanding of an object and take satisfaction in it, partly *through* that understanding, then we are in the presence of appreciation.

Dewey called appreciation an enlarged, an *intensified* prizing:

> This enhancement of the qualities which make any ordinary experience appealing, appropriable—capable of full assimilation—and enjoyable, constitutes the prime function of literature, music, drawing, painting, etc. in education.... They are not luxuries of education, but emphatic expressions of that which makes any education worth while.
>
> (Dewey 1916: 278–9)

Sometimes teachers falsely assume that if they tell quite a bit about a work of art, appreciation will naturally follow, though surely if they are paying attention to the pupils they won't keep believing that. But it is a lot easier to tell about Shelley's strange life and sad death and about his metrics and imagery than it is to bring the students to the point of wanting to re-read "Ode to the West Wind" purely of their own volition. And it is very much easier to test for factual knowledge than it is for appreciation, for, notoriously, appreciation can be easily faked. Of course the teacher too may fake her own appreciation, even supposing this to be her duty when a poem that is in the syllabus isn't one that much appeals to her, but even quite small pupils can often see through this guise. (It is not that the teacher is more easily taken in, but only that the student's faking is likely to be done in writing: "I enjoyed the Beethoven very much.") But here is a much sadder tale. Meeting his teacher a year after graduation from high school, a pupil, presumably trying to be nice, said to her, "I was so sorry that those school events near the end of our term meant we didn't get clear through *Hamlet*. I've often wondered how it came out."

Yet this is not to say, either, that appreciation is quite simply beyond reckoning, a mysterious something that occurs or fails to occur for quite unfathomable reasons. When it is genuine, teacher enthusiasm, *expressed appreciation*, sometimes helps. As Tolstoy might say, "It is infectious." Not just in a global way, but as referring to specific qualities in the work. "Notice how in this painting of 'The Lovers' Picasso, without doing much modeling of the faces at all, conveys by the very posture of the heads and bodies the different quality of the masculine and feminine love. Isn't that nice?"

But it would be stupid and insensitive to pretend that the teacher's own appreciation is going always to carry over to the students. There are usually a lot of things working against this consummation, however devoutly it may be wished. School-age pupils are even more likely to be influenced by their own *Zeitgeist*, by the powerful influence of their age peers, than even their elders are. (Isn't everybody?) With the best will in the world the teacher may simply find it impossible to cultivate a taste for the graffiti that so engage her pupils, to take delight in the heavy metal sound or even to see the humor in certain "sick" jokes. This in turn will tend to disqualify her, to a degree, as a judge and possible influence. (In this way a teacher not far removed in age from that of her pupils may have a distinct advantage.) Again only a very conscientious teacher may have the patience to acquaint herself with a number of "teenage novels"—even those highly recommended by the critics—in order to be able to recommend from first hand observation this or that book that may "speak to the condition" of her pupils. But then a teacher with even an ounce of realism will not suppose it necessary or even important to establish exactly overlapping areas of appreciation with the class. It will be quite an accomplishment if she is able to present the charms of Hawthorne and Hopkins, Brahms and Bartok, Whitman and Williams, Housman and Hardy, Michelangelo and Miró, sufficiently that these notables from the High Culture may take at least a modest place alongside her young associates' tastes in their own popular culture. Better still, perhaps, if she is able to direct their attention—and possible ultimate appreciation—to various features of this or that kind of art, so that they light up and become noticeable where before they had been invisible, but also in such a way that they may seem *worth* attending to in their contribution to the experience of the whole work: then she will be helping them toward an extension of their aesthetic lives whatever artists and works of art become their particular favorites.

Classes in "Art Appreciation" and "Music Appreciation" do not of course always succeed in broadening and deepening appreciation, but it is not clear that this alone differentiates them from other courses in the curriculum. Yet it is, finally, to be noticed that the educational aim of appreciation is one that extends beyond the aesthetic, or extends the word's meaning, something that was well observed by both Alfred North Whitehead and John Dewey.

Dewey wanted always to show connections between subject matters, and to bridge dichotomies, making them into continuities. He does this with respect to "the appreciation of art" and, say, "the knowledge of the sciences." The arts help us see what appreciation means: "Literature and the fine arts are of peculiar value because they represent appreciation at its best—a heightened realization of meaning through selection and concentration." (This is a meaty sentence to return to.) Then he adds, "But every subject at some phase of its development should possess, what is for the individual concerned with it, an aesthetic quality" (Dewey 1916: 292). We notice the moral word *should*: should possess. Teachers are delinquent to the extent that they do not at least become aware of this as a fact and work toward it as an accomplishment.

Dewey again: "This enhancement of the qualities which make any ordinary experience appealing, appropriable—capable of full assimilation—and enjoyable . . . . These are the chief agencies of an intensified, enhanced appreciation" (p. 279).

Mathematics, biology, chemistry, civics, history, home economics, physical education, religious studies—yes, all of them are there as appreciatable. At a minimum, this means (as we have seen) interesting, seen to be worthwhile, affording some enjoyment in the study thereof. Put another way, there are severe limits to what we can learn by sheer drudgery. We can perhaps learn fastest and most thoroughly what we understand to be essential for our very survival. (It is said that astronauts in training are superb learners.) Of course the computer lab may be enjoyable for its sociability and for finding the quirky message on your screen sent by a classmate across the way—what a development from old-fashioned note passing! But this is not yet appreciating the study of computers, which requires "a heightened realization of meaning through selection and concentration." As always, meaning is the central word in Dewey's discussions of what education is about.

Different as their philosophies are in many respects, Whitehead and Dewey come together on the central importance to education of appreciation. Whitehead too starts with a general characterization of art: "Great art is the arrangement of the environment so as to provide for the soul vivid, but transient values" (Whitehead 1925: 290). This point comes over into *Aims of Education* in the sentence "Our aesthetic emotions provide us with vivid apprehensions of value" (p. 63). As we have seen in a different context, Whitehead called attention to the importance of gaining an appreciation of the beauty of ideas and of the style in which these are most elegantly expressed. We come to appreciate the very "structure of ideas, but this means going beyond the somewhat diffuse appreciation of the amateur to the special studies" that alone can give any appreciation for the exact formulation of general ideas, for their relations when formulated, for their service in the comprehension of life (p. 19).

Appreciation, then, means a gaining access to, a participation in, the values of—anything at all. Its special quality comes out in the contrast with its antonym: depreciation. When we depreciate something we run it down, see its faults and deficiencies, contrast it unfavorably with other things. We find it not worth attending to, dwelling on. We dismiss it, try even to get it out of mind. That too has a place in life and education, but only if depreciation makes way for its positive opposite. To come to appreciate what had before seemed dull, boring, insignificant, confusing— in short, a long way away from where I *am*—is to make a leap upward in valuing, to add a cubit to that which alone makes life worthwhile, one's stock of values.

Back one last time to Whitehead. Although he has said, rightly, that fine art yields "vivid but transient values"—transient, for the excellent reason that no one can sustain for long the wonder, the excitement, much less that occasional rapture that attends upon our best moments with masterpieces—nevertheless the art works themselves abide as a source, a standing potential, for "more than a transient refreshment." Great art, Whitehead writes,

> is something which adds to the permanent richness of the soul's self-attainment. It justifies itself both by its immediate enjoyment, and also by its discipline of the inmost being. Its discipline is not distinct from enjoyment, but by reason of it. It transforms the soul into the permanent realisation of values extending beyond its former self.
>
> (Whitehead 1925: 290–1)

Unfortunately, by comparison science has yielded but little in the way of direct aesthetic value by seeming always to direct attention to things rather than values. Indirectly it has of course contributed a great deal to the fine arts themselves—consider for instance the importance of understanding tonal relations, something that goes clear back to the Pythagoreans of the fifth century BC, or more generally of acoustics. Think also of the multifold contributions of technology to the arts. Because of such advances the painter need no longer worry about the kind of destruction da Vinci's "The Last Supper" suffered; or think of the improvements in the manufacture of musical instruments—including a vastly extended area of timbres through the complexities of synthesizers; and of course there's the printing press! It is not that the study of physics, astronomy, botany, and other sciences cannot be a source of aesthetic delight. Far from it! Great scientific creators testify over and over as to the thrill of coming to see, to understand, some structure, some relation, some wholly unexpected regularity of happening, some high correlation of events that had never before been supposed to have any bearing upon each other. Both those fine moments, and their partial reproduction in the minds of students who come to see for themselves why that which is described by a natural law must be so, are instances of vividly realized value.

And yet, to say it one more time, among the aesthetic arts nothing excels the world's stock of masterpieces for dependable occasions of exquisitely distanced enjoyment—often but not always of extraordinary complexity. (There is the story of Einstein's returning a copy of James Joyce's *Finnegan's Wake* with the comment that he did not find the universe *that* complex.) This stock of masterworks, however, is scattered over a great variety of the world's cultures on every continent, and many of them may require quite unusual degrees of preparation if the works are to yield up their values.

But *preparation* for participation in aesthetic values is precisely what a great many people do not accept as necessary or even see the sense of. After all, anybody can walk through an art gallery glancing at the pictures and saying "I like that one, but I don't like this one." What's all this about preparation? Naturally we have to prepare if we are to understand why the seasons change or how DNA carries its intricate codes, but at Michelangelo's "Pietà" you have only to stare for a bit to see what is there. Is this not the supposition?

Perhaps it is the seemingly instant availability of the simplest and most nearly instinctual art that accounts for this assumption. An infant apparently does not need to *learn* to listen to a lullaby or the rousing effect of a tom-tom in time with the heart beat—this happens without study or guided experience. Yet the six-year-old typically wants to read a story herself and thus to depend less upon the oral reading of others for this particular kind of delight, and is willing (in all but a few cases) to invest some energy in learning to "de-code" those marks on paper. Yet how soon this kind of willingness can fade as the reading becomes more complex in order to grapple with difficulties and subtleties of the ideas.

A diplomat seconded to Bergen might find it necessary to go to a Berlitz school or a crash course in the language—for obvious, practical reasons— but Joyce taught himself Norwegian because he realized he was not getting the full value of Ibsen's prose in translation. And some students will take a course in music appreciation, taking the trouble to learn to identify themes and their variations, development, and recapitulation with at least a vague sense that this skill will enhance the satisfaction to be got from a Haydn symphony—something which they now guess to be possible from the avowals of more sophisticated listeners that such is indeed an achievement worth the effort. But is this not precisely the kind of motivation teachers can and often do provide? It has some similarity to the promise to the child, "You're going to *like* this," as the very first piece of fudge is about to be popped into the willing mouth—except that the reward in the latter case is much quicker and does not require any work. Yet the result in the one case as in the other is intrinsic value. The psychologist Abraham Maslow put it this way:

If I love Beethoven, and I hear something in a quartet that you don't, how do I teach you to hear? The noises are there, obviously. But I hear something very, very beautiful and you look blank. You hear the sounds. How do I get you to hear the beauty? That is more our problem in teaching than making you learn the ABC's or demonstrating arithmetic on the board or pointing to a dissection of a frog.

(Maslow 1971: 48)

Yes, the coming to hear the beauty of the Beethoven quartet constitutes a gaining of an intrinsic value, a gain probably mediated by a teacher. Is it possible that there is also an instrumental value involved? Chocolate gives energy. Can art give knowledge, say self-knowledge?

Part III

RELATIONS OF THE ETHICAL AND THE AESTHETIC

15

LITERATURE AS
ETHICAL

John Dewey has written:

> The sum total of the effect of all reflective treatises on morals is insignificant in comparison with the influence of architecture, novel, drama, on life . . . .
>
> (Dewey 1934: 345)

But then, in recognition of the fact that art is much more often accused of being a malign than a benign influence, he added:

> The first stirrings of dissatisfaction and the first intimations of a better future are always found in works of art. The impregnation of the characteristically new art of a period with a sense of different values than those that prevail is the reason why the conservative finds such art to be immoral and sordid, and is the reason why he resorts to the products of the past for esthetic satisfaction.
>
> (pp. 345–6)

True enough, but we should hurry to say that such artistic stirrings of new ways of being account only for "some" of the labeling of art as immoral, for it surely is not the only reason. When Tolstoy claimed that a very great deal of art (in all media) is immoral because it divides its audience into two very unequal parts, the elite who can understand high culture and the masses who can't, he was well aware that this source of immorality had been the wont of artists from ancient times. There was nothing new in such elitism and its disruption of the frail bonds of equality among all persons. So too with the Marxists of more recent vintage who claim that the very enterprise of art (except some "popular art") is antisocial by nature—and this again is nothing new in bourgeois lands.

The defense of art from this and other kinds of moral attack often preferred by artists was made succinctly by Oscar Wilde (1891): "There is no such thing as a moral or an immoral book. Books are well written or badly written. That is all." In other words, one can retreat to the notion of airtight realms: there is the moral and there is the aesthetic and never shall the twain overlap. But this retreat into formalism is surely reductive. Even Wilde and the whole art-for-art's-sake movement, though eager to protect their art from the strictures of the latter-day puritans of Victorian England, would have hardly supposed that "well written" is a judgment that can be seriously made by disregarding the "content" of the literary work in order to concentrate on the elegance or inelegance of the syntax. From the time of the ancient Greek and Indian epics, and in drama from the time of the first tragedies down through the ages, the literary arts have been blamed for their impiety, blasphemy, treasonableness, sensuality, and their provocation to libertarian and other sinful ways (and praised, as we shall presently notice, for the corresponding kinds of virtues).

It is, of course, notoriously difficult to know precisely what effect the reading of fiction and poetry has upon people. Today the issue is often joined as to the relation between television and film displays of violence and the rising incidence of violence among youth, and though hard evidence is hard come by, it is hard to doubt that wildly reckless driving, lashing out with fists, the use of hand guns and knives, and much other irresponsible and brutal behavior is not somehow legitimated—perhaps even made to seem everyday, by virtue of the high incidence of such drama—by the exposure of youth to such fare. Although the realistic visibility of such photographic art doubtless makes it all the more imitable by watchers, it must be assumed too that reading about murder, assault, robbery, war atrocities, explosions, ghastly accidents, cynicism, cruelty—all oftentimes presented in such a way as to seem not only exciting and adventuresome, but also delightful!—must somehow seep into the psyche of the gullible reader, and prepare the way there for acquiescence in such—even seeking it out—in real life. The word "gullible," though, is the big clue to the antidote. It is all very well to have films labeled as to their presumed suitability for young audiences, but this is a very limited protection indeed. More important is the preparation of precisely those audiences by the teaching of ways of getting more psychic distance between viewer and film. In short, the training of audiences is probably more effective than the censorship of the artifact. But far from easy!

Short of censorship, though, and even a concerted educational campaign, there is the need for criticism of antisocial and otherwise unethical art works. The easy mistake to make in this respect is the generalization from our observations of naive, moralistic, stuffy, and bigoted examples of criticism to a pronouncement about the necessity of keeping these domains wholly separate. For instance, a journalist inveighed against James Joyce's *Ulysses*, as follows:

> All the secret sewers of vice are canalized in its flood of unimaginable thoughts, images and pornographic words. The unclean lunacies are larded with appalling and revolting blasphemies directed against the Christian religion . . . .

In more recent times, one hears of indignant parents and over-zealously pious, patriotic, and defensive groups working to ban from the secondary school curriculum such books as *Huckleberry Finn*, *The Merchant of Venice*, *Madame Bovary*, and more generally all readings containing swear words, street language, references to extramarital sex acts, criticisms of one's government, generous comments about one's nation's current enemies, etc. Such criticisms may be opposed as provincial, intolerant, misguided, bigoted, chauvinistic, and priggish, but precisely because there are fictional works that fully deserve to be exposed as morally iniquitous, one should not forswear such criticism. And yet it would be equally naive and misguided not to realize that the age and developmental level of the audience must be taken into account in the choice of books for the curriculum. Perhaps "Little Black Sambo" does promote racial stereotyping, and some of Hans Christian Anderson's fairy tales quite unnecessarily terrify young children, or certain "torrid romances" unduly push the 10-year-old into adolescence. Or suppose a new book set off a wave of suicides among teenagers, as Goethe's *The Sorrows of Young Werther* did!

But there are books that merit denunciation by critics to lessen the iniquitous effects they may have even on adult audiences. For instance, Celine's *Journey to the End of the Night* has not infrequently been praised by advanced critics as an admirable novel, but Wayne Booth has brilliantly shown how in the novel or short story "the author's judgment is always present, always evident to anyone who knows how to look for it . . . . Then the question is about the soundness of that judgment."

> Though Celine has attempted the traditional excuse—remember, it is my character speaking and not I—we cannot excuse him for writing a book which, if taken seriously by the reader, must corrupt him. The better it is understood, the more immoral it looks. It is immoral not only in the sense that Celine cheats, though that is important; the world he portrays as reality contains no conceivable explanation of how anyone in that world could bring himself to write a book—even this book. More important, if the reader takes its blandishments seriously, without providing a judgment radically different from Celine's, the result of reading the book must be not only to obscure this sense of what is wrong with such an action as clouting a woman's face just to see how it feels but finally to weaken his will to live as effectively as possible. Taken seriously, the book would make life itself meaningless except as a series of self-centered forays into the lives of others.
>
> (Booth 1983: 383–4)

But there are also far more marginal cases. For instance, W. K. Wimsatt, Jr., a critic whose learning, sophistication, and literary sensitivities cannot be challenged, finds *Antony and Cleopatra* an immoral play:

There is no escaping the fact that the poetic splendor of this play, and in particular of its concluding scenes, is something which exists in closest juncture with the acts of suicide and with the whole glorified story of passion. The poetic values are strictly dependent—if not upon the immorality as such—yet upon the immoral acts. Even though, or rather because, the play pleads for certain evil choices, it presents these choices in all their mature interest and capacity to arouse human sympathy. The motives are wrong, but they are not base, silly, or degenerate. They are not lacking in the positive being of deep and complex human desire.

(Winsatt 1954)

Needless to say, other fully qualified critics leapt to Shakespeare's defense. Of course the present point is not about the adequacy of any particular criticism, but only about the appropriateness of the criticism of works we label as aesthetic according to criteria we may call moral or ethical. A further point is that if Wimsatt is right about *Antony and Cleopatra* making suicide romantically attractive, is this not a reason for according it a lesser place among the tragedies of Shakespeare than that occupied by those works not so marred, say *Macbeth* and *King Lear*? Wimsatt agrees, saying, "The greatest poetry will be morally right, even though perhaps obscurely so, in groping confusion of will and knowledge—as Oedipus the King foreshadows Lear" (Wimsatt 1954: 97)

But this point may be even better made, perhaps, when we turn to the question about works we may commend on both aesthetic and ethical grounds. And indeed this topic is central to this chapter's search for ways in which literature (and doubtless other kinds of works of art, though usually in much more devious and subtle ways) can work toward ethical growth.

But before getting far into this topic, let us scotch the supposition that what will be advocated is the restriction of the school literary diet to works of a uniformly positive, optimistic, upward-and-onward character. Plato himself came dangerously near to joining this "sweetness-and-light only" school, and not a few people alive today are infinitely at pains to shield children's eyes from any of the shadow side of reality. But such a view not only neglects the ethical value of showing evil to be evil (not neglecting here the power of satire) but sets the young person up for what may be the unbearable and inevitable shock of finding out how wholly unrealistic the school representation of reality is.

Given that, the present argument will be that ethical development can be furthered and promoted by the inclusion in the curriculum of fairy tales, stories, plays, and novels that have a prosocial, pro-individuality cast. These may be as simple as a nursery rhyme:

> One misty, moisty morning
> When cloudy was the weather,

I chanced to meet an old man
Clad all in leather.
He began to compliment
And I began to grin:
How do you do, and how do you do,
And how do you do, again.

We may go on to a Grimm brothers fairy tale, one which requires no commentary.

The Old Man and his Grandson

There was once a very old man, whose eyes had become dim, his ears dull of hearing, his knees trembled, and when he sat at table he could hardly hold the spoon, and spilt the broth upon the table-cloth or let it run out of his mouth. His son and his son's wife were disgusted at this, so the old grandfather at last had to sit in the corner behind the stove, and they gave him his food in an earthenware bowl, and not even enough of it. And he used to look towards the table with his eyes full of tears. Once, too, his trembling hands could not hold the bowl, and it fell to the ground and broke. The young wife scolded him, but he said nothing and only sighed. Then they bought him a wooden bowl for a few half-pence, out of which he had to eat.

They were once sitting thus when the little grandson of four years old began to gather together some bits of wood upon the ground. "What are you doing there?" asked the father. "I am making a little trough," answered the child, "for father and mother to eat out of when I am big."

The man and his wife looked at each other for a while, and presently began to cry. Then they took the old grandfather to the table, and henceforth always let him eat with them, and likewise said nothing if he did spill a little of anything.

Consider next that surpassingly great work, *Alice in Wonderland* (and *Through the Looking-glass*). Here is no namby-pambyness. The Queen is a disagreeable monarch, indeed, even if her "Off with his head" commands do not seem to have very serious consequences, and the caterpillar is a sour enough pedant, and Alice certainly has some quite unsettling, even frightening experiences; but what reader fails to envy her her adventures, meeting all of those extraordinary cats, eggs, mice, hares, and even humans. Alice herself of course is a thoroughly sensible little miss who miraculously retains her poise and equilibrium in a topsy-turvy world and has the gumption to correct, or try to correct, the odd logicians she meets. Thus when the dormouse is offered more tea, Alice says that he can't possibly have more when he hasn't had any yet, only to be set straight: "You can always have more, it's less you can't have." But best of all for our present purposes is the scene in which the Duchess says to Alice,

"You're thinking about something, my dear, and that makes you forget to talk. I can't tell you just now what the moral of that is, but I shall remember it in a bit."

"Perhaps it hasn't one," Alice ventured to remark.

"Tut, tut, child!" said the Duchess. "Everything's got a moral, if only you can find it." [11]

Child or adult, the reader puts down this book (reluctantly!) feeling caught between the hither and nether world.

Next there is Natalie Babbitt's *Tuck Everlasting*. The story opens conventionally enough with descriptions of an old woman and her husband, though we are struck with its being odd that the woman is off to see her children, as she is said to do every ten years. But then we are brought up short with the ending sentence of Chapter two: "For Mae Tuck, and her husband, and Miles and Jesse [the sons] too, had all looked exactly the same for eighty-seven years." We come to learn that this family had drunk the water of a secret spring that makes them "everlasting." A neighboring child gets a hint of all this and naturally wants to share their good luck—as she supposes. But we are forced by the author to ask whether this would be altogether a blessing.

Huckleberry Finn has had its severe critics (on ethical grounds), both naive and sophisticated, but at the very least it is an unsurpassed source of realization as to how deep the roots of racism can reach into the soil of a social environment. Mark Twain's ironic revelations of the contradictions between a churchgoing woman's protestations of virtue and her ready willingness to sell a slave and thus separating him from wife and family, is simple enough, but far more complex is the tension within Huck himself, torn between his ingrained assumption that Blacks are, in being inferior, natural slaves, and his delight and comfort in Jim's company and his gradual awakening: "I do believe he cared just as much for his people as white folks does for their'n. It don't seem natural, but I reckon it's so" (p. 131). And yet he can't quite shake the conflicting realization that he was "stealing a poor old woman's nigger that hadn't done me no harm" (p. 178).

A great many literary works raise more questions than provide answers, and of course this may be at least as important a function in ethical development as that of displaying virtue rewarded or the very quality of mercy or compassion or justice in a character. Or take the case of the Sherlock Holmes story, *The Adventure of the Devil's Foot*. This story of one Mortimer Regennis's theft of a highly poisonous root from Dr Sterndale, an eminent African lion-hunter, tells how the thief, for financial gain, poisons three persons, one of them the woman loved by Sterndale.

Sterndale, in turn, despairing of bringing the murderer to justice in the courts, takes the law in his own hands and kills Regennis. Sherlock Holmes, of course, solves what to everyone else is the mystery of who the murderer was, but then finally, instead of turning him over to the police, lets him make his escape back to Africa, saying to his sidekick, "I have never loved, Watson, but if I did and if the woman I loved had met such an end, I might act even as our lawless lion-hunter has done. Who knows?"

Here is food for thought, and one can easily imagine a young student audience deliberating about whether the great sleuth had this time acted wisely and rightly, and also about the very character of Holmes, displayed here and elsewhere. Was he mainly admirable, not alone for his detecting skill (who could doubt or fail to admire that?), but also as a non-loving person, and a cocaine addict to boot.[12]

It has often been remarked that villains and generally good but flawed characters, such as the protagonists of the great tragedies, are easier to create and more interesting than paragons of virtue. (The characteristic example is Milton's Satan.) We can easily believe in—that is, find both admirable and verisimilitudinous—such characters as Elizabeth Bennet in *Pride and Prejudice*, or Levin in *Anna Karenina*. But these characters are not saints and indeed *The Lives of the Saints* may make for piety but are hardly absorbingly interesting. Yet there is at least one example in world literature of a great novelist who dared go farther.

Dostoevsky has in his novels a number of saintly characters, both women and men, but for the most part they are subordinate to the great tortured, agonized protagonists like Raskolnikov and Ivan. However, he tried to develop two major characters of near perfection in moral character. One is Prince Myshkin in *The Idiot*, but after weathering many moral storms in Christ-like forbearance Myshkin is represented as finally cracking under the strain, as if to say that the actual world imposes too heavy a burden for the shoulders of a mortal saint to bear. In *The Brothers Karamazov*, on the other hand, the character of Alyosha is shown as growing toward moral perfection. Dostoevsky's marvelous accomplishment here has not been given sufficient credit by critics who have been understandably fascinated by the mercurial Dmitri and the tortured, intellectual Ivan. Alyosha is early presented as a young man seeking to become a kind of lay monk, one who will go abroad from the monastery to be a friend of God and man. He is good-tempered, gentle, kind, without cloying sweetness or passivity. However, he makes a great discovery, which is-that, for the accomplishment of the good, noble intentions are not enough. It also takes knowledge: one must learn how to be effectively good. To rescue those in distress may be to harden their hearts; to give alms may be to sink the indigent deeper in their quagmire. Above all, to be charitable may be to invite a self-debilitating kind of dependence upon authority. Love, Alyosha learns, is not just a diffused glow toward humanity; or if it is, then it is something less than the love required by God. Rather, love that has reached its full maturity must be of the indefeasible person; it must be of the concrete embodiment of freedom.

This statement of the growth and development of a character is, of course, severely abstracted from the tight drama of the story, but Alyosha remains a superlative example of how a character can be presented as approaching the ideal without sacrificing human warmth and intricacy. Some authors may be given high marks for their good intentions but blamed for their actual accomplishments. This is D. H. Lawrence's position about Galsworthy:

> It is when he comes to sex that Mr. Galsworthy collapses finally. He becomes nastily sentimental. He wants to make sex important, and he only makes it repulsive. Sentimentalism is the working off on yourself of feelings you haven't got. We all want to have certain feelings: feelings of love, of passionate sex, or kindliness, and so forth. Very few people really feel love, or sex passion, or kindliness, or anything else that goes at all deep. So the mass just fake these feelings inside themselves. Faked feeling! The world is all gummy with them. They are better than real feelings, because you can spit them out when you brush your teeth; and then tomorrow you can fake them afresh.
>
> (Lawrence 1950: 224)

But it is to be noted that Lawrence had no doubt but that it is the novelist's prerogative and even duty to get moral matters like this right, not just to avoid error (such as is betokened by sentimentalism) but more positively too.

According to Lawrence "The moral instinct of the man in the street is largely an emotional defence of an old habit" (1936: 521). But "If the novel reveals true and vivid relationships, it is a moral work, no matter what the relationships may consist in" (p. 130). This is quite an exceptionally interesting position, that the artist—and Lawrence makes clear that this is as true of a painter like Cézanne as of a literary artist—is a teacher, and what he teaches is knowledge, knowledge about human feelings and relationships.

The principal ways in which literature may serve the cause of ethics are more likely to be those that may be called "pre-moral." That is to say, there are certain skills or sensitivities that the reading of good literature may help us develop and which are part of the equipment needed to become ethically better, though any one of them can be used also to malign ends, or simply for that which falls altogether outside the ethical sphere.

The first is a cognitive matter; A. C. Ewing even calls it factual:

> We must not assume that, because we cannot . . . make our moral knowledge dependent entirely on inference, therefore there is no scope for inference or reasoning at all in Ethics. It does not follow,

because reasoning is not omnipotent, that therefore it is useless. We have to rely on something that may be loosely called "intuition," but to put ourselves in a position to make safe use of it we ought first to reason long and hard. It would be admitted by almost everybody that in order to determine what is right, in many cases at any rate, we have to use reasoning for the purpose of forecasting the probable consequences, this being a question of fact, not of values; but surely it is proper also to analyse these consequences and determine which elements in them are valuable and which are not . . . .

All ethical judgments seem to presuppose at any rate these three factors: (a) some empirical knowledge of the particular situation or object; (b) some more or less incomplete analysis of it; (c) the previous or simultaneous occurrence in the person judging of some desire or emotion relative to something good.

(Ewing 1929: 184, 194)

Next is the matter of empathy. The good writer displays empathy (or the notable lack thereof) in his characters, but also the vividness of her writing makes it easier for us readers to have empathy. (The hope, then, is that this may transfer to real-life situations.)

Here is a bit of Eudora Welty's fine story, *A Worn Path*. Phoenix, a very old, slight black woman, has to make a long hike across country to get medicine for her seriously ill grandchild. She will get the medicine (the bottle marked "charity" from a doctor's attendant) but will also beg some small change with which to buy a simple toy for the lad. But the trip itself is full of troubles:

It was December—a bright frozen day in the early morning. Far out in the country there was an old Negro woman with her head tied in a red rag, coming along a path through the pinewoods. Her name was Phoenix Jackson. She was very old and small and she walked slowly in the dark pine shadows, moving a little from side to side in her step, with the balanced heaviness and lightness of a pendulum in a grandfather clock. She carried a thin, small cane made from an umbrella, and with this she kept tapping the frozen earth in front of her. This made a grave and persistent noise in the still air, that seemed meditative like the chirping of a solitary little bird.

She wore a dark striped dress reaching down to her shoe tops, and an equally long apron of bleached sugar sacks, with a full pocket: all neat and tidy, but every time she took a step she might have fallen over her shoelaces, which dragged from her unlaced shoes. She looked straight ahead. Her eyes were blue with age. Her skin had a pattern all its own of numberless branching wrinkles and as though a whole little tree stood in the middle of her forehead, but a golden color ran underneath, and the two knobs of her cheeks were

171

illumined by a yellow burning under the dark. Under the red rag her hair came down on her neck in the frailest of ringlets, still black, and with an odor like copper.

Now and then there was a quivering in the thicket. Old Phoenix said, "Out of my way, all you foxes, owls, beetles, jack rabbits, coons and wild animals! . . . Keep out from under these feet, little bob-whites . . . . Keep the big wild hogs out of my path. Don't let none of those come running my direction. I got a long way." Under her small black-freckled hand her cane, limber as a buggy whip, would switch at the brush as if to rouse up any hiding things.

On she went. The woods were deep and still. The sun made the pine needles almost too bright to look at, up where the wind rocked. The cones dropped as light as feathers. Down in the hollow was the mourning dove—it was not too late for him.

The path ran up a hill. "Seem like there is chains about my feet, time I get this far," she said, in the voice of argument old people keep to use with themselves. "Something always take a hold of me on this hill—pleads I should stay."

After she got to the top she turned and gave a full, severe look behind her where she had come. "Up through pines," said she at length. "Now down through oaks."

Her eyes opened their widest, and she started down gently. But before she got to the bottom of the hill a bush caught her dress.

Her fingers were busy and intent, but her skirts were full and long, so that before she could pull them free in one place they were caught in another. It was not possible to allow the dress to tear. "I in the thorny bush," she said. "Thorns, you doing your appointed work. Never want to let folks pass, no sir. Old eyes thought you was a pretty little green bush."

Finally, trembling all over, she stood free, and after a moment dared to stoop for her cane.

"Sun so high!" she cried, leaning back and looking, while the thick tears went over her eyes. "The time getting all gone here."

At the foot of this hill was a place where a log was laid across the creek.

"Now comes the trial," said Phoenix.

Putting her right foot out, she mounted the log and shut her eyes. Lifting her skirt, leveling her cane fiercely before her, like a festival figure in some parade, she began to march across. Then she opened her eyes and she was safe on the other side.

"I wasn't as old as I thought," she said.

Phoenix herself has extraordinary empathy with her own surroundings, but the story-teller allows us to have extraordinary empathy with this character, giving us just the right bits of the old woman's talk on her solitary journey, and the right amount of description of how she walked, stooped, balanced, persisted, to make us participate in that experience.

Finally there is what literature does for us in the way of training our imagination. Shelley put it best in *A Defence of Poetry*:

> A man, to be greatly good, must imagine intensely and comprehensively; he must put himself in the place of another and of many others; the pains and pleasures of this species must become his own. The great instrument of moral good is the imagination; and poetry administers to the effect by action upon the cause. . . . Poetry strengthens the faculty which is the organ of the moral nature of man, in the same manner as exercise strengthens a limb. A poet therefore would do ill to embody his own conceptions of right and wrong, which are usually those of his place and time, in his poetical creations, which participate in neither.
>
> (Shelley 1821)

Of course it is not only imagination for the good—or more commonly, the better—that is assisted through the gifted writer's own imagination, she serving as our model, but also for how things can go wrong or how, in subtle ways, a character can be flawed, as in this brief excerpt from D. H. Lawrence's *The Rainbow*. A young woman, Ursula Brangwen, and her fiancé, Skrebensky, have spent their first night together, in an Italian kind of hotel in London:

> She knew he was awake. He lay still, with a concrete stillness, not as when he slept. Then his arm tightened almost convulsively upon her, and he said, half timidly:
> "Did you sleep well?"
> "Very well."
> "So did I."
> There was a pause.
> "And do you love me?" he asked
> She turned and looked at him searchingly. He seemed outside her.
> "I do," she said.
> But she said it out of complacency and a desire not to be harried. There was a curious breach of silence between them, which frightened him.
> They lay rather late, then he rang for breakfast. She wanted to be able to go straight downstairs and away from the place, when she got up. She was happy in this room, but the thought of the publicity of the hall downstairs rather troubled her.
> A young Italian, a Sicilian, dark and slightly pock-marked, buttoned up in a sort of grey tunic, appeared with the tray. His face had an almost African imperturbability, impassive, incomprehensible.

"One might be in Italy," Skrebensky said to him, genially. A vacant look, almost like fear, came on the fellow's face. He did not understand.

"This is like Italy," Skrebensky explained.

The face of the Italian flashed with a non-comprehending smile, he finished setting out the tray, and was gone. He did not understand: he would understand nothing : he disappeared from the door like a half-domesticated wild animal. It made Ursula shudder slightly, the quick, sharp-sighted, intent animality of the man.

Skrebensky was beautiful to her this morning, his face softened and transfused with suffering and with love, his movements very still and gentle. He was beautiful to her, but she was detached from him by a chill distance. Always she seemed to be bearing up against the distance that separated them. But he was unaware. This morning he was transfused and beautiful. She admired his movements, the ease with which he spread honey on his roll, or poured out the coffee.

When breakfast was over, she lay still again on the pillows, whilst he went through his toilet. She watched him, as he sponged himself, and quickly dried himself with the towel. His body was beautiful, his movements intent and quick, she admired him and she appreciated him without reserve. He seemed completed now. He aroused no fruitful fecundity in her. He seemed added up, finished. She knew him all round, not on any side did he lead into the unknown. Poignant, almost passionate appreciation she felt for him, but none of the dreadful wonder, none of the rich fear, the connection with the unknown, or the reverence of love. He was, however, unaware this morning. His body was quiet and fulfilled, his veins complete with satisfaction, he was happy, finished.

(Lawrence 1926:472–3)

It will be apparent that this woman's achievements are principally in recognizing the virtue and deficiencies of a man who strongly attracts her. But this is a great deal. Ursula is one who has very high standards. She knows that "Do you love me?" is such a shallow question as to invite a glib answer. She sees her lover's beauty, his quickness, his elegance in movement. He is extremely attractive. But that is not enough. She notices in herself a feeling of detachment from him, a "chill distance." He is domesticated. Worse yet, he seems "added up, finished . . . completed." The Sicilian waiter, pockmarks and all, has something that Skrebensky lacks, something slightly wild, undeterred by intellectuality, some strange connection with the unknown that her lover lacks. She knows she does not finally want to marry a man whose "Body was quiet and fulfilled, his veins complete with satisfaction . . . happy, finished." In Ursula's (and Lawrence's) book, those are serious faults, but they are rarely seen to be. We ourselves must be unfinished, searching, a little wild, with a connection to the mystery of life, to know these in—or not in—another.

Or take Jane Austen as a superb portrayer of women whom we both like and admire. Alasdair MacIntyre (1984:239–43) identifies Jane Austen's most praised virtues as constancy and amiability. Perhaps we are struck with the uninflated nature of these qualities: they are not exactly god-like perfections. Yet they are fairly rare, apparently very difficult to attain to in high degree, and, again it must be said, presented as highly attractive. For instance, one can easily imagine good-natured and doggedly loyal men and women who would hardly inspire emulation. But what an author of genius can do is to show us in detail someone that we would in ever so many ways like to be like—and some others about whom we say, "There but for the grace of God go I."

Through the imagination, fiction is a great extender of our experience. It puts us into an enormous number of situations we will literally never find ourselves in in our own real lives. And yet some of these imaginative realizations can come to seem somehow more real, more vivid and intense, than much of what happens in our ordinary existence. Although we may use the writer's imagination as a crutch, further impairing our own development, it can, especially with teachers' help, stimulate and provide a guide to our own imaginative capacities.

These skills and sensitivities here called "pre-moral" may even be employed for malign ends. We may intuit, empathize, and imagine in order to dupe more skillfully the ones we are dealing with, plot more carefully the burglary, seduce more cleverly our intended victim. This says that something more is needed to make sure these abilities do indeed contribute to benign accomplishments. That something more is caring.

Yet, after noticing these "pre-moral abilities," let us return to important aspects of the human situation that literature seems especially to confront us with. In her book, *The Moral of the Story*, Susan Resneck Park writes, "Because moral and values questions are inevitably at the core of the human experience, it is important that students learn to confront—deliberately, reflectively, and with caring—such questions" (Park 1982: 18–19). She concentrates her attention on three clusters of recurring ethical questions:

1 Though consciousness often occasions misery and freedom brings home the burdens of responsibility, literature over and over affords us examples of how unreflective—and thus unconscious—experience brings in its wake danger and devastation. Yet, somehow, recognition of the difficulties of consciousness and freedom tends to raise consciousness and heighten freedom.

2 "Again and again, regardless of time and place, literature gives life to the problems of being human. It dramatizes how people—given their cultural values, their individual aspirations and talents, and their

perceptions of the possibilities of freedom and self-realization—define themselves, make choices, and act" (p. 19). Sartre and other existentialists would bridle here at "define themselves," warning that that misguided attempt is precisely the root of most human woes, for the human being is historical, and as Nietzche said, "Only that which is without history can be defined." Perhaps the author will let us substitute the words "characterize themselves."

3 Literature helps us become aware of a larger human community, extending far into the past: thus in confronting this or that problem we are not alone, our dilemmas have precedents, and in turn the situations faced by fictional characters make us newly aware of our own.

The listing of the kinds of questions often raised by the reading of fiction, drama, and poetry in turn suggests how discussable are such works, and if well chosen how they are at once personal and detached, engaging and yet distanced enough to invite serious reflection.

16

ETHICAL
DEVELOPMENT
THROUGH WRITING

We do not write in order to be understood:
we write in order to understand.

Cecil Day Lewis's epigram may be challenged in what it denies. But teachers of writing have come to agree, though perhaps only recently, that we do write in order to understand. Or, more modestly, to reduce confusion, to understand better, to improve our understanding. But let not our academic caution or becoming modesty obscure the point: alike for us teachers and for our students, one great purpose of sitting down to write is to see whether we can convert a vague intuition, an inchoate glimmering, a sort of notion, an unformed feeling, into a realization, an expression, language that makes sense. Thus we will have gained clarity by *coming to terms* with that pre-verbal impulse—even, perhaps, giving a promising evanescence a local habitation and a name.

This important reason for writing and thus for teaching writing has affected our previous beliefs about how our teaching should proceed, but it is worth asking what sorts of topics, ideas, and problems are appropriate to writing-in-order-to-understand.

Socrates (nobody's model of a writer) in *The Meno* had a suggestion to make about this. In the famous scene of teaching a slave-boy geometry, precisely by not teaching in the sense of telling or showing but by asking questions, Socrates stimulated his pupil to think. Or, as Socrates thought, to search within himself for what he already in some sense knew in order to come to understand that the conclusions he had quickly jumped to were untenable. We remember that Socrates is then made (by Plato) to advance an exotic account of how we all have a store of knowledge on which we can call, everybody having come to know in a previous life what we subsequently have forgotten but can now, with help, begin to remember. But Socrates later admits that this is a speculation on which he would not stake his life, as he *would* on his belief that it is our duty to try with all the powers we can muster to understand that knowledge is possible and "to turn our minds on ourselves" (96A; 96B). Now, Socrates obviously did not mean that we can find out whether it is presently raining outside by looking inward: he was certainly not talking about empirical knowledge. What he *did* have in mind, the very things Aristotle was to call Socrates' forte, were logic on the one hand and ethics on the other. These, he was certain, are areas in which knowledge is possible (though often difficult) through thinking as hard as we can about what must be the case.

Mathematics teachers have always known this about their ultra-logical subject. When they pose a "story problem" about how many pounds of beans you can get for two dollars, the price being 73 cents a pound, they are not recommending a trip to the store. And in the ethical sphere both parents and teachers have had occasion to say to the erring student, "You know, deep down, that that isn't the right thing to do." But a lot of times our students, and even we ourselves, don't have the answer to an ethical problem right on the tips of our tongues, even our psychic tongues. Nor yet on the tips of our pens. Still, maybe we can get some light—by writing.

What if—three of us teachers asked recently—we were to challenge students to write either a true or a fictional (thus, with good management, fictionally true) story about an ethical problem? Though one could leave it wide open, we decided to provide some structure, yet not so much that the student would not have to find (or make up) some characters, a situation, a plot, (Hermes willing, a *perepeteia*) and a resolution.

What would be likely to happen? We of course didn't know, but thought something—something interesting—just might. We now think we might have put the assignments better, and will next time, but let's stick with what we did. Here is the first one: "Write about a true or imaginary situation where you have seen somebody who needed help, but where you felt conflicted or confused about whether you should help or not." The students were members of a Humanities class in the eighth grade of a small, middle/middle class suburban town in northern California.

Our first wonder was whether the students would find the assignment puzzling and ask a lot of questions. (They are far from shy.) But they didn't. It seemed intelligible enough—though nobody will be surprised that they varied in their interpretation. Indeed, some missed the point, so, yes, the assignment should be improved: for instance, there were a few who had their protagonist do something evidently wrong and then either feel bad about it or get off scot-free. Here are a few quick summaries of the fairly ordinary responses to the assignment.

Heidi wrote a story about a boy who tries to cook dinner for his working mother, but creates an enormous mess and comes to realize that he'd better leave the cooking to her. Andrea's protagonist accepts a prom date with a good friend so he will *have* a date, but finally realizes, when he showers her with flowers and candy, that she is leading him to believe she cares more for him than she in fact does. Matt has a policeman overreact by shooting a rape suspect. Far from being admired, he is tried for manslaughter. Frank has a boy, himself invited to a party, tell his friend who has not been invited and doesn't know of the party that it will probably be dull anyway, so he won't miss much. But the friend feels very bad about his lack of invitation, and his friend regrets having told him about it.

Such stories, with a few exceptions, stay fairly close to what these 13–14-year-olds or their acquaintances know from experience. Theirs are rarely extremely serious moral problems, but they do catch the point that our first impulse, if acted upon without reflection, may turn out to have been misdirected.

But two stories we thought to be unusually good, both as stories and as embodying ethical insight. By consent of the writers, here they are in full:

Not a Perfect 10

By Mike

Little Bobby Fisher walked along the Pier until he reached his friend Joey's houseboats. Joey lived on the houseboat with Parents and his younger sister. Joey was the same age as Bobby 7, and they both attended the Groverville Seaside elementary school. But today was a saturday and school was the farthest thing from their young minds. Today they were going to trade baseball cards. So when Bobby appeared outside the houseboat Joey was quick to welcome him in. And Bobby eagerly excepted this gesture.

So now with the two baseball card traders inside the action began. The two boys sat on opposite sides of the small card table that was set up in Joey's room. Both boy's immediatly started setting out their cards. Each boy had three piles. In one pile there were the cards he had doubles of in another were the cards of players who weren't all that good, and in the third pile their were the cards of the superstars (the tough ones to get). Neither boy usually traded from this pile but instead they put it out as sort of bragging rites. Now with the sides laid out the battle began. First the boy's went through all of their doubles and some small trades were made. Each boy argued a little over who got the better deal but in reality it was all about even. Then Joey suggested that he go and get them both a Coke from downstairs and Bobby agreed that that was a good idea and Joey went to get the Cokes.

When Joey left Bobby continued looking though Joey's superstar pile untill he came upon a Billy (the sleazeball) Ryan card from 1985. Bobby wanted this card dearly because it was the only card he had yet to get for his 1985 collection. But Bobby new Joey would never trade any card from the superstar pile. So he acted fast and switched this one card into the not good pile. When Joey returned they drank their Coke's and continued tradding. When old sleazeball came up in the has been pile Joey didn't even notice so he traded it away for almost nothing. Bobby was happy and headed home soon after proud of his clever idea.

As Bobby ran up his front steps he noticed his older brother's things in the front hall. Bobby darted in the house and ran into his older brothers (older brother home from colledge for Spring brake) room and told him his clever plan that got him this great card. Bobby's older brother pointed out the error in young Bobby's way.

Bobby upset because he had done wrong and because he knew he couldn't keep the card decided to give it back immedialy. He headed back to Joey's house and reluctently told Joey the whole story. The true story. How the two piles had fallen on the ground and goten all mixed and how only when Bobby got home did he discover sleazeball was a superstar. WELL NOBODY'S PERFECT.

By Nora

Dear Johnathon;
I came accross a very strange story last week I think you will enjoy. It seems that there was once a very small towne called Hegarty. Only 15 people lived there and they all new eachother. How could they not. Each worked very hard, but the one person who worked the hardest was the priest. Not only was he the priest but he was in charge of all the church duties. That wouldn't have been so bad but they had a very large church. Hegarty used to be a center of trade and hundreds of people lived their. Then a large storm ruined their harbor. So the people decided instead of building a new town they would merely move somewhere else where they would be happier. Except for 15 people everyone left.

But back to the priest (Father Donovan). He worked very hard. He cleaned the stain glass windows, visited the poor and the sick (old charlie), taught sunday school, gave sermons, did every single thing it took to run the church. Even though no one ever came to church. Not once in the past 5 years. Everyday the priest would start by saying that today people would come, they would care, but no one ever did.

One day, the Devil was reading his paper and one of his pet cats came and told him about Father Donovan. The Devil, never one to miss an opportunity, decided to go pay the Father a visit. He told the father that he would make people flock to his church, but the first person to enter the church would be his. The Father would not hear of it and the devil spent the rest of the week trying to convince him.

Finnaly the devil tried a new approach. He told Father Donovan that he would be doing the wrong thing for the right reason so that made it O.K. The good father adgreed and the deal was to take place the next morning, Sunday. But that night the father had a dream. The mother of the condemmed person was crying at his feet. It was then that the father realized that he had made a grave error.

He called for the Devil so that he would try to change his mind but he could not.

"A deal is a deal" the Devil said, "why should I let you out of it." With that the devil left.

Morning came and the church bells rang. All 15 people were walking down the road toward the church. Before the father let them in he laid a cat on the egde of the threshhold. He then poured a bucket of water on the cat, and the cat ran into the church. The Devil appeared, overjoyed at being able to claim a cat instead of a medlesome human.

"Hello there my little smopsy," thats what the devil called cats, "how about some milk."

And the devil never bothered the town of Hegarty again. As for Father Donovan's church, it's full every sunday and after services everyone goes on a picnic.

> Sincerely,
> Anna

Mike's story rings true. The scene is well set, the motivation is convincingly established, the "crime" is elegantly described, and the denouement has a little surprise without any loss of verisimilitude—quite the contrary. To be sure, the story does not *quite* meet the assignment, for what the hard trader did was not something he considered right, but rather something perhaps not really wrong, which he then, with his older brother's help, comes to repent of. But that which keeps the protagonist this side of "perfect ten" represents a very deft stroke on the part of the author, and we readers say to ourselves, "Yes, I too might have let myself off the sharpest hook in just such a way."

Nora's story certainly went well beyond her (and our) experience. It might almost be an early Borges, but this was not the only evidence that this 13-year-old had a powerful imagination. In the discussion she said that yes, she had heard something about stories that employed the Faust motif, though she did not use this expression, but rather something more like "a pact with the devil." But as a fine variation on the old theme it seemed to us an exceptional piece of work on all counts. The present point is the ethical one, and to learn from a dream the fallacy of doing a wrong for the sake of a good result can hardly be improved upon. It has something approaching the shock of recognition we have in the presence of William James's noble insistence that if the hypothesis were presented that millions of humans would be

> kept permanently happy on the one simple condition that a certain lost soul on the far-off edge of things should lead a life of lonely

torture, what except a specifical and independent sort of emotion can it be which would make us immediately feel, even though an impulse arose within us to clutch at the happiness offered, how hideous a thing would be its enjoyment. . . ?

(James 1956: 188)

Nora scored again, though not quite so signally, in the next assignment, when the challenge was put in this fashion: someone is in need of help, yet finally the protagonist does not provide it. Nora imagined a country in which the surprising discovery was made that an "old" creature of five months was becoming six rather than the usual four months old. Indeed, even when this person got to be 13, it would still be possible to reverse this unprecedented process, but the protagonist thinks this would be to "mess around with life" and refuses. Hm.

Owen wrote a poem about being approached by a Berkeley panhandler asking for 50 cents, but the "I" rubs together the quarters in his pocket, tells the pleader he is broke, and goes on to buy some comic books which prove boring, fit only for almost immediate discard. He feels himself "guilty of cruelty."

Matt wrote the only other poem in this batch and it too proved to be good. Here the setting was Lima (Peru, where the author later said he had been two years before), and again there is a beggar, this one able to speak only with his eyes. A woman tourist is tempted to give him the dollar in her pocket, a king's bounty, but then decides that this "would only temporarily solve the problem/That so many people felt," and she walked on, feeling "black inside" and "Hiding from reality." In this instance the discussion was interesting, as people recognized that it was not simply an excuse that the woman had given, but a truth: helping one person would by no means solve the problem of poverty. And yet they could understand too how one would feel in the presence of "those penetrating eyes," for it is rare indeed that one can do more than meet, in some measure, another person's immediate need.

Two students wrote about the needs of a person whose wheelchair had overturned. Heather and her friend held back for fear their offer would further embarrass the handicapped one. And (another) Matt wrote of a boy who, downright afraid of persons paralyzed, hangs back when one needs help; a woman steps in and does the job, and the young man feels at once sorry he had delayed, and relieved to be saved the pain of involvement. Again an uneasiness or embarrassment was a factor in preventing Elie's character from providing some consolation to a three-year-old crying for his mother. Finally he does, but the father appears and explains that the mother has in fact recently died.

The third assignment was designed to introduce a conflict between parent and child: write about a case in which a young person feels that something his mother or father has told him to do is basically *not* a good thing to do.

To this challenge there were no responses that could be considered outstanding, but there was a pretty general rising to the bait: 13-year-olds—*bonjour*, M. Piaget—know that parents can be wrong, and perhaps take some small pleasure in catching them out. Conflicts of values figure strongly in these stories. Thus Leah has a mom telling a young son to take an apple from a grocery store, even threatening him in case he is unwilling; the boy remembers her admonitions never to steal, and is of course confused. Christine tells a story of a very young girl who, though she remembers a warning never to talk to strangers, gives a motorist directions to the swimming pool—for had the same parent not also told her to be helpful to other people?

Sometimes the story would not pronounce outright on the iniquity of parental guidance, but only raise a question. Thus Meredith overhears a mother telling a very young child that her pet lizard is away visiting a friend: why should she not tell the truth, that the lizard is dead? Still, the girl *is* quite small, so *perhaps* the mother is right.

But in some cases the parent is pinned to the moral wall. Matt Z. has a talented kid forget, for once, to do his project, due tomorrow. His mom offers to call him in as sick, and thus save him from a bad mark, though requiring him to promise not ever to do it again. He promises, but the author wonders if the next time a lie might be even easier, and pretty soon become a habit. Furthermore, the culprit didn't even feel very guilty: wasn't his mother condoning the transaction? Andrea's story is similar, but in this case with the student not accepting the mother's offer: that would be *cheating*.

Some student writers opted for an unresolved ending. Heidi has a girl overhearing her parents quarrel, which sets her to reflecting gloomily that divorce these days is common. However, her parents had always insisted that they were different and would never part. Still, something in her wants to confront them. She is not sure she can trust what they say. Mike has a complex plot about a rich teenager, left alone by his traveling parents who seem to have forgotten both Thanksgiving and his birthday. He offers a ride to some obviously poor people who are walking home in the rain, and is impressed with how little self-conscious they are about having no car and but a modest home. When he has grown up and has his own wife and children he is offered a much better-paying job, which will require him to be away from home much of the time, but also give him the money better to provide for his family. Which is the better choice?

But what is to be made of this? Giving this kind of assignment appears to have certain advantages:

1   It encourages students to remember or invent—perhaps most often a combination of the two, if one may trust certain comments made in discussion—moral occasions, events, situations. *Their* choosing them

may well mean that the emergent problem rings true to the student, and probably so too to his or her contemporaries. Thus the students are forming their own agenda, which includes a choice of the kinds of people involved, some sort of conflict, some sort of resolution, or at least outcome. This contrasts with textbook or teacherly problems that may, as Dewey was forever pointing out, be far more problematic to the adult than to the pupil.

2 It sets a kind of frame for the writer to improve the probability that what comes out will have a moral quality to it. Or, if it doesn't, this will set the stage for a discussion of some of the distinctions that can be drawn between, say, manners and morals, or between allowable differences of taste on the one hand and moral obligations on the other.

3 The responses that emerge exhibit something of the possible variety of concrete situations that fall within the abstract formulation.

4 Discussion allows for the emergence of other possible courses of action than the one the writer prescribed for the protagonist. "Yes," a student would say, "but that kid in your story had more choices than the two you described. What if. . . ?" Is this not often precisely the trouble with what appear to be dilemmas: such an appearance locks one into choices, both of which are highly undesirable, neglecting the possibility of other dilemmas?

On another occasion, we would want to extend the try-out over a considerably longer period of time, partly to see whether there is any development that individual students show in their sensibility, their skill at empathy, their capacity to imagine more satisfactory courses of action and better penetration into the motivation of their characters. What we are always given, Ortega said, is a person *and* his circumstances. But circumstances alter cases. Our students over and over presented cases that could be abstractly summarized as "Moral rules don't always work out," or "This shouldn't be taken completely literally." One student had her protagonist get around the "Don't talk to strangers" rule ingeniously, by simply pointing her finger, in answer to a question, rather than talking. But another pupil strongly suggested that talking, to the extent of saying, "Down a block and then left," didn't violate the spirit of the rule. Others doubted that the admonition not to fight or to steal must prevail in all cases.

Development doesn't happen in the twinkling of an eye, or if it seems to, it probably will wash out unless conditions are favorable for reinforcement. So, yes, something like this experiment needs a stretch of time to work itself through. At the same time, we encountered after three assignments the beginnings of restiveness. It was fine up to that point, but now they wanted a change, a shift to more open-endedness or a problem that lay well outside the ethical realm (though this realm is far more commodious than is often thought). But over a course of a semester or a year, there might well be a kind of rondo of assignments with those of an ethical cast representing the theme to which a group returns.

We would probably want to extend the discussions, at least of the more provocative stories, far beyond what we did this time. Perhaps we were too eager to get a number of stories out before the group, and thus curtailed, or at least insufficiently encouraged, lingering on a given story to draw out more of its suggestiveness, its assumptions, its possibilities for change, and what particular feelings were aroused in a character or reader.

We would like to make the move not just from writing to discussion, but then (on occasion) from discussion to more writing. It seems to be the case that some students in particular respond to this kind of stimulus. At the lonely desk, the ideas may not flow for them as they do in the social context. And, as we all know, students learn from each other—learn, for instance, a certain daringness from the more daring, freely imaginative members of the group. Or learn that stories need not be on exalted themes. V. S. Pritchett once said about his early struggles to become a writer that he was blocked by an inflated notion of what writing must be about. Beginning to read what the professionals wrote, he would say to himself, "Oh, I didn't know one could write about *that* kind of thing"—that is, something quite ordinary, such as had happened to him, too, dozens of times. For this requires development of one's imagination, to see that the ordinary need not be banal.

It might help to sharpen and extend the questions, perhaps pointing out the specifically ethical quality of the desired consideration, to forestall cases like that of the writer who found the mother of the family *wrong* in wanting to shorten her daughter's dress because she did not understand graduation to be a formal occasion.

The sort of writing here described can of course be taught at virtually any age level. Studies of child development show that younger children tend to focus on others' need for help, while older children often begin to think about the requirements of justice; teachers will keep this in mind as they compose their assignments, as well as the demonstrated fact that children differentiate between positive and negative morality, which is to say the acts that are prosocial or in the interest of distributive justice, on the one hand, and those that consist in refraining from wrong acts on the other. Further, there is the distinction between obligation and that which is above and beyond the call of duty. A distribution of writing assignments in these several respects may be advisable in order to give students some notion of the spread of moral situations.

Of course students may be invited to write about real happenings—like those told of in newspapers or which they know at first hand—but the fictional approach may give children more freedom to use their imaginations as well as to move outside of the restraints of personal inhibition.

Of course short stories and novels are abundant sources of ethical problems, as we have already observed; and episodes in history—for example, the dropping of the atomic bombs on Japan, various aspects of the British involvement with India—may at once give a certain distance to the writing-pondering and yet appeal by their importance and reality. Mention of this in turn prompts the remark that this use of writing to raise consciousness of ethical matters may prove as applicable to social studies and the natural sciences as to the humanties.

Rounding, then, on our opening, we would want to express our feeling that Socrates and Plato may well have exaggerated the extent to which young people inherently know mathematics and ethics. And we would not go quite all the way with the neo-Platonic sentiments of a Wordsworth, apostrophizing the young child:

> Thou, whose exterior semblance doth belie
> > Thy soul's immensity;
> Thou best philosopher, who yet dost keep
> Thy heritage, thou eye among the blind,
> That, deaf and silent, read'st the eternal
> > deep,
> Haunted for ever by the eternal mind . . . .

> (Wordsworth: 'Ode: intimations of immortality')

Eight-year-olds, and those who are 13 and 17, *do* often have better ideas on ethical subjects than adults credit them with. Still, surely Socrates was right in always saying that these ideas need sorting out by dialogue—including (we add) the internal dialogue that is writing. And not ideas only, but also feelings.[13]

Part IV

OTHER GREAT VALUES

17

THE VALUE OF
KNOWLEDGE

Doubtless most people, challenged as to why they seek schooling, or education, more broadly, would say that it was in the interest of gaining knowledge; and if in turn the value of knowledge was brought into question, the answer would come that "knowledge is power" or that knowledge affords access to desirable kinds of work, and thus money, perhaps higher status, and (again) power. We gain knowledge and are motivated to gain knowledge in order to . . . . Even if the knowledge be so specific and contained as that of how to change a fuse or fill out a tax form, still this is worth knowing, in order to restore electrical power and not be penalized by the tax collector.

This is the kind of knowledge that is synonymous with skill, "know-how". Gilbert Ryle, in distinguishing knowing how from knowing that, has argued that at least since the time of Socrates the former has been severely subordinated—by theorists, not by the practical people of the world—to the latter. There seems to be something so much more lofty, dignified, even sublime about knowing that such and such is true than knowing just how it works or what to do about it if it doesn't. He calls this the "intellectualist legend,"that all cases of knowing how can be assimilated to knowing that, which means an emphasis upon rules and their observance, theory and its verification, or criteria and their employment. Socrates, in his trial for having introduced new gods and corrupted the youth of Athens said that the news of the Delphic oracle's having declared that there was nobody wiser than Socrates puzzled him, for he was intensely aware of his own ignorance and of the genius of the various statesmen, artists and others. Yet, when he came to ask the political leaders about the true nature of Justice, or the artists about the essence of Beauty, he found them to be literally dumb. They knew quite a lot about public administration or chipping marble, but they were short on theoretical knowledge, abstract knowledge, and thus, after all, they could not be called wise. (He went on to say that though *he* did not have theoretical knowledge either, he at least *realized* that he did not, and therein stood his only claim to wisdom.

Ever since, and no doubt a long time before, mere practicality has been associated with a kind of knack, some adeptness one picks up here or there. The advice, then, is to ground yourself thoroughly in theory, though it may take many years, and then you can, probably fairly quickly, acquire the know-how, the skill for applying theory to practice. Ryle thinks this distinction between theory and practice is very much overdrawn and that it rests to some extent upon an untenable distinction between the sorts of things we do "in our heads" and those we do "hands on," the latter of course being menial as distinct from mental. He goes on to assert that:

> The boxer, the surgeon, the poet and the salesman apply their special criteria in the performance of their special tasks, for they are appraised as clever, skilful, inspired or shrewd not for the ways in which they consider, if they consider at all, prescriptions for conducting their special performances, but for the ways in which they conduct those performances themselves.
>
> (Ryle 1949: para. 8)

The invidious distinction between skill and theoretical knowledge is of course preserved in the schools and (even more so) in the universities. Was it G. B. Shaw who said, "Those who know, do: those who don't know, teach"? To which another miscreant added,, "And those who don't know how to teach, teach others how to teach." So within institutions of learning the devotees of the most abstract disciplines enjoy the highest status, while those who are very much on the applied side are ranked lower in the hierarchy of learned scholars. It is finally left to the humorist to expose the absurdity inherent in this distinction; thus Mark Twain has someone (himself?) saying during the First World War that he had decided that the best way to rid the allies of the German submarine menace was to boil the ocean. When someone then had the temerity to ask how that could be done, he haughtily replied, "I have the ideas; it's for others to put them into practice."

All of this is not to deny that there is a distinction—though far from absolute—between theory and practice, knowing that (or propositional knowledge) and knowing how (or skill). It is common to have one with little of the other. Thus I may be quite competent at doing long division, but not really able to understand why the algorithm works—given accurate calculations. And I can understand the general idea of non-Euclidian geometry, highly abstract theory, without being able to carry out a Lobachevskian proof. I can know the hydrostatics of swimming and not be able to swim. I can be a competent driver and not know the least thing about an internal combustion engine. I can know all about musical harmony and yet be stone-deaf from birth. Or, in Bertrand Russell's example, a blind man can know the whole of physics (if anyone can know the whole of physics).

School subjects in some cases divide themselves between these two kinds of knowing. A woodworking class may be as little theoretical and as much skills-oriented as imaginable. A biology class may, in not having a laboratory or any "natural study", be almost completely theoretical. A class in choral singing may involve no musical theory, and a class in political theory (or civics) may not require any participation in civic or governmental duties. Commoner though is the sort of class in which there are alternative concentrations on the one or the other. In a class in logic or mathematics, typically one will study the rules and then do a number of problems. Again it is easily possible to be better at one or the other, as with the student who can state and explain a set of rules but, perhaps because of carelessness, poor memory, or impatience, fails to solve many of the problems. One may have a knack for perspective drawing but be quite unable to explain the principles thereof, even though the teacher has gone over them in detail.

Even more to our prevailing point, each of these ways of knowing has its value and both are valuable—potentially. Offhand, it might seem that the two kinds, with respect to their value, split between intrinsic and instrumental value, but that is not so. The reason why it can seem so is that the use of our skills is in the interest of a product. Because Tom is a skillful carpenter he is able to make this table—the very model of what a kitchen table should be. It is level, its legs are of a length, its parts are soundly joined, and so on. His skill produced this and I value it. I value his skill because of its results, but it's the results that matter most. On the other hand, Jill is a political theorist. She helps me understand the essential differences between the British and the American structures of government. It is very unlikely that this is going to lead to any reforms of either, or change my acts as a voter, but I very much enjoy coming to understand what before was still a little obscure. That sounds entirely intrinsic. But of course I have set it up to seem so. Let us now grant that this treatise may come to the attention of an MP or a Senator, and it helps them understand a possible change, something that would improve the legislative processes of their own government. Now, that abstract knowledge is getting applied, is beginning to have some instrumental value. But in the case of Tom's table, though I don't need such a table, I very much like its looks: it is a thing of beauty—of its kind. It doesn't pretend to be Chippendale, and rightly so, but it has its own kind of fineness that I have learned to recognize. It thus has intrinsic value.

But now consider the two kinds from the point of view of the maker. Tom is able to sell his table for a handsome profit, or has the pleasure of pleasing his mother when he presents it as a gift, or he simply installs it in his own kitchen and day after day finds that it truly works as the nearly ideal place on which to set, and from which to eat, a meal—all instrumental. But Tom is that enviable carpenter who loves his work. He's seldom happier that when he, having sawn a board, begins to shape it more finely to fit it snugly into position. He draws his hand over the planed surface and feels a shudder of satisfaction go down his spine. If he didn't do this kind of work for a living, he'd do it as a vocation sheerly for the sake of the delight of working in wood. Of course by no means all skills afford this satisfaction, or they do so in much lesser degree than the case just imagined. Generally I prize my driving skills only for their allowing me expeditious transportation: they enable me, if all goes well, to get to my destination quickly and safely and at not too high a price. Only very occasionally do I find myself simply enjoying my driving. Maybe it's because I have a new and better car, or maybe it's because it is a fine day, the road is smooth, the traffic light, and I like getting away from the hurley-burly. Some things I do, and (let us say) do relatively well, but which I'd like very much to be spared doing at all, like washing pots and pans or fixing the broken lock on the door or writing a bread-and-butter letter. Yet I do like cooking in clean vessels, having the secure feeling of a well locked door, and seeing the smile of gratitude later on the face of my pleased letter recipient.

Jill likes both writing and teaching her subject, but she also is very much gratified by pleasing her students and readers, and whatever indicates that such is the case will be a new reward for her activity.

Socrates taught clear thinking, as in the definition of a difficult concept. It is a fair guess, from Plato's account, that he liked this teaching even better than his stone work. He also devoutly believed that clear thinking "pays off" in right moral conduct: if we have thought straight, we will act as good citizens or good friends should act. Thus the intellective is in the service of the moral. Aristotle later made it more specific that knowledge has two kinds of value. It is obviously often practical, enabling us, for instance, to decide intelligently between two courses of action. This he called a practical virtue. But there is—he thought a higher—virtue that is intellectual. This is contemplation, as when we finally comprehend what it is that links the forming genius of a Phidias with the unhewn block of marble, as a perfect illustration and thus clarification of the abstract relation between form and matter. Contemplation may or may not have any practical ends, but it is an activity marvelously worth doing for its own sake, and it is the sign of a highly developed human being to be able to take satisfaction in this kind of use of one's leisure.

R. S. Peters has been one of those who has especially emphasized the role of schools in getting pupils into the habit of engaging in worthwhile activities. He writes, for instance, that education, especially at the higher levels, "consists largely in initiating people into this form of life—getting others on the inside of activities so that they practice them simply for the intrinsic satisfactions that they contain and for no end which is extrinsic to them" (Peters 1963: 56).

There's no end to the multiplicity of instrumental values that knowledge may have. A college student comes around to her teacher to say that she must withdraw from his class. He wonders why. She replies, "My father says that paleontology almost never comes up in polite conversation." We now have a clue as to this critic's criterion by which knowledge is to be accorded value.

Yet that we humans differ radically in both the size of the place that knowledge (of any kind) occupies in our system of values and in the kind or kinds of knowledge we especially value or disvalue, is something known, not necessarily in these terms, by every teacher. When the English class finishes its unit on grammar and starts on poetry, a good part of the class takes new heart, but there will be some who think that now there has been a falling off, for there is something solid and dependable about grammar (or so it is thought), but literature is airy-fairy. But then there are those in the class who do not see much value in either or yet others who prize them both. In the university, classes on marketing may draw many hundreds of enrollees, but elementary Sanskrit only a tiny handful. Even in kindergarten, some pupils will light up when the teacher pulls down a map, but the hearts of others will fall, for it means putting away the blocks that they are just managing to build up to surprising heights.

Some people delight in the abstractions of mathematics, formal logic, theoretical physics, or, in a different way, metaphysics. Others shy away from high abstraction in order to get to the knowledge of concretes, like the perception of just this shade of blue or hearing the strange chord from a Debussy quartet. But, one may ask, is the latter kind of thing knowledge at all? The answer is that it is at the very least knowledge-as-acquaintance, the direct confrontation in experience with qualities. It is not, perhaps, knowledge about, which is again knowledge that, but now with a different antithesis. There is a vast difference between *knowing* Matthew Arnold's "Dover Beach" and knowing the Pythagorean theorem, though part of the knowing in either case may be partly a matter of memorization, and both are cases of penetrating the meaning of symbols and their syntax. Yet the first kind of knowing yields (in the fortunate case) aesthetic appreciation, but the second kind yields a very different kind of appreciation, that of the relation of lines and spaces within a right-angled triangle. Knowledge which has people as its content or object varies enormously as one moves from anthropology and sociology to psychology (within which there is the range from psychoanalysis to experimental psychology, and to human physiology, and then to a kind of knowing that is not in the curriculum at all, the way we know this person or that—and that too, as we have been reminded, differs from the knowing which occurs inside friendship and that of more casual or distanced acquaintance. My physician may in a way "know me well" but mainly as a body, and my dentist may know my mouth "backwards and forwards." But my mother knows or knew me once in as different a way as may be imagined.

But we differ too in what for us counts as knowledge. Those who are accustomed to the knowledge available in mathematics or that somewhat different way in the sciences in which highly exact measurement is employed may (though not necessarily) have little patience for the knowledge displayed by art historians, at least when they leave behind dates and places for interpretations of formal qualities. The psychologist may quickly grow impatient with philosophy simply because it is so little empirical and thus the scientific methods of verification have therein little or no applicability. In short, all of us have our preferences and our regions of indifference, boredom, or even indignant rejection. The poet may make his unflattering appraisal of the scientist as in Walt Whitman's poem:

> When I heard the learn'd astronomer,
> When the proofs, the figures, were ranged in
>   columns before me,
> When I was shown the charts and diagrams,
>   to add, divide and measure them,
> When I sitting heard the astronomer where
>   he lectured with much applause in the
>   lecture-room,
> How soon unaccountably I became tired and
>   sick,
> Till rising and gliding out I wander'd off by
>   myself,
> In the mystical moist night air, and from
>   time to time,
> Look'd up in perfect silence at the stars. . .

Somewhat similarly Wordsworth scorned those who would "peep and botanize on their mother's grave."

But the scientist may be no less irritated with the poet. Whitman's astronomer would doubtless have turned away in amusement or disgust from Coleridge's Ancient Mariner, who recounted how

> From the sails the dew did drip—
> Till clomb above the eastern bar
> The hornèd moon, with one bright star
> Within the nether tip.

Here is a miracle to go along with that of the sun standing still (so to speak) while Joshua fought his famous battle. And then there's Keats's "On First Looking into Chapman's Homer":

> Then felt I like some watcher of the skies
> When a new planet swims into his ken;
> Or like stout Cortez when with eagle eyes
> He stared at the Pacific—and all his men
> Looked at each other with a wild surmise—
> Silent, upon a peak in Darien.

Even the elementary geographer says, "Did he forget, or would Balboa have spoiled the rhythm?"

Often enough the nine-year-old will turn from a lesson in geography to one in literature, and on to astronomy, and its mathematics, with something like equal interest and satisfaction; all too often, that same student eight or 10 years later will have decided (perhaps because he felt he had to decide) for one of those subjects (or its first cousin) and against the rest. Whitehead famously described the "rhythms of education": the time of Romance, when stories are told about the famous explorers, say Columbus' finding a whole new continent, or Archimedes' discovery in his bath of the theory of displacement, or of Galileo looking through his telescope. No necessity of choosing among subjects at this point—for all are fascinating, as stories should be. But then comes the sobering discovery that in the geography class one is tested on mean annual rainfall in the main cities of South America, and the relation thereof to their economy—and for some students the charm begins to tarnish. This is the period of Precision: facts and figures, theories and evidences, proofs and refutations, logical argument and counter-argument. Still, in secondary school, students are expected to take mathematics *and* literature, history *and* biology, even if there is beginning to be a distinction between those who settle for a general knowledge of one subject in favor of more specialization in another.

It has been said that Leibniz (1646–1716) was the last person of whom the claim might be made that he knew everything there was to be known. Of course no one believes that this was the case, even in those primitive times, and in any case we know that this man, who invented the integral calculus, was a doctor of jurisprudence, a diplomat, and a metaphysician (among other interests), valued the technological gadgets of his patron's residence above the works of even the great painters—from which one might deduce that he did not really *know* art!

But in any case, it was not long after that that Leibniz's kind of versatility fell out of favor, or rather was abandoned as impossible, such was the proliferation of knowledge in practically all fields. Of course even by the turn of the 20th century a William James could still be painter, physiologist/psychologist, and philosopher, and half a century later a Robert Oppenheimer would take time off from theoretical physics to study Sanskrit, but it was also the case that advanced historians no longer claimed to be historians of the whole reach of British history, but concentrated on the Roman occupation of Britain or the Victorian era. Even in the much shorter length of American history one academic historian was characterized as a "Late-Age-of-Jackson man." And the old stories continue apace about the doctoral dissertation on the left hind foot of the centipede, and so on.

In 1883 Herbert Spencer propounded the question "What knowledge is of most worth?", a query made important by the necessity of specialization—and increasingly, of what kind of knowledge is going to be included in the school and college curricula as well as what kind of research will be funded by governmental and private monies. Spencer answered his own question

195

by saying that the natural sciences were of the most worth, by far, for even the fine arts are founded on science, as is apparent in the study of the chemistry of pigments and of the glue which holds violins together. Spencer argued that five categories of knowledge derived from the answers to the question of what we need to know in order to live:

1 What we need to know for direct self-preservation.
2 What we need to know in order to secure the necessities of life, food, shelter, etc.
3 What we need to know about the rearing and disciplining of offspring.
4 What we need to know in order to maintain social and political relations.

So far, these kinds of knowledge are scientific, natural or social. (Spencer was trained as an engineer, but counted himself a sociologist.) Only with the fifth and least essential category do we possibly bring in the humanities:

5 What we need to know in order to fill out our leisure time interestingly.

But the poet and school inspector Matthew Arnold disagreed, telling the story of a pupil in one of the technical colleges who, asked to explain Macbeth's question to his wife's physician, "Can'st thou not minister to a mind diseased?" offered for paraphrase, "Can you not wait upon the lunatic?" Whereupon Arnold wrote:

> If one is driven to choose, I think I would rather have a young person ignorant about the moon's diameter, but aware that "Can you not wait upon the lunatic?" is bad, than a person whose education had been such as to manage things the other way round.
>
> (Arnold 1885: 127)

Proclaiming that the great desideratum for the student is to gain knowledge of "the best that has been thought and said" in the world, Arnold took his stand on the tradition of the Great Books, which, though some of them obviously are in the fields of mathematics and the sciences, are heavily slanted (on most reckonings) toward literature, philosophy, and history.

Similarly Cardinal Newman wrote that a university education:

> aims at raising the intellectual tone of society, at cultivating the public mind, at purifying the national taste, at supplying true principles to popular enthusiasm and fixed aims to popular aspiration, at giving enlargement and sobriety to the ideas of the age, at facilitating the exercise of political power, and refining the intercourse of private life . . . . It prepares [a man] to fill any post with credit, and to master any subject with facility . . . . He has the repose of a mind which lives in itself, while it lives in the world, and which has resources for its happiness at home when it cannot go abroad. He has a gift which serves him in public, and supports him in retirement, without which

good fortune is but vulgar, and with which failure and disappointment have a charm.

(Newman 1852: Discourse 7, Section 10)

Such rhetoric sounds to the modern ear both charming and old-fashioned,
perhaps charming because so old-fashioned, but redolent of times that are
gone forever. Especially in a time when in America approximately half the
secondary school population goes on to university or at least some kind of
advanced tutelege, such claims for higher education border on the embar-
rassing. Nevertheless, the advocates of the liberal arts, sometimes in retreat,
sometimes in attack, continue to argue for grounding all technical and
vocational education in knowledge which is liberal both in the sense of being
designed for the "free mind" and in being liberating from parochialisms of
time, place, and a premature narrowing of interest to the directly practical
matters associated with the vocational and professional. Sometimes a distinction is made between "liberal" and "general" education, the latter term
being reserved for the level of education which is thought desirable for all
students regardless of their more specialized destination, whereas "liberal
education" is thought of as ranging from the elementary to the advanced
degrees in any subject that may be pursued for the sake of the value of the
knowledge itself rather than simply for its application—which brings us back
once again to the chapter's starting place. Although the teachers who day
after day exhaust their energies trying to bring classes up to a reasonable
mastery of the three Rs may be forgiven for failing to get involved in the
debates about the ideal number of A-levels or the requisite scores on
comprehensive achievement tests, the potential values of both breadth and
depth of knowledge remain an essential concern of teachers at all levels.
Once again: it is not just having a battery of skills and knowledge that is
sufficient; rather, skills and knowledge as appreciated, prized, and enjoyed—which is to say as valued, intrinsically and instrumentally—are at the
heart of the teaching enterprise.

But back to different ways of knowing. Outside the academic disciplines
too there is ample recognition of varying degrees of "knowing." We may say
we know something and discover that we did not, that it just was not true,
and that may be a disillusionment (thus a disvalue) or it may even be a relief,
as when we find out that a distressing rumor was unfounded.

There is the kind of "knowing" that all animals have, which is called
instinctual, like that of birds who *know* which berries to eat and how to
combine twigs to form a nest. Humans are somewhat short of that kind of
knowing, but they often have a sense of knowing that which they can give
no proof of or offer any empirical evidence for. Thus we say, "I just knew"
or "I know that my Redeemer liveth." And that may be a rewarding experience even though others might have their doubts about the veracity of the
claim. Then there is the kind of knowing that is true memory. Each of us has

memories that nobody else shares, except indirectly through our own report. Yet everyone has had the sense too of memories that have played tricks on us. But often we are not concerned with exactness in this area. We say that we remember our first tricycle—it is a fond memory and that's that. Other times we are concerned to try to get a validation of what we think we remember, whether something as current as the date of our next visit to the dentist or something that happened years ago and that has somehow emerged into a new consciousness and importance.

Short of knowing is the finding of something to be plausible, and that may have a value. Or we like a fantasy in fiction that we praise by saying that it has verisimilitude even though it could not have happened in reality. And most of us enjoy imagining, or day-dreaming, perhaps pretending that such and such is true, when we know it is not.

And then there is the undoubted satisfaction of the process of inquiry, more especially (but not exclusively) when it eventuates in a discovery or insight. Thus we speak of coming to know, though again this may be an exaggeration, such that the more accurate account would be of coming to suspect or coming to find fairly probable.

Obviously most of any person's body of knowledge—all the things she does in fact know, a stock from which a mental retrieval system usually works reasonably well—is in ready reserve and not in use or at all applicable at the present time. Then we may cherish our knowing quite a lot, say, about the Wars of the Roses, so that in case the subject comes up we can call upon this knowledge-in-store.

We noticed above two of the aspects or moments in Whitehead's "rhythms" of education. Yet, in addition to the period of romance and the period of precision, he calls our attention to the period of synthesis. This cannot come before the other two, for obvious reasons, and yet in a sense it is a return to the generality of the first, but now with a degree of erudition, a comprehensive outlook, and above all, a capacity to bring things together—as he so well puts it, "to see the forest by means of the trees" (Whitehead 1932a: 24–5). Not many people enter into this cathedral farther than the alcove, and no one does it in many different subjects; yet it is the natural and desired consummation of the earlier periods and phases, and the most richly rewarding. Though history and philosophy are the great synthesizing subjects, which is to say those that assume the accomplishments of other empirical and formal studies to try to achieve a larger whole, right within each of the disciplines there are ample opportunities too for the synthesizing of more partial kinds of knowledge, as in those notable instances when Darwin brings his studies of a particular species of plants and animals into the compass of a general theory of evolution that embraces the whole organic world; when Einstein develops a *general* theory of relativity; when Hegal or Toynbee manages to encompass the many histories of nations into a *pattern* of history, universally; or—to show that this is by no means an achievement merely of fairly recent times—when Thomas Aquinas produced in twenty stout volumes his *Summa Theologica*.

In addition to the intrinsic and instrumental values of having knowledge and coming to know, there are moral concerns within this area. An obvious example is in the knowledge—even quite factual in nature—that is necessary for appropriate moral behavior, as in the case of the sort of information that is given in sex education courses or in the case suggested by the whining complaint: "But I didn't know the gun was loaded—I don't even know how to tell."

Then there is the regrettable absence of psychological knowledge as betrayed by such a plaint as "I didn't think that would hurt her feelings." This suggests an extension of the area of responsibility. Just as ignorance of the law is said to be no excuse, so now we are beginning to understand that, at least for an adult, failure to come to know oneself or one's close associates even in unconscious dimensions of the personality may result in serious, preventable harm. Thus: "I didn't even imagine that I could get so furious!" Offered as an excuse for having acted out of "uncontrollable anger," this response may sometimes mitigate punishment in a court of law, but the question remains, *"Why* didn't you know? Such knowledge of yourself is available—you could have known." (See Erich Neumann, 1969.)

Yet a more familiar relation between knowledge and obligation lies in the vice of plagiarism and, more broadly, falsification of data. When C. P. Snow was making a transition from his career as a physicist to the profession of writer, he published a novel called *The Search*. In it, a character who is a crystalographer, in consternation over not having an experiment "come out right," makes the fatal decision to falsify his data.

What comes out forcibly is the absolute if unwritten rule that obtains within science and scholarship, requiring complete regard for the truth in reporting observations, in data analysis, in drawing conclusions, and in proper acknowledgement of sources. Lord Snow knew very well—what is perhaps not fully understood in all circles—how great a shock wave spreads over a professional community when an accusation is made that a psychologist has apparently invented case studies, "cooked" the data, and "doctored" the statistics in favor of a claim about human intelligence. Or when one anthropologist finds reason to believe that a predecessor in the field has knowingly misrepresented an ethnographic situation. Or, again, if a psychoanalyst has falsely claimed a cure. Or, commonest of all, when an investigator borrows without acknowledgement an idea or theory from a colleague. The *New Yorker* sometimes runs what it calls its "Funny Coincidence Department," two columns of print which are virtually identical, but written by two authors separated by several years. The mathematician and comic singer Tom Lehrer raises a laugh by his advice in a song called "Lobachevsky" to:

Plagiarize,
Let no one else's work evade your eyes.

Yet, in the real world, plagiarism and the other kinds of falsification are by no means laughing matters, for the ill effects are not confined to someone's not getting credit for his own achievement. Beyond this, there is the serious offense of proliferating misinformation and wrong theory, for the publication of one paper may well serve as the basis for many other conclusions drawn in good faith by other investigators. Furthermore, and perhaps worst of all, is the planting of the seed of doubt and suspicion in many minds, for obviously there is little possibility for the average reader of scientific accounts to verify the reputed findings. Rather one says, in effect, "This is obviously a reputable scientist, who therefore is careful and scrupulous, so I am justified in trusting what he reports." And when it turns out that there has been falsification, one's trust in this kind of investigation is weakened.

The implications of this for the school setting are in one sense obvious, and indeed it is the rare teacher who has not taken occasion to caution students about such misdemeanors as "borrowing" from another's work; but what is not always noticed is that this whole subject opens up a rich relevance of moral education to (particularly) the teaching of the natural and the social sciences. The teacher of chemistry (say) may need reminding that moral education need not be left to the others, when a few case studies of notorious lapses on the part of fellow scientists can easily and fruitfully be introduced to the fledgling chemists.

The good teacher enjoys knowing, coming to know, and facilitating the coming to know in others. But finally—here we hark back to the earlier discussion of the way appreciation applies right across the curriculum–the great test of a teacher's ability must be accounted in her knowing how to conduce toward students' coming to value knowledge and coming to know for its own sake, intrinsically. For in this alone lies any promise of the students' pursuing knowledge beyond the confines of classroom requirements or the practical needs of home and work. How prized are those teachers of whom we can say, retrospectively, "She not only taught me a lot, but helped me toward learning how to acquire new knowledge and to love doing just that. From her I learned to want to learn."

Yet, as Bertrand Russell said, with one eye on bored erudition and the other on indolent ignorance, "To learn without ceasing to love learning is difficult" (1932: 162).

18

VALUES IN WORK

The good life is a life of free and productive activity, a life in which men's active essence is actualized without alienation.

(Karl Marx)

Some people seem to think that vocational education is something new, whereas in old and better times education was uniformly "liberal." Yet it is doubtful if there has been any time or place in which in some important sense schooling (not to mention other forms of education) was not in considerable measure preparatory to a vocation. In ancient times, beyond literacy lay skill in rhetoric, and rhetoric was thought to be the most useful kind of learning, not alone for political power, but for getting ahead in virtually any kind of profession. In the Middle Ages, university training, with its heavy emphasis in Europe upon mastery of Latin and, with that, knowledge of philosophy, theology, and other writings, had as its reward, beyond the sheer delight of such study, appointment and advancement in the clergy.

Late in the 17th century John Locke composed *Some Thoughts Concerning Education*, in response to a request from a wealthy gentleman for advice from the learned doctor on how to educate his son. Locke understood that the young gentleman would be entrusted with many duties in the management of the family fortune and estate, and wrote accordingly, listing four proper outcomes of a proper education: virtue, wisdom, breeding, and learning. But these too are eminently practical acquisitions. Wisdom, for instance, is not considered here as contemplation upon the eternal verities or even a deeply judicious understanding of the good life and one's duties in society. Instead:

Wisdom I take in the popular acceptation, for a man's managing his business ably and with foresight in this world. This is the product of a good natural temper, application of mind, and experience together, and so above the reach of children.

Nevertheless, one can prepare children for what later they must learn "from

201

time, experience, and observation, and an acquaintance with men, their tempers, and designs . . . " (Locke 1693: ss. 139–40).

Even Rousseau, motivated especially to preserve the natural innocence and merriment of children in their growing up, and thus training them to keep their distance from a corrupt and inevitably corrupting society, believed that the course of study directed by his tutor would equip Emile, when he came of age, to fulfill any vocation with competence. In turn Sophie's upbringing and education, equally "natural," would naturally prepare her to accomplish her destiny, to answer to her calling, that is, to become Emile's companion and wife, which then of course meant motherhood as well.

Until relatively recently, people were trained to become school masters and mistresses almost exclusively by following the regular curriculum up to secondary school graduation, thus equipping them—so it was assumed—to "pass along" this knowledge to the young. Lawyers and civil servants were not trained, say at Oxford or Harvard, in their specific fields of future endeavor, but in the liberal arts which trained them to learn "on the job," from law offices, hospitals, and (say) foreign service to become skilled in their professions.

In short, it has been rare at any time for education to have been mainly praised and sought out for the satisfactions inherent in reading, writing, thinking, and solving problems dissociated from a private or public career, even though it has been common to assign the liberal arts a high value for helping men and women to spend their leisure time agreeably and well.

Work and leisure: such, for who knows how long, has been the most convenient division of life's days and weeks and years. The distinction might be even more generally made between necessity and freedom, between what we feel we *have* to do and the times that are "our own" to fill as we choose. For the child the required part consists of school and chores, or other parentally directed activity; the rest is: play—and loafing time. Conventionally, these two periods are closely associated with the pleasurable and the painful, but it is not quite that simple. The youngster may, secretly or openly, like school (and even some of the work at home) and may find that in a long vacation the time begins to hang heavy, making the return to school the more welcome. But in virtually all cultures some such distinction between work and free time is made, even though the blocking out of time may be much less rigid than in highly industrialized societies. Today we read with heavy heart of the child labor associated with the industrial revolution, when many urban children, even early in life, were strapped to a job of such demands that between periods of work there was time for almost nothing but sleep, and so too with adults. From historians and novelists we learn of times when, say, miners would, much of the year, go underground in the pre-dawn and emerge above ground only after the sun had sunk. It is no wonder that workers were as keen to reduce their work day as to increase their wages, for even a nursery rhyme tells us about the effects of all work and no play.

In recent times, with the growing proliferation of kinds of work, an increasing amount of effort has gone into the matter of deciding what kind of work to elect to do (provided always that kind is to be had) and then how specifically to prepare therefor. So deeply entrenched in the minds of most people, especially those who are well along in their schooling, is the belief that one must be specifically educated (or at least trained) for one's life work, that just recently governmental bureaucracies, financial companies like banks and brokerage houses, and even engineering firms have gone out of their way, for instance by advertisements in university campus publications, to "remind" those specializing in the liberal arts that they too are employable, that one need not be technically prepared in public administration, economics, and technology in order to explore opportunities for a career previously thought to be wholly out of bounds.

Naturally enough, young people dream of the possibility, however far-fetched, of being able to find their life work, the work which will provide them the means for setting up a household, etc., in doing exactly what they already like to do best. Thus, who can estimate the number of boys (and just now a rapidly escalating number of girls) who think that the greatest fate in the world would be to become a professional athlete? Playing football or basketball, tennis or golf being something they find wholly delightful, they imagine what it would be like to be a professional in such a sport, and, with eyes upon the most celebrated models of the day, regard it is a job with unbelievably high pay! Though even a quick calculation of the ratio between those who do in fact earn their living in this way and those who aspire to reveals that one's chances are much like those of winning a lottery; in the one case and the other, hope persists—and very possibly other preparation is too long delayed. Of course, the odds are far better for those who like to cut and shape their friends' hair of being "hair stylists" and of those who like caring for sick animals to be, or far more likely work for, veterinarians, and those who love to type and work office machines of becoming secretaries. But to say nothing of the rate of disillusion for those who thus become what seemed natural for them, how many people "in the job market" settle for work because it was pretty much all that was available when it was needed and expected; and with no surprise that it was not exactly what they wanted, it would do to provide a living. Compensation then is found in what one does in one's spare time, after work and during vacations, with the money which the job itself, boring, routine, perhaps soon replaceable by a robot, yields.

Probably most people in European/American cultures would say that work is what one does—or is the price one pays—in order to have the necessities of life and to support one's leisure activities. Aristotle, on the other hand, quoted with approval the saying of one Anacharsis: "Play in order that you may work," adding in support that "amusement is a form of rest; but we need rest because we are not able to go on working without a break, and therefore it is not an end, since we take it as a means to further activity" (*Nichomachean Ethics*, X, vi).

This position is very similar to that of the much celebrated and deplored "Protestant work ethic," which, however, was preceded by very similar Roman Catholic doctrine, going back to as early as the sixth century when St Benedict pronounced both intellectual and manual work a religious duty: "Idleness is the enemy of the soul and therefore, at fixed times, the brothers ought to be occupied in manual labor, and, again at fixed times, in sacred reading" (rule XLVIII). Work was thought of as a discipline necessary to strengthen the soul. Thus, in severe contrast to the long supposition of aristocratic, landholding classes that manual work is essentially ignoble and thus fit only for slaves, it is here "conceived of as ennobling rather than degrading, as a way of serving God" (Neff 1968: 4).

But Luther, Calvin, and Protestants generally went well beyond prescribing work for the monastic orders, saying that it is essential for all in being character-building. Whereas the devil finds work for idle hands to do, "the moral ideal became that of the sober, prudent, and industrious Christian, who could pile up credit with the Lord by hard labor and 'good works' in the world below" (Neff 1968: 49).

In turn this ethic was made the butt of ridicule by the peculiar American phenomenon, the "flower children" of the 1960s, who associated work—more especially of course the work of business—with the hated "military/industrial complex." Instead of working one should "tune in, drop out . . . . " From the perspective of about three decades, this protest can be seen to have exposed some of the joylessness and righteous self-satisfaction that is often bound up with a relentless push for advancement in status and increased money. Many of these young people began asking questions that their parents—particularly their fathers—had failed to ask about life's meanings. Especially those of the rebels who combined this attack with a defense of civil liberties and a strong protest against a war in Vietnam that was to come to seem in retrospect, even to a great many of its earlier defenders (or overlookers), unwarranted and senseless, were by no means indulging merely in youthful negativism. Yet the deliberate dropping out of the world of work did not last long, more especially for those who were near the end of the time when their middle class parents would support them in their new lifestyle. More recently the increasing number of beggars and panhandlers in urban centers, not only in Mexico, Brazil, and India, but also in Britain and the United States, represents some combination of regional falling off of jobs, a decline in governmental support for public services (including care for the emotionally disturbed and the mentally and physically retarded), and some residue of persons who though able-bodied do indeed find it preferable to beg than to work.

Of course most people regard work as a necessity. And a great many of us work at different things from what we used to. It is not just that we are no longer hunters and gatherers—that goes without saying. But consider the large-scale reduction in simple manual labor: digging ditches, hand-tilling the soil, chopping wood, scrubbing floors and pans, darning socks, ironing stacks of clothing, peeling potatoes, churning milk. Machines, and recently electronically driven machines, have obviously changed the nature of work. Who knows to what extent the reduction of the drudgery of housework has contributed to the large-scale increase of women in the "work force"? Yet one may conjecture that still more important are (1) the rapidly escalating sense among women that the role of housewife represents a distasteful subordination to the male, (2) the belief that a second income will far outweigh the sacrifices of certain aspects of family life, and (3) an inner urge to look beyond the home for further development of their own potentiality.

Add to this the apparent fact that professional and management-level people are working longer hours a day and a week than formerly, and the picture becomes clearer that the earlier supposition that technology would gradually allow all people to reduce their work time to, say, 25 or 30 hours a week has gone by the board, even though it is obvious that working class hours have been seriously cut back from the prevailing rates of 50 years ago. Perhaps for the upper middle classes the principal motivation for spending so much time at work is to be able better to afford more costly travel, more expensive automobiles and living quarters, and the like. It is interesting too that in the United States the mandatory retirement age has advanced significantly in recent decades, a clear indication that a sizable portion of the population wants to keep working, into the late 60s, and 70s, instead of relaxing into retirement. Again it is not easy to separate the motivations for this, between keeping income at a higher level or the sheer interest in the work itself—or, indeed "workaholism."

Nevertheless, the popularity of retirement communities, recreation vehicles, and tours designed for "seniors" are among the indications that retirement continues to have its charms. One may assume that its appeal is strongest for the same group who eagerly look forward to weekends and holidays, and dread Monday morning blues. These facts in themselves do not indicate hatred of work, or even of one's present job, for work can be interesting but so demanding that one needs and wants relief from it, as when teachers greet each other with TGIF—Thank God it's Friday.

Yet, it must also be said, obvious though it be, that for a very large proportion of the population, work—the work they do and know—is disagreeable, something they would very much rather not do, and thus do only out of the necessity for earning a living. Indeed a fair proportion of people apparently assume that that is the very nature of work, and would be surprised that anybody thinks otherwise, or even incredulous of anyone like the professor who at his retirement dinner said, "If I had had the means,

I should gladly have paid Harvard, rather than having Harvard pay me, for all these years of teaching here."

Now, of course those who dislike—even loathe and despise—their jobs are with great frequency trapped into jobs that it would be hard, even with the best disposition in the world, to find agreeable. The standard example is work on a production line, as in an automobile assembly plant. Turning the same screw, slipping in the same small part, over and over all day long, can be nobody's idea of intrinsically rewarding work. And yet, some years ago, when under a foundation grant, arrangements were made to exchange workers between a Swedish and a Detroit automobile plant, giving the Swedes some months of experience on the most rationalized system imaginable, and giving the Americans a chance to participate in a highly flexible plan, wherein groups of workers would do their own planning as to who would do what, with opportunity for exchanging responsibilities, the Americans afterwards on the whole expressed a preference for their own accustomed way, not just because it was accustomed (if one can trust their report) but because it at least allowed them to think their own thoughts, dream their own dreams, *while* working—rather than having to think and plan and decide. This will serve as at least a reminder that people differ in these respects as in most others.

Still, teachers and counselors concerned with career planning make a good deal of the importance of (1) knowing what various possible jobs are like; (2) what is the best preparation for being employed and succeeding in jobs one is attracted to; and (3) learning to adapt to the presented realities and (of course within limits) even modify the work itself in accordance with one's own personal characteristics. Obviously the possibilities for this latter adjustment vary enormously with the work, but in all but the very most clockwork performance some accommodation is possible—and sometimes rather more than one might know or admit to oneself.

Perhaps the single most important goal for a teacher to work toward has to do with the basic attitude toward work. Though no one can be promised a job custom-made to one's own requirements and heart's desire, one should at the very least come to adopt a pro-work attitude. A good starting place is a distinction between work and labor.

In his fine book *Work, Leisure, and the American Schools* (1968), Thomas F. Green argues that labor is distinguished by its presenting vocational activity as done out of sheer need to survive and furthermore that it accomplishes nothing of enduring value. What is done must simply be done again, and thus it means continuing frustration, like that of Sisyphus, doomed to push a rock up a hill with no hope of reaching the top, or Kafka's protagonist who is trying to reach the castle but finds that the roads always diverge just as the goal is in sight. Or again, we look at the seabirds on the shore and, beautiful though they appear to us, we think of their activity: hour after hour, day after day, seeking food, eating it and seeking for more; in short "laboring" in order to stay alive in order to . . . . Green concludes this point by writing, "Necessity and futility are therefore the two fundamental and interconnected features of labor" (p. 19). By contrast, if we *perform* a labor, we *produce* a work. If labor is slavish and unfulfilling, like breaking rocks in an unending field of boulders, work may be exemplified by one who chisels and carves a piece of marble to produce a handsome table or statue. Hannah Arendt puts it this way: "the word 'labor,' understood as a noun, never designates a finished product, the result of laboring, but remains a verbal noun . . . , whereas the product itself is invariably derived from the word for work . . ." (cited in Green 1968: 21). Thus the laborer is bound to the job, whereas the one who works has a degree of freedom—the work itself is freeing—as is characteristic of the skilled artisan or artist or any professional.

Yet all of this is not to romanticize work. An essential lesson for every youth is that no kind of work is one long stream of delights and fascinations. Every job has its tedious moments, its routines, its setbacks, its times of discouragement and very likely some long stretches in which one is engaged in activity one would be ever so grateful to be spared. The physician grows weary of treating hypochondriacs and conducting a long series of routine physical examinations. No nurse delights in making beds and emptying bedpans. The civil engineer may have to spend days or weeks under the blistering desert sun. The scholar may plough through book after book in search of an elusive item and come up empty-handed and bone-tired. The creative artist characteristically pays for his vaunted freedom to do as and when he wills by stretches of dryness, when the ideas seem to have run out and the bank account too.

Yet work, genuine work, taps one's own resources, calls out and develops one's potentialities, affords the possibility of doing something at least a little out of the ordinary—something worthwhile, something one may be pleased with, proud of. Nearly everyone likes to think that his or her work matters, not only to oneself but to others, however few.

One of Karl Marx's greatest contributions lay in his insight into the conditions for alienation of the worker (or for that matter the laborer), namely those frequent conditions in which one not only cannot see how what one does contributes anything important to a product, but furthermore in which there is a disproportion between what one has done and the market value of the product. This is what he called *exploitation*: the sense, the feeling of being exploited is a primary cause for falling into that dismal state of alienation, which is isolation, separation off from one's livelihood. (Nietzsche was to add that alienation is the feeling of meaninglessness, that things—life itself—have lost their value.)

It must be noticed too that work which is itself dully repetitive, even tiring drudgery, may take on meaning a context which makes it a genuine contribution to someone's welfare. Think, for instance, of the volunteers who somehow always come forward in times of emergency: a flood, an earth-quake, a disastrous train wreck, a large-scale explosion: then a person may stand for many hours ladling out soup or diverting traffic or digging in rubble. Such work will have its rewards solely in the feeling that one is being of some help to those in great need.

Green, indeed, goes so far as to say that "the meaningfulness of a task lies not in the work, but in the worker." He adds that "some people may find even cosmic significance in a task that, to others, would seem mean and inconsequential" (p. 25). This is undeniable, but so is it that some people may fail to find even the tiniest meaning in, say, laboratory research aimed at analysis of the AIDS virus. All the same, it may be more fruitful to think of significance, meaning, and value in terms of an interaction between attitude and, to the degree it can be isolated thus, the act itself. Scrubbing floors is doubtless a useful thing to do, and there are occasions when one might think it about the most important task possible; still, it is generally to be classified as drudgery; whereas, fortunately, all but a few six-year-old children quickly grasp the satisfactions to be had in learning to read—though it may be hard!

There will never be a way of automatically—or electronically—matching up a person's personality with a job, to get something like a perfect fit; nevertheless, considerable progress has been made in psychological instruments which can serve as an aid to the careers counselor. The best known of these tests is the Strong-Campbell Interest Inventory. In the manual for this widely used test, six types of human personality, as they relate to kinds of work, are described. They draw on John Holland's *Making Vocational Choices* (1973). These types are: realistic, investigative, artistic, social, enterprising, and conventional, and the assumption is that there are kinds of work suited to each type. Very briefly, these are the characterizations of the types:

Realistic persons are strong, with good motor coordination, mechanically inclined, preferring practical, concrete tasks such as those associated with the mechanic, electrician, crane operator, tool designer.

Investigative persons are oriented toward scientific inquiry, being intro-spective and not very social, preferring thinking to doing; they work independently, are confident of their intellective abilities, and dislike repe-titious tasks.

Artistic persons like relatively unstructured situations that call for free decisions, with emphasis upon self-expression, and, like the investigative ones, are not especially sociable, but strongly introverted.

Social persons contrastingly, like to work in groups, have good verbal, communicative skills, solve problems interpersonally, and tend to be ideal-istic and humanitarian. Many teachers fit in here, but also school administrators, counselors, recreation leaders, and social workers.

Enterprising persons have sociable verbal skills "suited to selling, domi-nating, and leading." They are power and status oriented, and tend to be aggressive, self-confident, and cheerful. Obviously these persons are suited to become business executives, campaign managers, buyers, and merchandisers.

Conventional persons like order and system, avoiding ambiguity and interpersonal problems. They tend to be efficient, practical, and obedient. Jobs suiting them are those of accountant, business education teacher, clerk, and bookkeeper.

Of course, like all type tests, this one rarely yields pure types, but a good bit of work has gone into correlating them. Examples of low correlation are Realistic/Enterprising, Investigative/Enterprising, Artistic/Conventional, Social/Artistic. These vocational interests have also been related to success in school subjects. Use of such a test by a skilled counselor can often open up to those thinking about their future career possibilities that might not at all have occurred to them on their own, but can also expose unrealistic choices.

But, short of this combination of expertness of counseling buttressed by good diagnostic tests, there is much left for teachers and others to do, helpfully, in collaboration with a young person, whether for someone contemplating some remaining years of education and training before looking for work, or for a person much nearer to the process of job application.

Especially important, in terms of vocational education, is the middle ground between the unique individual and universal truths about work. Fortunately, there are ways of likening groups of people with respect to work, and of likening work tasks with respect to the sorts of interests and skills they relate to. (This is so even though ultimately an utterly distinctive human being will be performing work that is not *exactly* like that anybody else is performing.) Thus we can say to a young person, "Mathematics has more to do with preparing to be an engineer or an accountant than does music," or "If you think you might like to be a pharmacist, see how you like chemistry." So much is obvious. That is, we help pupils see both what are some of the preparatory stages for a certain kind of work, and how one can test one's own interest and aptitude for that work by one's performance in certain school subjects.[14]

Given the fact that some students seem to like pretty much everything they do in school and others practically nothing, it remains that most of us find some subjects much more appealing than others, first and last. What students often want to know, somewhere along the line, is: "What can you do with a specialization in English literature, botany, physical education, religious studies, etc.?" And teachers can often help with these matters. But suppose the question is more vague: "I don't seem to know *what* I'd like to do, what I'd be best at—just have no idea. How do I find out?" Once again, one is looking for a match-up between a *kind* of work and a *kind* of person. Often the most useful path is, as in so much else, that toward further self-knowledge. Aptitudes are important, of course, but also interests, ideals, and values. Given the fact that people differ even radically on questions such as how important they consider work to be, in relation to the other aspects of life, how they feel about work of evident social service, whether, on the whole, they like to work by themselves or in close relation to others, how they feel about the relative importance of job security and opportunity for big financial rewards, and so on. The following little exercise is useful in sorting out some of these matters. (This one was devised for university students, but it could be easily adapted for younger audiences.)

A. I could not be truly satisfied for long with a job unless it: (rank order)

  (a) offered opportunity for very substantial monetary rewards—much above the average for college graduates.

  (b) was one in which I felt I was making a very substantial contribution to general human welfare.

  (c) was one of very high status, such that it is generally accepted that this is one of the highest and most honored of callings.

  (d) had so many fascinating characteristics that almost anybody would envy the person fortunate enough to be in such a situation.

  (e) was so interesting and fulfilling in itself that one really would not require a great deal of leisure.

  (f) was so challenging that it called out the full extent of my capabilities.

  (g) left me an abundance of time and energy, as well as a reasonable amount of money, for doing the things I care most about.

  (h) provided ample opportunity for advancement toward a position of above average responsibility.

  (i) was one in which I would be recognized for my achievements and appreciated.

  (j) afforded me a high degree of security, so that as long as I was performing competently, I would not have to fear losing my position.

  (k) involved a great deal of social interaction.

  (l) (another characteristic that would not be at the bottom of your list: specify)

B. If I became suddenly independently well-off (e.g. by winning a lottery), I would spend most of my "working hours" doing:

  (a)

  (b)

One gets the impression that a vast number of school leavers *fall* into whatever job (if any) they end up in with an absolute minimum of exploration either of the job market, what particular lines of work they like and what they require by way of qualifications, or of what they themselves are best suited for and would find most satisfaction in doing.

Not, of course, that personality is an "ever-fixèd mark." One has to allow too for the possibility one may come to like a job that was at first distasteful, that one may change in ways that the job indicates, and that one may even modify the work closer to the heart's desire.

When people are asked by pollsters or acquaintances whether they like their work, the answer is often yes, but it is hard to tell what is behind this agreeable response. Perhaps one doesn't like to be put down as a complainer; or there's the reminder that there are far worse jobs; or anyway it has its good moments and maybe these at least slightly outweigh the bad or indifferent. Yet it is not to be forgotten that many people, by hook or by crook, by planning, careful preparation, and conscientious searching, or by luck, have found a job that they like very much, enjoy doing a very large percentage of the time, and feel various satisfactions, such as working with good companions, having a sense of accomplishing something socially worthwhile, feeling challenged and brought out by the nature of the work, and by consciousness of one's own special competence, of doing the job well. And there remains the ideal achieved by workers in jobs ranging from low to high status and remuneration that work and leisure may coalesce.

A well known poem of Robert Frost makes the point incomparably. It tells the story of two itinerant lumber workers who come upon the narrator thoroughly enjoying splitting blocks of beechwood in his own yard. But their presence makes him aware that what he is doing for the fun of it is for them a livelihood and their claim finally wins out. The poem, "Two Tramps in Mudtime," ends on the separation between work for gain and work for the love of it:

> But yield who will to their separation,
> My object in living is to unite
> My avocation and my vocation
> As my two eyes make one in sight.
> Only where love and need are one,
> And the work is play for mortal stakes,
> Is the deed ever really done
> For Heaven and the future's sakes.

19

THE CROWNING
VALUES: FRIENDSHIP
AND LOVE

"Without friends no one would choose to live, though he had all other goods." So spoke Aristotle in his essay on friendship, which he regarded as an essential part of his *Nichomachean Ethics* (Book 8). Has friendship come down in importance in our "post-modern" society? Some say so and cite as evidence that in the *Encyclopaedia Britannica* of 1810 there were twenty columns devoted to "Friendship," but by 1879 they had disappeared and have not been seen since, without much else in the way of articles and books taking their place. Of course talk about a subject can decline without a similar decline in the thing itself, but one might suppose there is reasonable correlation between the two. (Love as a topic has fared rather better in recent times.) That original authority, Aristotle, listed three kinds of friendship: that which is pursued purely for pleasure, that pursued for profit or gain, as in the case of "business friends", and the highest and best, that which is pursued for its own sake (and not with pleasure or profit as an aim) and which is good for those who share it. Further, it seemed clear to Aristotle that only equals could be true friends, friends in the best sense, which for the ancients (at least) ruled out friendship between ruler and subject, father and son or more generally the elder and the younger, wife and husband. (Aristotle did not dwell on any distinction between love and friendship, and would not have made any sense out of "man's best friend.")

Even bad men can be friends for utility or pleasure, but only good men can be friends for the very sake of friendship. So says Aristotle—but of course times have changed. What is the status of friendship today in European and American societies?

For one thing, the word "friend" seems to have become somewhat debased. Someone is spoken of as a friend, even as "my good friend," or "a very close friend" and we come to find out they have not been in each other's homes, do not keep in close touch and in short seem hardly more than acquaintances. But is that not more of a male than a female phenomenon? Or is it more generally a tendency of extroverts?

In any case people are known to differ in the extent to which they value friendship. A 1981 Gallup Poll asked, "How important to you is having friends?" Fifty-four percent answered "Very important", which was the same percentage who believed it very important to give time to helping people in need, but compared relatively unfavorably to these other values deemed very important: family life (82 percent), good self-image or self-respect (79 percent), personal satisfaction (77 percent), freedom to do what I want (73 percent), living up to my full potential (71 percent), having an interesting, enjoyable job (69 percent), sense of accomplishment and lasting contribution (63 percent), and following God's will (61 percent); but friendship ranked higher than having an exciting, stimulating life, following a strict moral code, having a nice car, home, and other belongings. It was significantly ahead of having a high income (37 percent), enough leisure time (36 percent) and social recognition (22 percent). (Survey 87-G.)

Religious scripture too tells of fast friends, such as that between Khidr and Dhulgarnein in the Qur'an. Male friendships have fairly frequently figured prominently in literature, especially in tales of comrades-in-arms, from Achilles and Patroclus on down through the ages. Friendships made in school and university figure too, as with Hamlet and Horatio. For boyhood friends one thinks of Tom Sawyer and Huck Finn. There are tales of male friendship crossed by the new presence of a girl or woman. But where are the stories of long-lasting mature relationships in civil society? Is it the lack of drama in such friendships that has kept them out of plays and novels? The social sciences of recent times contain but few studies of male friendships too.

Are friendships among men significantly different in nature from those among women? One writer, Louise Bernikow, speaking of camaraderie among men, says:

> Their eyes are forward, like the eyes of men marching to war, fixed not on each other but on what is out there. They are shoulder to shoulder. Female friends are more often eye to eye. It is the creation of "us" that is important, we *two*—and in this very different arrangement lie the great depths and the great rapture of our friendship.
>
> (Bernikow 1980: 119)

This writer, among a number of others, mainly coming from a feminist persuasion, feels that at this time in American society, as in some elsewhere and at other times,

> women find each other the most interesting people around, . . . find new thinking, new ways of looking at the world, in other women far more than they do in men.

She remembers a time in school days when a telephone call from a man, suggesting a date, would be an occasion for quickly breaking a previous engagement with a female friend, but she suggests that this is changing:

I have come to feel my own life as one in which women are an enormous delight, at least most of the women I know, and that to cancel an appointment with a woman because a man had called would not only violate my expectations and hers, but is unthinkable and would diminish my life.

Bernikow adds, "The man beside me is envious. He does well, I think, to be so" (p. 153). Her further point goes beyond the intrinsic value taken in such friendship to include a deep utility too. Speaking of the difference in the way "life has evolved" for men and women, she comments that women "have been brought up to be relational people and to embody feeling, to develop the affective parts of themselves. . ." (p. 119).

But "Women must belong to themselves before they can be friends to one another; culture conspires against it. Female friendships that work are relationships in which women help each other belong to themselves. . ." (p. 143).

It is often remarked that men who are "bonded" with each other are very likely to share activities with each other, such as sports, whether as players or spectators. There is often even a fairly strong sense of competitiveness among such friends, but the element of competition serves more as a link than a divisive force.

It would seem that by and large schools do little to teach or promote the value of friendship beyond bringing potential friends together in a joint enterprise and affording them a little time, around the edges of direct instruction in regular school subjects, to be together. As in every field and subject, some people need little or nothing by way of motivation, special occasion, or directed teaching to develop their own capacity for and their enjoyment of friendship, but others need help.

To be sure, there are always certain teachers who have a knack and propensity for, say, bringing some young people out of their native shyness, or even timidity, and getting them to be better "mixers," even to the point of taking the initiative in inviting a closer relationship (than the relatively formal one of classmates) with this person or that. That this sort of thing is typically by the way and occasional does in no way diminish its value; yet one wonders if somewhat more systematic attempts might be made to include this kind of teaching and learning more directly in the classroom. To be sure, friendships are rooted in mutual *liking*. Like love, it is either there or it isn't, and no third person (such as a teacher or parent) can make it happen:

> I do not love thee, Dr Fell.
> The reason why I cannot tell,
> But this I know and know full well:
> I do *not* love thee, Dr Fell.

What the teacher can do is to facilitate situations for the discovery of compatibilities and liking. One thing that militates against this happening in more traditional school settings is the emphasis upon competition, and hence upon "doing one's own work"—lest there be cheating, or at least a confounding of teacher appraisal of this person's achievement or that. But as was noticed in the chapter on prosocial learning, learning can be better, more conducive to various values, when it is cooperative, shared, mutually supportive. And are not those the qualities that particularly make for and characterize the relations between friends? Friends are precisely those from whom we are particularly geared to learn, for their instruction—whether it is so labeled or not—is so freely, generously, and unselfconsciously given. With whom better than a real friend can we try out our notions, our ideas, our (perhaps half-baked) theories, our feelings, our attitudes, knowing that friendship permits, even encourages, criticism and correction in the interest of sounder belief, more finely tuned judgment? The space in which friends exist is an area of safety, allowing the running of risks without fear of unintended offense. In short, friends teach each other, learn from each other, and join their forces the better to learn from one another, comparing notes about the mentor, the book, the work of art they share.

If we hear real news, get word of a breakthrough, encounter a fresh explanation of a baffling phenomenon, have a sudden instinct, raise a puzzling doubt, do we not think immediately of one whom we want to tell—or of course more than one, for who is to set an absolute limit on the number of friends we have? To be sure, we differ in this respect too. There are some who pour so much into their single friendship as to have—so it seems—nothing much left to share, at least with that degree of intensity, with another. Then, only if that friend disappears from the scene is there a possibility of another. But others may have—pick a number—a dozen genuine friends (not acquaintances *called* friends);[15] and if challenged on this proliferation may respond, "Different friends address different parts of oneself: anybody who is thought to share all of one's interests, and you theirs, is not a friend but a clone, or anyway an identical twin. Now, for instance, there is no one I'm closer to than Karen, but she has no time or tolerance for sports, while I love them. I don't blame her for this, nor she me for lacking patience for gardening. Hence each of us goes to another for companionship in this or that respect."

It might be thought that the introversion/extroversion distinction is highly relevant with respect to this distinction between few/many friends types, but it must be remembered that introverts are by no means reclusive, typically, but generally value friendship no less their "opposites." Because of their inward orientation, they may be somewhat slower to make friends, but their sharing of the deeper aspects of themselves may be stronger, so that their friendships may have a special intensity. Furthermore, introverts and extro-verts may particularly prize each other for their very differences, thus again having a compensatory point of view to offer, which can be a rich source of learning for both—and not necessarily of a purely intellective kind.

In these days of increasing acknowledgement of what are now called "sexual preferences," it is still not uncommon for same-gender friends to *be* friends without sharing a sexual orientation. Other psychological factors may enter into same-gender relations. Since male homosexuals are often characterized as having a "mother complex" (but this does not mean that those with such a complex are homosexual) it is interesting to note that C. G. Jung finds that there are positive effects of this way of being:

> Thus a man with a mother complex may have a finely differentiated Eros [that is, a propensity for relating and synthesizing] instead of, or in addition to, homosexuality. (Something of this sort is suggested by Plato in his *Symposium*.) This gives him a greater capacity for friendship, which often creates ties of astonishing tenderness between men and may even rescue friendship between the sexes from the limbo of the impossible. He may have good taste and an aesthetic sense which are fostered by the presence of the feminine streak. Then he may be supremely gifted as a teacher because of his almost feminine insight and tact. He is likely to have a feeling for history, and to be conservative in the best sense and cherish the values of the past.
>
> (*CW* 1, para. 164)

Non-romantic male/female friendships again have a special quality, along with limitations. Men and women often prize each other for their help in understanding the other gender point of view—on anything at all. If each is well grounded in a love relationship with a regular partner, there may be a particular feeling of "safeness" in this kind of friendship. But some would insist that inevitably there is an erotic coloring present, however slight.

Here is how one mature woman described her way of being with male acquaintances in contrast with a close relationship with another woman:

> There is more of a surface quality to it, repartee. Exchanges are often on practical subjects. Feelings are not strong. I can be open but only to a point, when I answer a question in a way so that I won't be asked to go on. In other words, I have serious reservations about what I will divulge of a personal nature. I am only semi-revealing; I often short-circuit my response. I have a sense of not wanting to be fair game. I always assess the tone of the conversation and decide how far I want it to go.

The degree of guardedness in this response is impressive, and especially so when contrasted with this same person's description of her relationship with her own best (woman) friend:

We share similar aims in life, similar understandings about life, questing, and relationship. We also share similar values, e. g., around honesty, humor, trust, or how to raise children. I always feel *accepted* by my friend; thus I don't have to worry about whether something I divulge will put a strain on our closeness. We accept each other as a process of shifts and swings and changes, yet as retaining a continuity that constitutes ourselves.

Another thing is what might be called *responsiveness*. I say something to her, knowing that I will be heard. She'll take it in and respond, relevantly, feelingly. In turn, if I say something to her, I like where she takes it—though it might be a surprise, and indeed often is. In this way she makes me see my ideas better, see where they might lead. Thus I get clearer about them, and modify them accordingly.

True friends can open themselves to each other, reveal their fears, their self-criticisms, their weaknesses, knowing these will be taken seriously—one doesn't just want them waved away as if they aren't real—but also that somehow they will not be held against one.

A popular author (Judith Viorst 1977) has distinguished the following kinds of friends a woman might (and usually does) have:

1 Convenience friends: a next-door neighbor, mother of one's child's best friends, *et al*.
2 Special-interest friends: those we see only for tennis or at a bridge club, or for a special kind of shopping.
3 Historical friends: those we knew at some previous time of life.
4 Crossroads friends: connected with a crucial period of one's life.
5 Cross-generational friends: those who are the age of one's parents or one's adult children.
6 Part-of-a-couple friends: those we never see alone.
7 Non-romantic men friends.
8 Very good friends: those with whom one shares—practically everything.

As we have seen, friendship does not at all have to be justified by its instrumental value, though such can be a great addition. Mainly we prize, and rightly prize, our friends, our relations with our friends, for the experienced quality of our times together. Friends are precisely those we often want to be with, and the shared times and occasions tend to be—nothing is good every minute—strongly gratifying. Indeed, we cherish our friends too in their absence, remember particular times when in companionship we enjoyed something we were similarly experiencing, or even more directly enjoyed each other, our talk, our exchanged looks, the touch of our hands.

But friendship too has its contexts. Sometimes we may feel that we are too busy, too singularly devoted to some project, to have friends, and such as exist must be held in abeyance. Other times we feel a great need for friends, or for new friends: at crucial moments we want our friends to "rally around" and give us the support we need. Yet if we have moved to a new community, it may be loneliness that makes us more than commonly aware of the gap left in our lives by the absence of friends, and of the need to seek friends near at hand in this community.

For most people, the first exposure to friendship is within the family. Mother and father are very special cases, such that friendship seems not relevant to the parent/child relationship, though of course, later in life, strong and genuine friendships can develop between son or daughter and mother or father. But sibling relationships, especially with those close to one in years, can—though they do not do so necessarily—furnish the first model of what it is to have a friend, a playmate, someone you can normally count on for support. Later, to say of one not related by blood, "You are a brother to me" (or sister) is to make a very strong avowal of friendship.

Within the context of a neighborhood, many people discover their first friends outside the family. The propinquity of those of similar age will then make the sprouting of friendships possible, perhaps even easy. To be sure, only gradually do children learn to take the point of view of the other—surely a prime requisite for friendship properly so called: Piaget noticed that often children who seem to the adult to be engaged in conversation are doing little more than politely taking turns in the talk, with little attention paid to what the other is saying. But then one begins to sort out the many relations that one forms with others: each person within the family is different but shares the family bond; slightly more distant relatives, aunts and uncles, cousins, grandparents, constitute the extended family. Various other adults impinge at least slightly upon the child, but most of them only casually in the early years: a nursery school teacher, one's pediatrician, shopkeepers, the parents of one's playmates, and so on. To many of these one learns to adopt an attitude that is little more than politeness. But entering into a regular school makes one of its largest impacts by virtue of the immediate presence of a sizable group of contemporaries: the dynamics of those forming relationships are indeed very complex and soon children begin to make such distinctions as those between friends and "best friend," or even possibly "best friends." Now, more negative feelings become more prominent, notably jealousy, though this may have been very powerfully experienced—as all the world knows—at the appearance of a rival sibling. But schoolchildren are very often caught up in an almost vicious competition for friends, particularly in that honorific status of "best friend." Feelings are bruised, envy is aroused, rejection is experienced and of course there is the wondrous elation of having one's deep affection reciprocated: "You are my best friend."

As we have seen, in studies of children's play, boys are found to spend more time arguing about rules or infractions of them than are girls, but they typically settle their dispute and keep the game going. Girls' play, however, is likely to be disrupted by any such disputes, though "best friends" will tend to exit together, still in harmony, and each may be peremptory or even cruel in excluding another girl on the ground that "You are not my best friend."

In the early school years, in most cases, there is much less differentiation of friends with respect to different interests in and aspects of one's life: the closest friends may go right across the whole board of one's interests, concerns, values. That alongside these intense values, positive or negative, academic concerns pale is perhaps known to all but the most distant parents and even some teachers.

Further complications arise here, as in practically everything else, with the onset of puberty. What may have been a period of antipathy to the opposite sex, or at least a strong ambivalence, fades to make way for a new set of rivalries with respect to favored opposite-gender partners, which in turn lends a new color to same-gender friendships: now there is more to confess, to hide, to ask about, fret about, boast about, be ashamed of, and certainly to be nervous, even anxious, about.

More differentiation among functions of friends appear: there is the friend in the glee club, the friend on the basketball, football, or debate team, the friend who is a better dancer or cannier in courtship rituals and from whom there is so much to learn. Even the friend who makes studying algebra more palatable.

In boarding school or in college residence halls, again friendships take on another dimension. For the day-pupil school friends and neighborhood friends may be quite different, but in the school or college where one lives around the clock there can be no such distinction except at times of holiday. The very absence of parents and probably (at least at times) of a sibling makes a big difference in the quality of the friendships. Conversely, the loneliness of the friendless boy or girl may be even more intense, such that erratic behavior begins to manifest itself, which often furthers the person's alienation from the community.

Still further changes are made by entry into the world of work, with differences made by the type of work it is—and again temperamental differences will be important, some people much preferring work that contains a good deal of sociability, others opting—to the extent that option is available—for work of a more solitary nature, or at least where one's associates are but few. Friends are now chosen and sustained according to new criteria. For instance, in the military, notably so in times of war and other dangerous pursuits, friends may be prized for their dependability and their courage.

With marriage and the forming of other relatively stable live-in relationships, yet other considerations come into view. Women who are housewives may complain justly that they have fewer opportunities to form friendships than do their husbands; hence the relationships between couples may be mainly determined by the business or professional bonds between the men. Nevertheless, in this kind of situation, friendships among women may be stronger, because less based in Aristotle's utility, than those of the men. Children born into these households will in turn affect friendships, sometimes interfering, sometimes strengthening them.

But with the dramatic changes in household economies in post-industrial societies, especially with respect to the striking increase in women entering the work force, these generalizations must be changed. Now women too have friendships based in their workplace and their calling, with the woman oftentimes taking even a dominant role in the choice of couple-friends.

In turn, the mounting divorce rate implies yet other powerful influences upon friendships, crises in which friends become unusually important, the dissolving of many of the couple-friendships. In these poignant times women seem very often to express more need and get more help from friends than do men.

In the "second half of life," once again friendships tend to change. In the 40s and thereafter, it seems, there is commonly more introspection, more wondering about the meaning of life (as distinct from "getting ahead," "carving out one's niche," and the like). Consequently friends may spend more time exchanging reflections about what is important (according to new standards), and friends who do not share these interests may drop away, with friendships forming around new-found interests perhaps centering on spiritual, political, psychological, or altruistic issues. Now, women of any age who are not employed often turn to volunteer activities and this in turn means new associates and, among them, new friends.

Stereotypical pictures of the friendships of the later periods display women crocheting together, and bearded pards leaning over a chess board or smoking their pipes from their porched rocking chairs. But of course friends are by no means always of an age, and older people may often seek out and enjoy the friendship of those considerably younger than themselves, the latter also enjoying and inviting such relationship. But old age too means, naturally, the disappearance of those who have been friends, and, with opportunities for making new acquaintances diminished, not a few people experience an intensification of loneliness, though it is not to be forgotten that solitude is not experienced by all as unpleasant—for those given to contemplation, quite the contrary. But in the time of dying, many people experience a loss of interest in their old friends, even in those closely bound to them through the years by ties of blood or marriage; to those around them they may seem to have redirected their thoughts elsewhere, which in turn may be experienced poignantly as a rejection by those newly excluded.

Beyond this sketch of some of the typical vagaries of friendship relations along the course of a life, mention must be made of another kind of context for friendship: the community itself, the town or city, or as the Greeks said, the *polis*, the political entity in which one lives. In his *Ethics*, Aristotle put it this way:

Friendship seems too to hold states together, and lawgivers to care more for it than for justice; for unanimity seems to be something like friendship, and this they aim at most of all, and expel faction as their worst enemy; and when men are friends they have no need of justice, while when they are just they need friendship as well, and the truest form of justice is thought to be a friendly quality.

(Nichomachean Ethics, VIII, 1155a)

According to this way of thinking, then, it is friendship that is the very foundation of community, a radically different way of thinking from that of those who, like Hobbes, picture humans forming communities to protect themselves from external and internal disorder and threat.

Sophocles, in *Philoctetes*, has his main character, who has been stranded on Lemnos for ten years, say, "You left me friendless, solitary, without a city, a corpse among the living" (cited in MacIntyre 1984: 135). In this speech we see once again a dramatically persuasive utterance of the importance of friendship and of the community which supports it.

But what then of Dido's lament after her lover Aeneas' final departure: "You've gone, you've gone." Not friendship but love has gone. In French *aimer* can be translated as either "to love" or "to like". Somehow it seems especially strange that the French (of all people) should not differentiate between these ways of feeling by distinct words. And yet no one would deny that the concepts are intricately related and oftentimes overlapping. But they are not always. One may be "head over heels in love" and yet in serious moments realize that one does not like the other very much—in the sense of sharing many interests, trusting, being eager to confide—or even trust.

But as many thinkers (!) remind us: loving and being in love are by no means the same, and it is at least interesting that a growing number of psychologists believe that the latter is a particularly unsound and even dangerous state. In any case, that state is not relevant to the present study, and love itself may at first seem an odd inclusion in a work on the teaching of values. Yet love is one of the most esteemed of religious values and a great many people count their capacity to love and their fortune in being loved incomparable blessings. There still may be a question of whether love is something having to do with learning and teaching: it is surely not frequently encountered in the curriculum of schools. That question can, however, be better approached after a brief discussion of love itself. Brief not because the subject is a simple one, but for the opposite reason: it is so complex that one despairs of saying much that is worthwhile about it in fewer than several thousand words. Nevertheless, it is too important to omit from our present considerations.

We like some of our acquaintances, but the ones who become friends are typically the very ones we particularly like. (Contrary cases are to be imagined, such as the person who is rejected by the persons he likes best, and thus has to fall back upon those he likes less in order not to be friendless altogether.) Those friends we are the closest to we may not hesitate to speak of as persons we love, though some persons are skittish about this emotion-laden word except for immediate members of one's family (and possibly not even all of *them*) and one's beloved. But this is only the beginning of the difficulties of characterizing love and loving. Thus we may say we love our mother, father, son, daughter, sister, brother, grandparent, cousin, aunt, uncle (other blood relatives and in-laws), "romantic" other, favorite teacher, pupil, spiritual guide, therapist, pet, the Virgin Mary, Jesus, Mohammed, Shiva, Tara, and others. (Listen to the mother saying to the child, "No, dear, you do not *love* chocolate, you can only love persons"; but then the child overhears her mother say over the telephone, "I just *love* my garden.") In these several cases do we have meanings of "love" that are so disparate as to confound the attempt to find the common denominator? Still, as Wittgenstein might have insisted, they have a family resemblance.

Then there is the question of being unsure about whether we love or not.

Do you love your brother?
Of course.
Really?
Well, maybe not, to be candid.

But again the "out" is that one isn't sure of what it means to love.

Some definitions have been offered. Here is one: love is "the will to extend oneself for the purpose of nurturing one's own or another's spiritual growth" (Peck 1978: 119).

This does indeed say something important about love, but it surely does not define it! The emphasis upon *will* interestingly—and in part persuasively—moves beyond the feelings to a kind of determined and active process, specifically the nurturing one. That is, loving, to be authentic, must go beyond having a glow of pleasure and more generalized satisfaction in the other's company. Love which is purely passive, requiring no effort or activity, hardly deserves its name. Furthermore, "nurturing spiritual growth" does sound like an idea to work toward. And yet cannot one be so nurturing toward and with a person one surely does not *love*? Or has "love" now come to mean something that, say, a teacher feels toward all her pupils, a pastor toward all his parishioners, a therapist toward all her clients? If it is answered that Jesus required all men to love their neighbors, one remembers the wry remark that it is the neighbors precisely whom one cannot love—and not all one's students either, though one tries to be concerned with their welfare, their mental and spiritual growth. Is the feeling part of love to be consigned to a subordinate place, a kind of disposable accompaniment to this willed activity?

And what shall we make of that part of the sentence which speaks of "nurturing one's own *or* another's . . . growth"? Are we now speaking of self-love, and once again—Dr Peck's orientation is clearly Christian—there is that about Jesus' commandment that says love the other "as oneself"?

There seems to be a virtual unanimity among writers on love that loving oneself is an absolute prerequisite for loving another. The evidence is clear that anyone who consistently and abjectly derogates himself is not yet ready to love another; or, put positively, it is indeed the case that a positive, though realistic, self-regard is essential to other-love. But is there something else in the way of attitude toward oneself, something that is truly *love*, that is needed? "Love" seems to be best reserved for a relation (not always reciprocal) between two persons, and not an intra-psychic phenomenon. This may become more apparent if once again the question arises of what love for another most importantly consists in. Here is a list of proposals:

Freud famously said that love is an overestimation of its object. The statement still makes a smile come to our lips because everyone has had occasion to ask about an acquaintance in the throes of an infatuation, "What does X see in Y?" And of course when falling out of such an infatuation one is altogether likely to wonder what one *had* seen in the other—or at least what had made one elevate the beloved up above the stars. There are two appropriate responses to this phenomenon:

1   This seeming exaggeration is typically something that happens precisely in the case of an infatuation, or in an instance of falling in love. Falling out of love does often mean if not a disillusionment, at least a more sober assessment of the other.

2   However, this seeming overestimation is not always to be explained away as a projection upon the other, a kind of blind wish that the person really was all these wonderful things. It may be that the eye of the lover does indeed see more deeply into qualities that remain obscure to the uninvolved. Furthermore, being the recipient of the admiration of the lover surely does tend to bring out the very best traits in the one loved, as if to say, it's a case of living up to one's billing.

But a perhaps deeper way of looking at this aspect of the love relation is to think not in terms of an objective assessment, one that pretends to command universal agreement, as when one pronounces upon the inestimable quality of Shakespeare's *The Tempest* or Mozart's 'Symphony in G Minor', or the profundity of Einstein's General Theory of Relativity; but rather in terms of why this person is so very much "right for me." Now, this way of assessing pays close attention to individual differences. One may say or dumbly feel that one's beloved most marvelously and amazingly complements one. Or, perhaps better put, that he or she is an astonishing combination of compatibilities (some of them at least grounded in shared interests, traits, and dispositions) and complementariness.

The well-known speech attributed to Aristophanes in Plato's *Symposium* makes the point especially well by way of a concocted myth, to the effect that once upon a time we all had four legs, four arms and double the number of other physical traits that we now have. Since these primordial creatures were very swift and strong, they threatened the gods, who had them sliced in two and rounded off. Since that time, the story concludes, we have all been going around looking for our other half.

If we add to the tale our belief that even originally the two halves did not match entirely, but in a number of respects were very different from each other, we are ready to adopt it as speaking a profound truth: that the lover feels to be united with the beloved would produce a far more rounded, more nearly complete and full being than either could be alone.

On such a reckoning, it is no longer surprising that lovers are amazed and delighted at the profound difference between them right along with being highly gratified at how much "we two share in common."

This sense of a "greater whole" is also eminently compatible with a concomitant aspect of love: an exceedingly high degree of solicitude for the other, a powerful interest in the other's welfare, even to the point of being willing to undergo any number of sacrifices in behalf of this goal. Now, perhaps, is the time to reintroduce love as "the will to extend oneself for the purpose of nurturing one's own and another's spiritual growth," for that is an important part of the enlightened lover's desire for the other—and not completely unselfish either, for in important ways such growth resounds to one's own satisfaction (within this larger and now expanding whole) and indeed itself probably conduces to one's own growth—and vice versa.

But there must be a strong feeling component as well before we are willing to call the relationship *love*. It is, in the first instance, quite simply a great delight in the other's company and a low tolerance of extended absence. It is further a desire for yet greater intimacy than whatever presently obtains, with commonly a strong erotic quality therein in the case of man–woman lovers (or with homosexual couples, *mutatis mutandis*.) There will be, too, an almost insatiable desire to *know* the other person, of which carnal knowledge is part, for the "one flesh" of the marriage ceremony does connote a kind of knowledge: carnal lovers do indeed know something about the other that can be known in no other way.

Although sexual intimacy is desired by lovers and when achieved adds a dimension to the mutuality of their knowing each other, let it not be supposed that sexual intimacy constitutes love, or even that sexual union even guarantees intimacy. Some psychologists who have especially worked with teenagers have concluded that often sexual conjoining may be used as a way of forestalling the threat of intimacy rather than, as with maturer relations, a means to it, or a consummation of previous kinds of intimacy.

This in turn brings to the fore another characteristic feature of the early stages of the attraction: a certain fear—possibly stronger, most often, in the case of the woman than the man?—that commitment to the other entails a serious element of risk. A sense of a powerful vulnerability is present because in declaring one's love, becoming more intimate, thus revealing more and more about oneself, one is opening oneself up to hurt, even profound hurt. It does, after all, happen that a person is powerfully attracted to another who turns out to be unscrupulous—and how can one be sure?

Such are not the only shadow parts of love, for there are dangers too in the neglect of friends and family, distraction from the goals of schooling or career, and so on. But usually these come to be reckoned the legitimate price one pays for a priceless treasure.

Yet again lovers often testify to each other their respective wonderment that "you should be able to love the likes of me." This feeling does not necessarily indicate a strong disparagement of oneself (which has been found to be incompatible with the love of others), but only the feeling that "I am getting the better of the bargain." If, secretly, the other's response is "Yes, you are," the relationship is almost surely doomed. Or at least its ideality is doomed, for though so far the assumption has been that the subject of inquiry has been *healthy* love, no one doubts that there are various degrees of ill-health associated with human pairings. For instance, there is sometimes (not infrequently?) to be found a kind of love that is grounded on one side by the need for adulation, and on the other by—adulation. Some have noted such to be the case when a woman is quite exceptionally beautiful and also expects and seemingly needs continual homage to be paid to this reality; or again, in the case of a man of commanding presence, perhaps by virtue of an intellectual brilliance or immense force of personality. But it can of course work the other way around too, with the man possessing the physical attractiveness and the woman the spiritual power. (In our changing Anglo-American cultures, these "other way arounds" are surely becoming steadily more common.)

Another less than completely mutual love is exemplified by those instances in which one person is more attracted by the other's weakness than by their strength, thus meeting a powerful need to be the support, the helper and comforter of the weak or afflicted. This is by no means necessarily unhealthy. It is doubtless good that there should be this kind of need and feeling, but in its asymmetry it departs from the love previously sketched.

C. G. Jung has argued that in a marriage, or perhaps in any love relationship, there is a virtually inevitable asymmetry because of the fact that one of the partners is "the container," the other "the contained." What this means, at least in terms of the need for a human relationship, is that the contained feels so well satisfied within the status quo that all erotic and other needs for affection are taken care of, whereas the container requires more than the partner provides to make life agreeable. This does not necessarily mean "infidelity" but does mean a dispersion of energies that is at least often resented by the partner, who may be puzzled and irritated not to be found sufficient. (see "Marriage as a Psychological Relationship," in *CW* 17.) On the other hand, both may be content with this difference in their expectations and actuality.

This point prompts a serious caveat about the previous attempt to describe "true love." As in so much else, what is a virtually perfect relationship for these two people may turn out to be disastrously inadequate for another couple. But this in turn puts new emphasis upon the need—in the various games of love—for more and more self-knowledge and a capacity for knowing the other self. Matches may be made in heaven, but suppose one guessed that heaven favors those who are willing and able to assess their own propensities, weaknesses and strengths, interests, potentialities, and downright needs in *relation* to a similar inventory of the other. So stated, this sounds unduly a matter of stock-taking and intellective judgment, so it must be added that this kind of activity is far more a matter of feeling than of conceptual thinking. Neither does it preclude the element of mystery that is so commonly found in the authentic love relationship. Mystery's presence need not be a deterrent to concerted inquiry, but it properly serves as a reminder that one's findings are, at best, going to be incomplete.

Finally, let us return to the question of the relevance of this brief excursion into the values and disvalues of love for the teaching/learning process. That lovers teach one another has been testified to since the days of Socrates, but it is seldom honored by more than a nod of agreement. They teach each other first (perhaps sometimes only) by "modeling" their own best developed ways of being-in-the-world. This especially speaks to the reciprocity and compensatory balancing previously alluded to, part of the attraction being so often with respect to those ways in which one lover feels surpassed by the other. (This may be there even in cases that seem to a couple's acquaintances as a seriously discrepant relationship, for the seemingly more powerful one may have just as much need for the other as the other way around.) But one lover can teach the other too by helping cultivate underdeveloped interests. Thus, though a businessman may say he is content to stay home and read the *Wall Street Journal* or the *Economist* while his wife looks after the cultural side of the family by going to the opera, she may gradually whet his interest in the music, and he hers in fiscal investments. They modify and correct each other in various ways, for instance with respect to sensitivity to the needs of others, the pleasures of altruism, and the expression of affection and concern.

Yet a lot depends upon the learning that takes place before the establishment of the relationship. This is not the place to crawl into the thorny thickets of sex education, but teachers who are concerned with *love* can find many opportunities for engaging students' attention with the historical sociology of love, the anthropology of love, the philosophy of love, and the psychology of love. One of the very most important entryways into a consideration of love relationships is through poetry, drama, and fiction. Stendhal has a character say that he does not know how to carry on a love affair because he is still ignorant of novels. Here is the testimony of a great novelist to the exceptionally important insight he and his fellow artists have had into a realm upon which but little light has been cast by the social sciences.

We now need to return to self-liking and self-loving, asking whether it makes sense to count *oneself* as loved one or friend—in any other way than that (unusual) one in which, perhaps after a period of self-criticism, one might say, "I'm again feeling very friendly toward myself," or something of the sort.

Friends are surely those whose company we enjoy and who, in their absence, we miss and want a reunion with. But people differ very considerably with respect to how much they "enjoy their own company." This seems to correlate highly with the difference between introverts and extroverts. It is not quite so simple as saying introverts *do* enjoy their own company, for some seem to think rather that they are—as one would be in the case of a tiresome roommate or officemate, or overstaying houseguest—*saddled* with the intrapsychic "other." But, assuming they have a generally beneficent attitude toward themselves, perhaps it makes sense to say that introverts enjoy their own company, spend relatively frequent, or long, periods of time in inner conversation, do a lot of self-monitoring, and indeed will relatively often happily forgo the company of a separate other for being by and with (but not beside) themselves. (Yet the question remains as to whether they approve of themselves.)

This way of thinking of course entails a reflexive relationship, as in such a saying as "I asked myself . . ." or addressing to oneself a question, "Well, what do you think of that?" William James found it handy to play upon the grammatical distinction between the personal pronouns *I* and *me*, in making a distinction between parts of the human self. As he thought of it, the *me* is the accumulated part of the self, what one has become and what one amounts to as a result of all the things one has done, thought, felt, etc. This, then, would be the self as describable by oneself or another, perhaps in answer to such a question as "What sort of person are you (is he)?" ("Myself" works in the same way, as when Heraclitus said, "I searched into myself.") But the *I* is the executive aspect of the self, the one that is on the knife-edge of the present, tilting toward the future. Then the *I* is the inquirer, the asker, the asserter, the predictor, the reminder, the praiser, the scolder (etc.) *of* me or myself.

In this way of thinking, learning to "get along with oneself," "getting better acquainted with oneself" (in obedience to the ancient command, "Know thyself") and being on quite friendly terms with oneself, thus enjoying (often—not necessarily always) internal dialogue, not only make sense, but could be thought of as a way of being that a person might well be counseled to cultivate. As Buber said, "To be able to go out to the other, . . . you must be with yourself" (1947: 20). This is not altogether different from the counsel to "meet some new people, strike up a new friendship," or even to cultivate those attitudes and skills that will have such results.

Consequently, it would be far from ludicrous—though certainly unusual—for a teacher to try to help someone cultivate the art of "self-friendship." However, being in love with oneself would generally be regarded as unhealthy and thus inadvisable, even worse than (according to some, as noticed above) being in love with someone else. But of course one can respect, admire, or be proud of some part of oneself, such as one's disposition, mind, body, or some aspect of any of these. For instance, body-building is an activity conscientiously pursued by some portion of the population in many cultures, past and present. Serious body-builders will talk (if you let them) about specific goals of their self-development, this or that part of the musculature, typically, that wants cultivating; and when this is done, up to a certain level or standard of attainment, then such a person might be said to be pleased, and when this applies fairly generally to the body, to like one's body very much. The sort of body thus aimed at tends to be quite different from those cultivated by the ones who set out to enhance their physical beauty, but in the latter category we think of some movie stars and models and professional athletes (of both sexes) who very much like what they see in the mirror and may even spend what to others would seem an excessive period of time thus gazing and enjoying. The reader will at this point already have thought of the proper end of such attitudes in the Greek myth of Narcissus: drowning. But this is of course the extreme. Up to a certain point, liking some aspects of oneself is surely part of what is meant by positive self-esteem, to which we now turn.

Whether or not it be true that only those who love themselves can genuinely love others, there appears to be total agreement among students of moral and ethical development that those infected with low opinions of themselves, along with a tendency to minimize their own abilities and even to have deep-rooted doubts about their personalities, characters, and selves, are going to be neither attractive companions nor persons who function well along a large range of ways of being. Now, although of course there are persons who have fallen into a mannerism of speaking slightingly of their own abilities, and there are whole cultures which seem to approve of deprecating talk both about oneself and—especially among certain Asians—about one's offspring, often enough we see that this is a pose meant to be seen as just that, whereas deeper down there is a considerable degree of confidence and even a reasonable self-pride. But, even outside clinical offices, it is by no means unusual to encounter those who appear to be so lacking in a sense of self-worth and ability as to seem virtually doomed to fulfill the very prophesy their attitudes proclaim. Today teachers are aware as never before that, for instance, a child will almost surely not be able to learn to read, or read at better than a minimum level, as long as his or her self-esteem is at such a low level. Alfred Adler's "inferiority complex" is now

228

seen as no joking matter, but a stark fact with serious effects in and outside school. (The opposite extreme, "the superiority complex," is not presently at issue.)

Thus for the last decade or two there has been a strong surge of interest in what is variously called "positive self-concept," "healthy self-esteem" or, in one branch of pop psychology, "I'm OK, you're OK", the big point of which is that you are not likely to seem to me OK until or unless I already seem OK to myself.

So-called "attribution theory" in academic psychology has closely examined the reasons people give for their various failures. Thus, if a pupil is asked why he thinks he did poorly (as he did) in a recent test, he may say things like "Bad luck," "I hate school, so I didn't really try," or "The test (or teacher or examiner) was unfair." All of these let the failer off the hook, and thus perhaps decrease the likelihood of lowering his self-esteem, but they also militate against an improvement on subsequent tests. "Frankly, I didn't work very hard—I was just unprepared" may itself, of course, be just an excuse, but at least it is looking in the right direction for improvement. Yet there is danger here too, for what if one genuinely believes that that was the trouble, works hard next time—and still fails: will self-esteem now fail to slip?

To be sure, these considerations go well beyond performance on academic tasks. The socially unpopular student may use similar attributions for his maladroitness.

No one doubts that the best cure for low self-esteem is relevant success, and this can readily introduce a benign cycle, more success following on the boost in self-confidence stimulated by the first success. So much is commonsensical, though not always remembered in school practice. However, caring teachers have always tried to show students that "my care for you" is not contingent upon excellent performance, and have usually gone out of their way to find something to praise in a pupil's performance. (Even descendants of Don Juan often say, "Every woman has some attractive feature to praise": presumably their reasoning is that such praise raises self-esteem and thus makes the other more loving.)

Beyond adapting school tests to students' ability, establishing a "safe" environment where mistakes are not lethal, helping students learn the efficacy of "working harder" and giving direct help on basic skills such as thinking, problem-solving, and study habits, good teachers often try to give students confidence that certain important goals are achievable by all members of a class. Yet it is increasingly believed that still more effective in raising the self-esteem of those who are low achievers is reducing the emphasis upon competition, substituting cooperative learning, which in teaching cooperative skills is also directly an instance of ethical, caring instruction. (See Covington, 1989: 72–124.)

What D. C. Briggs says about parents applies as well to teachers: "Focused

229

attention—direct involvement—'all-hereness'; it is a quality that gets love across. It nourishes self-respect at the roots because it says, 'I care.'" (Briggs 1975: 65). So too with what she calls establishing a climate of trust, which says in effect, "'You can count on me to help you meet your needs. I am not perfect but you can depend on my being honest with you—even about my imperfections. You can afford to be imperfect too . . ." (p. 80).

All of this is relevant to an increment of value in helping students take satisfaction in learning activities. At the risk of belaboring the obvious, let it be said yet again that the teacher who helps preserve in the pupil the young child's delight in coming to know (how and that) is both increasing the quantity of experienced value and opening up potentialities for further value ahead. The very condition of welcoming challenge, in the confidence that one can (probably) meet that challenge, is itself high on the list of values indigenous to the school setting. Finding value (new or old) is itself a matter of esteeming some person, object, process, or act. A general esteem for oneself, consonant with judicious self-criticism, appears to be the kind of value that conduces to many others.

Finally, we cannot leave the subject of the values of human relationships without attending to the distinctive contributions of Martin Buber to this subject, notably his distinction between two basic kinds of relations named by the "word-pairs": *I–It* and *I–Thou*. His primary point is that most commonly and necessarily each of us brings some small part of ourselves to address and regard some small part of another. It is not even a matter of rudeness or inconsiderateness or callousness that he is talking about when we relate to another person without taking into full account his or her humanness, for, amid the daily demands of getting on with our work and with the busy commerce of life, it seems we must often regard each other as "its," objects, or rather as highly limited subjects. I can quite courteously accept the package the delivery man puts into my hands or respond to an inquiry over the telephone or answer a routine business letter, and yet not go beyond the very specific quality of the other person that is relevant to the immediate situation. But in so doing I am asked not to forget that in such encounters I am equally limiting what is present in the "I". If he is the messenger, I am nothing more than the receiver, nor do I wish to be more. I am told the time and I say, "Thank you," and nothing more is involved.

Thus, for Buber, there is an *It* world, which is spatial, temporal, and causal, and there is the *Thou* world of inclusive relationships. Though we could not as humans fail to occupy the *It* world, if we should fail to be part of the other world, that of the *I and Thou*, we would be failing to live up to our human potentiality.

But there are possible misunderstandings of Buber's message. For instance, the *Thou* is not necessarily a human. It may be a horse—and indeed as a young man his intimate fondness for a horse remained a great relationship in his memory. But one can even look upon a tree as a *Thou*, which thus calls out in us the fullness of our being, for when I respond to a *Thou*, I do so with the wholeness of my self. And then, above the human, there is God, the ultimate *Thou*. But in the case of worldly love

> I, the lover, turn to this other human being, the beloved, in his otherness, his independence, his self-reality, and turn to him as to one who is there turning to me, but in that very reality, not comprehensible by me but rather comprehending me, in which I am there turning him. I do not assimilate into my own soul that which lives and faces me, I vow it faithfully to myself and myself to it, I vow, I have faith.
>
> (Buber 1947: 29)

There are also approximations to the full *I–Thou* relationship. Not only cannot the tree respond to me as a *Thou*, but so too with a young child, who, though her love may be wholly genuine, is not able to include me, her other, wholly into her own comprehension, for essential to this relationship is the inclusion of the other's response to oneself. Not only does the *I* bring the fullness of his own being to the fullness of the other, but he also identifies with the other as a recipient of the *I*'s attentive regard. Two people are in what Buber calls a dialogical relationship when each of them is an *I* for whom the other is a *Thou*, but without limiting the independence of that other.

It is this kind of prevalent relationship that is the basis for a community, as distinct from a collectivity. And it is this kind of relationship that characterizes education at its best, though Buber believes that necessarily teacher and pupil are on a different footing:

> In order to help the realisation of the best potentialities in the pupil's life, the teacher must really *mean* him as the definite person he is in his potentiality and his actuality; more precisely, he must not know him as a mere sum of qualities, strivings and inhibitions, he must be aware of him as a whole being and affirm him in his wholeness. . . .
>
> But however much depends upon his awaking the *I–Thou* relationship in the pupil as well—and however much depends upon the pupil, too, meaning and affirming him as the particular person he is—the special educative relation could not persist if the pupil for his part practised "inclusion," that is, if he lived the teacher's part in the common situation. Whether the *I-Thou* relationship now comes to an end or assumes the quite different character of a friendship, it is plain that the specifically educative relation as such is denied full mutuality.
>
> (Buber 1958: 132)

It seems somewhat strange for Buber to put these limitations about education once the pupil has the maturity to practice the "inclusion" that is essential to reciprocating the teacher's *I-Thou* way, but this should not obscure the main point that Buber is making: that it is essential for the teacher to be an authentic *I* to the pupil's *Thou*, thus bringing the wholeness of herself into the situation, not being there just as an expert in biology or as disciplinarian or as the preserver of the cultural heritage or in any other such limited role.

The teacher, for Buber, is the "selector of the effective world" for the pupil, the instructor and corrector, and whether the instruction has to do with history or science or the aesthetic or the moral, "if the educator of our day has to act consciously he must nevertheless do it 'as though he did it not.' That raising of the finger, that questioning glance, are his genuine doing" (1947: 94). The teacher does not select her pupils: they are, as the existentialists like to say, "flung" before her as all of us are flung into the world. And they are, of course, of various kinds. But the teacher must be able to practice "experiencing the other side"—the side of the pupil— "if teaching is to be genuine" and must ultimately help the pupil also to experience the other world, so that he too may assume his rightful place as an *I* in the world of *Thous*. But for this to happen there is an essential understanding required of the teacher:

> Only in his whole being, in all his spontaneity can the educator truly affect the whole being of his pupil. For educating characters you do not need a moral genius, but you do need a man who is wholly alive and able to communicate himself directly to his fellow being. His aliveness streams out to them and affects them most strongly and purely when he has no thought of affecting them.
>
> (1947: 105)

In his fine little book on caring Milton Mayeroff writes "Caring, as helping another grow and actualize himself, is a process, a way of relating to someone that involves development, in the same way that friendship can only emerge in time through mutual trust and qualitative transformation of the relationship" (Perennial Library, New York: Harper & Row, 1971: 1). But caring is also a feeling of warm affection in the presence, or even in the thought and image, of another. It involves a concern for, a devotion to the other, and its genuineness is tested by acts of helpfulness and consideration, prompted at times by sympathy, at times by a desire simply that 'things will be well' for the other. It has its antitheses not only in malice and hatefulness, but also in indifference, callousness, and an impulse to bend the other to one's own wants and ends.

Caring can exist between persons of any age, gender or status. But I can care, too, for my school, my community, my country—and must, if I am to realize my humanity, care for things that are unable to return my feelings of care: a book, an idea, a mountain or bay, a lilac bush, a rug, the pool I swim in—for to care for many things, some of them deeply, is a requisite for full humanity.

20

CONCLUSION

What we are generally after in our schools is an improvement in the quality of the lives of students and in turn of the other lives they presently (and will in the future) affect. This requires attention to values of various kinds. Here the word "ethical" has been used to describe those intentions, decisions, and acts that have as their purpose living well—more immediately living *better*—in oneself and for others. In the moral sphere this means a number of obligations which we as social creatures have. The fact that we are *human*, social beings means that we are able to take the point of view of the other, reckon the probable consequences of our potential actions, sometimes even those distant in time and place. Yet beyond these actions that our duty prompts, we seek to extend our access to and participation in aesthetic and cognitive values and those that afford friendship and love, work and play, and the spiritual dimensions of life.

Although, as Whitehead reminds us, we can all profit by the "habitual vision of greatness," the contemplation of exalted ideals must not be allowed to eclipse less dazzling virtues. For instance, a case can be made out for teachers having a vital concern to develop a general competence in their charges. Now, "competence" is not a value that sends chills and thrills up and down the ethical spine, but it requires only a moment's reflection to understand how much we prize this quality in others (and are pleased when we ourselves exhibit it). There is of course the competent swimmer or carpenter or driver, but more generally a competent person is one who "shows himself *to be up to those tasks* which *life presents to him*" or "*to be able to do what is required*" (Brezinska 1988: 76). Everyone has had the experience of looking around, in moments of need, for just that kind of person, the one who can be depended upon to come through, to handle the situation, perhaps to take charge, or at least not to collapse into ineffectuality but rather to rise to the occasion.

Or again "moderation" has been praised as a virtue from of old, and often our earliest memories of ethical instruction may be in parental cautions not to overdo—sweets or noisemaking or rough play. But this undramatic virtue may serve as a reminder too that not all people usually, or any of us always, want to *maximize*, to squeeze every last possible drop of enjoyment out of our quest for various satisfactions. Economists have begun to recognize that not every person interested in selling her house or negotiating a contract is strenuously seeking the highest possible price or salary. Often enough, people want only a fair price or a decent recompense. We do not require that *every* meal be a glorious feast, every kiss a swooning delight, but are content with what is good without being marvelous. Even this kind of moderation needs to be learned—though of course not overlearned. Yet a mark of the person who is high on the human development process, the so-called individuated person, the self-actualizer or self-realized one, is a capacity for "peak experiences," but also the taking of satisfaction in a multitude of "little things": the sudden glint of sunlight on a passing butterfly, the soft smile of an old woman, the synchronicity of trying to think of a name and then having someone with the same name call. In this respect more than others, it is surely the teacher's example that teaches, the exhibit of her capacity to be, in Henry James's requirement of a fine novelist, "one on whom nothing is lost." (See Slote 1988.)

The child—the student of any age—wants to find in the school, the individual classroom, an environment that is at once replete with safety and interest, and which, normally under the sensitive guidance of a teacher, leads to growth, a fulfillment of one's potentialities that promise realization of value.

There are those educators who prize above all classroom management; others who emphasize, almost to the exclusion of all else, the sharpening of intellective skills and the acquisition of great bodies of knowledge. But here the accent has been differently placed, upon how "each individual embodies an adventure of existence." In Whitehead's words:

> Education is the guidance of the individual toward a comprehension of the art of life; and by the art of life I mean the most complete achievement of varied activity expressing the potentialities of that living creature in the face of its actual environment.
>
> (Whitehead 1932b: 61)

As with all art, this most comprehensive of arts will always bear the stamp of its individual creator and exemplar. The good teacher is not concerned to reproduce clones, but to recommend in word, gesture, and larger patterns of action some of the goods of life that have come her way, and even some others that she still aspires to, on the good report of an author or friend. Yet, a pattern of living well is not a rag-bag of discrete delights: such is not a pattern at all. Neither does it have the regularization of a schedule. At its best it will exhibit a rich variety of *kinds* of values, some few of which receive a particular cultivation with correspondingly deep rewards. It will be marked by continuities, overlaps, and surprising interrelations. It will have a place for both the values of solitude and those of sociability. And somehow through all its complex variety there will be the unifying recurrence of a few themes, so that looking back one may say, "Such has been my way."

The reader will have discovered in this work less prescription than recommendation, fewer definitive answers than suggestive queries, more exposure to a variety of points of view than of dogmatic decision as to which one is right. And yet there has been also no pretense of neutrality on the major issues of valuation. It will have taken no unusually discerning eye to tell that the book's author is fonder of ethical than of moral issues, has an especial love of beauty in art and nature, and believes that the best teachers are those who find ways of extending and enriching value-enhancing experiences in the lives of pupils. The choice of words in the subtitle *Caring and Appreciation* is meant to throw a highlight on the cultivation of these ingredients of the value-full life. *Caring* has first of all to do with a way of being toward other persons. One who cares for and about others is one who is endowed with, and who has doubtless had help in developing, a capacity for genuinely liking, and in at least a few cases loving, others and (more positively) helping them, without abridging their own freedom, toward fulfillment of their possibilities for living well. The caring person's way of being in the world is contrasted not only with malicious behavior and attitudes but also with indifference, the shrug, someone's turning his back on another. If the establishment of justice is the noblest of human pursuits, the nurturing of one's own propensity for caring is the most humane.

Yet caring is directed not only at other human creatures but at a selection of creatures great and small, at plants and rocks, rivers and the sea. If we smile at the over-sophisticate's complaint that he was bored by the solar system, we are more moved by Kant's awe of "the starry heavens above" no less than for "the moral law within." If, as has been said, our ultimate fate is to turn away from the whole world in the acceptance of our own death, we can have little admiration for one who prematurely gives over concern, affection, and caring for and about a multitude of persons, happenings, things.

The transition from caring to *appreciation* is swift and easy. Indeed, they might almost seem the two sides of the same attitude and way of being. If "appreciation" seems to be especially apropos of beauty, we recognize also the appreciation we feel for our friends, fair and not-so-fair of face and figure—or perhaps even character. But authentic appreciation connotes discrimination and a sensitive capacity for apt judgment and not just a fixed smile of approval on every sight and sound.

Caring and appreciation are learnable and teachable. The argument here is that their cultivation should be the unifying container of the curriculum.

NOTES

1 Recently some investigators have noticed that adult teasing sometimes undermines children's self-confidence and esteem and confuses them by a felt mixture of playfulness and serious disapproval.

2 A similar point could be made about philosophers' typically heavy emphasis upon abstract principle. Blum, himself a philosopher, recalls William James's observation that in each moral act there is both an abstract principle and a concrete context and agrees "that every moral situation also has a particular actor, target, and situation that should not be ignored" in concentrating upon Kantian maxims or principles (Kagan 1987: xx).

3 This is cited in Barry Chazan (1985: 50). This latter work is recommended for an unusually clear exposition of Values Clarification and the Kohlbergian program, among other "approaches."

4 In turn, Carol Stack (1989), an anthropologist, argues that Gilligan is herself generalizing about women from a mainly white sample, whereas her own investigations suggest that many black women rate justice very high (and many black men rate care high).

5 Yet this too can be set aside by a repressive government, as was shown in the 1989 massacre of students in China.

6 Compare Italy and Germany in the 1930s.

7 Russell was brought up by his grandparents. His grandfather was Prime Minister under Queen Victoria and a friend of John Stuart Mill.

8 Bertrand Russell was imprisoned for his pacifism in World War I, was denied the right to teach at City College of New York on the grounds that his books were immoral, and was one of the most famous dissenters from Anglo-American policy during the Cold War period.

9 I here quote my own words in *The Quest for Beauty* (Jarrett 1957: 181)

10 These and other ways of interpreting "expression" are analyzed by Guy Sircello (1972: 10–13).

11 Dare we correct the stern duchess? It's not "the moral"—which is to say, an edifying capsule—that should be sought, but something far deeper and subtler.

12 I have here borrowed from a paper of my former student, Peter H. Kahn, Jr, "Growing in awareness of moral situations through literature: Sherlock Holmes—The Adventure of the Devil's Foot."

13 Karen Randlev and Peter Kahn, former students, shared in the teaching episodes described in this chapter and have been very helpful in considering the evaluations thereof and in making suggestions for future changes.

14 Lest this seem not worthy of mention, let me add that nowhere is youthful innocence more intense than in knowledge of what one really *does* in a vast

variety of jobs, and in what by way of academic or technical preparation is required for this or that vocation. At one time I was counseling young men being discharged from the armed forces, helping them get ready for re-entry into civilian life, including further schooling and eventual careers. Over and over I would have a conversation with one of these men along the following lines:

"What sort of work do you find interesting? What would you like to prepare for?"

"I think I'd like to go into medicine. That'd be very interesting."

"I expect you found your school classes in biology among your favorite subjects, then."

"Oh, no, I couldn't stand biology—all that mucking around with frogs and so on. I did like woodwork and glee club."

15 A recent magazine column claims that President Bush's computer, under a file entitled "Close personal friends," has 10,000 entries!

REFERENCES

Aiken, H. D. (1965) 'The concept of moral objectivity,' in H.- N. Castaneda and G. Nakhnikian (eds) *Morality and the Language of Conduct*, Detroit: Wayne State University Press.

Aries, P. (1972) *Centuries of Childhood*, Harmondsworth: Penguin.

Aristotle (1961) *Poetics*, trans. S. H. Butcher, intro. Francis Fergusson, New York: Hill and Wang.

—— (1984) *The Complete Works of Aristotle*, ed. Jonathan Barnes, rev. trans., Bolling Series LXII 1 and 2, Princeton, NJ: Princeton University Press.

Arnheim, R. (1969) *Visual Thinking*, London: Faber & Faber.

Arnold, M. (1885) 'Literature and Science,' in *Discourses in America*, London: Macmillan.

Aronson, E. (1978) *The Jigsaw Classroom*, Beverly Hills, Calif., and London: Sage.

Attfield, R. (1987) *A Theory of Value and Obligation*, London: Croom Helm.

Babbitt, N. (1975) *Tuck Everlasting*, New York: Farrar, Straus, Giroux.

Berger, P. (1983) 'On the obsolescence of the concept of honor,' in S. Hauerwas and A. MacIntyre (eds) *Revisions*, Notre Dame, Ind.: University of Notre Dame Press.

Bernikow, L. (1980) *Among Women*, New York: Harper & Row.

Bernstein, B. (1973) *Class, Codes and Control: Applied Studies towards a Sociology of Language*, Vol. II: *Language and Education*, London: Routledge & Kegan Paul.

—— (1974) *Class, Codes and Control: Theoretical Studies towards a Sociology of Language*, Vol. I: *Primary Socialization*, revised edn, London: Routledge & Kegan Paul.

Bettelheim, B. (1950) *Love is Not Enough*, Glencoe, Ill.: Free Press.

—— (1987) 'The importance of play,' *Atlantic Monthly*, March.

Blum, L. (1987) 'Particularity and responsiveness,' in J. Kagan (ed.) *The Emergence of Morality in Young Children*, Chicago and London: University of Chicago Press.

Booth, W. C. (1961) *The Rhetoric of Fiction*, Chicago: University of Chicago Press.

Bourdieu, P. and Passeron, J. C. (1977) *Reproduction in Education, Society and Culture*, London: Sage.

Bowles, S. and Gintis, H. (1976) *Schooling in Capitalist America*, New York: Basic Books.

Brezinska, W. (1988) 'Competence as an aim of education,' in B. Spiecker and R. Straughan (eds) *Philosophical Issues in Moral Education and Development*: Milton Keynes and Philadelphia: Open Court Press.

Briggs, D. C. (1975) *Your Child's Self-esteem*, Garden City, NY: Dolphin.

Bronfenbrenner, U. (1969) *Two Worlds of Childhood*, London: Allen & Unwin.

Brown, D. and Solomon, D. (1983) 'A model for prosocial learning,' in *The Nature of Prosocial Development*, New York: Academic Press.

Buber, M. (1947) *Between Man and Man*, trans. R. G. Smith, Boston, Mass.: Beacon Press.

—— (1958) *I and Thou*, trans. R. G. Smith, New York: Scribner.

Bullough, E. (1957) 'Psychical distance as a factor in art and aesthetic principle,' in E. M. Wilkinson (ed.) *Aesthetics*, London: Bowes & Bowes.

California State Department of Education (1988) *Moral and Civic Education and Teaching about Religion*, Sacramento, Calif.: California State Department of Education.

Carroll, L. (1946) 'The Mock Turtle Story,' *Alice's Adventures in Wonderland and Through the Looking Glass*, New York: The Macmillan Company.

Castaneda, H.- N. and Nakhnikian, G. (eds) (1965) *Morality and the Language of Conduct*, Detroit: Wayne State University Press.

Chazan, B. (1985) *Contemporary Approaches to Moral Education*, New York: Teachers College Press.

Cohen, D. K. and Rosenberg, B. H. (1977) 'Functions and fantasies: understanding schools in capitalist America,' *History of Education Quarterly* 17(2).

Coles, R., Seel, J., Becker, J., and Hunter, J. D. (1989) *Girl Scouts Survey on the Beliefs and Moral Values of America's Children*, New York: Girl Scouts of the United States of America.

Collingwood, R. G. (1938) *The Principles of Art*, Oxford: Clarendon.

Cornell, J. B. (1979) *Sharing Nature with Children*, ed. G. Beinhorn, n. p.: Ananda.

Covington, V. (1989) 'Self-esteem and failure in school: analysis and policy implications,' in A. M. Mecca, N. J. Smelser, and J. Vasconcellas (eds) *The Social Importance of Self-esteem*, Berkeley and Los Angeles: University of California Press.

Cummings, W. K., Gopinathan, S., and Yasumata Tomoda (1988) *The Revival of Values Education in Asia and the West*, Oxford: Pergamon.

Damon, W. (1988) *The Moral Child: Nurturing Children's Natural Moral Growth*, New York: Free Press.

De Laguna, G. (1927) *Speech: its Function and Development*, New Haven, Conn.: Yale University Press.

Dewey, J. (1900) *The School and Society*, fifth edn, Chicago: University of Chicago Press, 1905.

—— (1916) *Democracy and Education*, New York: Macmillan.

—— (1934) *Art as Experience*, New York: Minton Balch.

Dickinson, E. (1862) *The Complete Poems of Emily Dickinson*, ed. Thomas H. Johnson, Boston: Little Brown & Co., 1890.

Dunn, J. (1987) 'The beginnings of moral understanding: development in the second year,' in J. Kagan (ed.) *The Emergence of Morality in Young Children*, Chicago and London: University of Chicago Press.

——(1989) Public lecture, University of California, Berkeley.

Durkheim, E. (1956) *Education and Sociology*, trans. S. D. Fox, New York: Free Press.

—— (1970) *Essays on Morals and Education*, ed. W. S. P. Pickering, London: Routledge & Kegan Paul.

Egan, K. and Nadaner, D. (eds) (1988) *Imagination and Education*, New York: Teachers College Press.

Erikson, E. (1968) *Identity, Youth and Crisis*, New York: Norton.

—— (1980) 'Reflection on Dr Borg's life cycle,' in N. J. Smelser and E. Erikson (eds)

Themes of Work and Love in Adulthood, Cambridge, Mass.: Harvard University Press.

Ewing, A. C. (1929) *The Morality of Punishment*, London: Kegan Paul, Trench, Trubner.

Freire, P. (1971) *Pedagogy of the Oppressed*, trans. M. B. Ramos, New York: Herder.

—— (1985) 'Cultural action and agrarian reform,' in *The Politics of Education: Culture, Power and Liberation*, trans. D. Macedo, South Hadley, Mass.: Bergin & Garvey.

Freud, S. (1933) *New Introductory Lectures on Psychoanalysis*, trans. J. H. Sprott, London: Hogarth Press.

Gilligan, C. (1982) *In a Different Voice*, Cambridge, Mass.: Harvard University Press.

Gombrich, E. H. (1962) *Art and Illusion: a Study in the Psychology of Pictorial Representations*, new edn, London: Phaidon Press.

Gordon, J. C. B. (1981) *Verbal Deficit: a Critique*, London: Croom Helm.

Green, T. F. (1968) *Work, Leisure and the American School*, New York: Random House.

Hartshorne, H. and May, M. A. (1928) *Studies in Deceit*, New York: Macmillan.

Hauerwas, S. and MacIntyre, A. (eds) (1983) *Revisions*, Notre Dame, Ind.: University of Notre Dame Press.

Havighurst, R. J. (1953) *Human Development and Education*, New York: Longman.

Hearne, V. (1987) *Adam's Task: Calling Animals by Name*, New York: Knopf.

Herndon, J. (1972) *How to Survive in your Native Land*, New York, Bantam.

Hersh, R. H., Miller, J. P., and Fielding, G. D. (1980) *Models of Moral Education*, New York: Longman.

Holland, J. (1973) *Making Vocational Choices*, Englewood Cliffs, NJ.: Prentice Hall.

Hughes, T. (1857) *Tom Brown's Schooldays*, London.

James, W. (1907) *Pragmatism*, New York: Longman.

—— (1956) 'The moral philosophies and the moral life,' in *The Will to Believe and other Essays in Popular Philosophy*, New York: Dover.

Jarrett, J. L. (1957) *The Quest for Beauty*, New York: Prentice Hall.

Jung, C. G. (1959-79) *The Collected Works of C. G. Jung*, 23 vols, Princeton, NJ: Princeton University Press; London: Routledge.

Kagan, J. (1984) 'Emergence of self,' in *Annual Progress in Child Psychiatry and Child Development*, New York: Brunner & Mazel.

—— (ed.) (1987) *The Emergence of Morality in Young Children*, Chicago and London: University of Chicago Press.

Kahn, P. H. (1988) 'Growing in awareness of moral situations through literature: Sherlock Holmes – The Adventure of the Devil's Foot,' *Ethics in Education* 7.

Kay, W. (1974) 'Morality and social class,' *Journal of Moral Education* 3, 19 February.

Kegan, R. (1982) *The Evolving Self: Problems and Process in Human Development*, Cambridge, Mass.: Harvard University Press.

Kirschenbaum, H. (1977) *Advanced Values Clarification*, La Jolla, Calif.: University Associates.

Kohlberg, L. (1980) 'High school democracy and educating for a just society,' in R. L. Mosher (ed.) *Moral Education: a First Generation of Research and Development*, New York: Praeger.

Kohn, A. (1988) 'P is for prosocial teaching,' *Boston Globe Magazine*, 6 November.

Lawrence, D. H. (1926) *The Rainbow*, London: Heinemann.

—— (1936) 'Art and morality' and 'Morality and the novel' in *Phoenix*, London: Heinemann.

—— (1950) 'John Galsworthy,' in *Selected Essays*, Harmondsworth: Penguin.

REFERENCES

Lepley, R. (1949) *Value: a Co-operative Inquiry*, Westport, Conn.: Greenwood Press.

Levinson, D., Darrow, C. N., Klein, E. B., Levinson, M. H., and McKee, B. (1978) *The Seasons of a Man's Life*, New York: Knopf.

Locke, J. (1693) 'Some thoughts concerning Education', in *On Politics and Education*, London; (ed.) H. R. Persimmon, New York: Van Nostrand, 1947.

Loevinger, J. (1976) *Ego Development*, San Francisco: Jossey-Bass.

Lorenz, K. (1967) *On Aggression*, trans. M. K. Wilson, New York: Bantam.

Lunn, A. and Lean, G. (1964) *The New Morality*, London: Blandford Press .

MacIntyre, A. (1967) *Secularization and Moral Change*, London: Oxford University Press.

—— (1984) *After Virtue*, second edn, Notre Dame, Ind.: University of Notre Dame Press.

McPhail, P., Ungoed-Thomas, J. R., and Chapman, H. (1972) *Moral Education in the Secondary School*, London: Longman.

Maslow, A. (1971) *The Farther Reaches of Human Nature*, New York: Viking Press.

Mayeroff, M. (1971) *On Caring*, New York: Harper & Row.

Mecca, A. M., Smelser, N. J., and Vasconcellas, J. (1989) *The Social Importance of Self-esteem*, Berkeley and Los Angeles: University of California Press.

Mill, J. S. (1859) *On Liberty*, London.

Mosher, R. L. (ed.) (1980) *Moral Education: a First Generation of Research and Development*, New York: Praeger.

Murdoch, I. (1970) *The Sovereignty of the Good*, London: Routledge & Kegan Paul.

Musgrove, P. W. (1978) *The Moral Curriculum: a Sociological Analysis*, London: Methuen.

Neff, W. S. (1968) 'Work and human history,' in *Towards Social Interpretation of Work*, New York: Atherton Press.

Neumann, E. (1969) *Depth Psychology and a New Ethic*, New York: C. G. Jung Foundation.

Newman, J. H. (1852) *The Idea of a University*, London.

Niblett, W. B. (ed.) (1963) *Moral Education in a Changing Society*, London: Faber & Faber.

Noddings, N. (1984) *Caring: a Feminine Approach to Ethics and Moral Education*, Berkeley and Los Angeles: University of California Press.

—— (1989) *Women and Evil*, Berkeley and Los Angeles: University of California Press.

Park, S. R. (1982) *The Moral of the Story*, New York: Teachers College Press.

Parker, D. H. (1931) *Human Values*, New York: Harper.

Peck, M. S. (1978) *The Road Less Traveled*, New York: Simon & Schuster.

Peters, R. S. (1963) 'Reason and habit: the paradox of moral education,' in W. B. Niblett (ed.) *Moral Education in a Changing Society*, London: Faber & Faber.

Piaget, J. (1965) *The Moral Development of the Child*, trans. M. Gabin, New York: Free Press.

Pinkevitch, A. P. (1929) *The New Education in the Soviet Republic*, New York: John Day.

Plato (1937) *The Meno* and *The Symposium*, in *The Dialogues of Plato*, trans. B. Jowett, New York: Random House.

Rader, M. (ed.) (1960) *A Modern Book of Aesthetics*, New York: Holt Rinehart & Winston.

Radhakrishnan, S. and Moore, C. A. (eds) (1958) *A Source Book in Indian Philosophy*, Princeton, NJ: Princeton University Press.

Raths, L. E., Harmin, M., and Simon, S. B. (1966) *Values and Teaching: Working with Values in the Classroom*, Columbus, Ohio: Merrill.

Read, H. (1961) *Education through Art*, London: Faber & Faber.

Rieff, P. (1959) *Freud: the Mind of a Moralist*, Garden City, NY: Doubleday & Co.

Robinson, J. (1963) *Honest to God*, Philadelphia: Westminster Press.

Rogers, C. (1969) *Freedom to Learn*, Columbus, Ohio: Merrill .

Russell, B. (1932) *Education and the Social Order*, London: Allen & Unwin.

—— (1945) *A History of Western Philosophy*, New York: Simon & Schuster.

Ryle, G. (1949) 'Knowing how and knowing that,' in *The Concept of Mind*, London: Hutchinson.

Sanford, N. (1966) *Self and Society: Social Change and Individual Development*, New York: Atherton Press.

Schweder, R. (1987) 'Culture and moral development,' in J. Kagan (ed.) *The Emergence of Morality in Young Children*, Chicago and London: University of Chicago Press.

Sheldon, W. H. (1954) *Atlas of Men: a Guide for Somatotyping the Adult Male at All Ages*, New York: Harper.

Shelley, P. B. (1821) *A Defence of Poetry*, in J. H. Smith and E. W. Parks (eds) *The Great Critics*, revised edn, New York: Norton, 1939.

Simon, S. and Olds, S. W. (1976) *Helping your Child Learn Right from Wrong: a Guide to Values Clarification*, New York: Simon & Schuster.

Sircello, G. (1972) *Mind and Art: an Essay on the Varieties of Expression*, Princeton, NJ: Princeton University Press.

Slote, M. (1988) 'On seeking less than the best,' in B. Spiecker and R. Straughan (eds) *Philosophical Issues in Moral Education and Development*, Milton Keynes and Philadelphia: Open Court Press.

Smelser, N. J. and Erikson, E. (eds) (1980) *Themes of Work and Love in Adulthood*, Cambridge, Mass.: Harvard University Press.

Snow, C. (1987) 'Language and the beginnings of moral understanding,' in J. Kagan (ed.) *The Emergence of Morality in Young Children*, Chicago and London: The University of Chicago Press.

Snow, C. P. (1958) *The Search*, New York: Scribner.

Spiecker, B. and Straughan, R. (eds) (1988) *Philosophical Issues in Moral Education and Development*, Milton Keynes and Philadelphia: Open Court Press.

Stack, C, B, (1989) 'Different voices, different visions: gender, culture and moral reasoning,' unpublished paper, University of California, Berkeley.

Stent, G. S. (ed.) (1980) *Morality as a Biological Phenomenon*, revised edn, Berkeley and Los Angeles, University of California Press.

Taylor, P. W. (1961) *Normative Discourse*, Englewood Cliffs, NJ: Prentice Hall.

Telfer, E. (1980) *Happiness*, New York: St Martin's Press.

Tolstoy, L. (1896) *What is Art,*? trans. A. Maude, London: Oxford University Press, 1930.

Trotsky, L. (1942) *Their Morals and Ours*, New York: Pioneer.

Turiel, E. (1983) *The Development of Social Knowledge: Morality and Convention*, New York: Cambridge University Press.

Twain, M. (1884) *The Adventures of Huckleberry Finn*, London: Penguin.

Vasari, G. (1550) *Lives of the most Excellent Architects, Painters and Sculptors*, trans. A. B. Hinds, New York: Dutton, 1927.

Véron, E. (1878) 'Aesthetics,' trans W. H. Armstrong, in M. Rader (ed.) *A Modern Book of Aesthetics*, New York: Holt Rinehart & Winston, 1960.

Viorst, J. (1977) *Redbook*.

Vitz, P. C. (1986) 'Religion and traditional values in public school textbooks,' *Public Interest* 84, Summer.

Voltaire (1759) *Candide*, Paris.

Walser, R. (1988) 'In search of a child's musical imagination,' in K. Egan and D. Nadaner (eds) *Imagination and Education*, New York: Teachers College Press.

Weil, S. (1983) 'The Iliad or the poem of force,' in S. Hauerwas and A. MacIntyre (eds) *Revisions*, Notre Dame, Ind.: University of Notre Dame Press .

White, J. T. (1909) *Character Lessons in American Biography for Public Schools and Home Institutions*, New York: Character Development League.

White, R. W. (1967) 'Ego and reality in psychoanalytic theory,' *Psychological Issues*, Monograph no. 11, New York: International University Press.

Whitehead, A. N. (1925) *Science and the Modern World*, New York: Macmillan.

—— (1932a) 'The aims of education,' in *The Aims of Education and other Essays*, London: Williams & Norgate.

—— (1932b) 'The rhythmic claims of freedom and discipline,' in *The Aims of Education and other Essays*, London: Williams & Norgate.

Whitman, W. (1967) *Complete Poems and Selected Prose and Letters* (ed.) Emory Holloway, London: The Nonesuch Press.

Wilde, O. (1891) *The Picture of Dorian Gray*, London.

Wilkinson, E. M. (ed.) (1957) *Aesthetics*, London: Bowes & Bowes.

Williams, B. (1985) *Ethics and the Limits of Philosophy*, Cambridge, Mass.: Harvard University Press.

Willis, P. (1977) *Learning to Labor*, New York: Columbia University Press.

Wilson, J. (1961) *Reasons and Morals*, Cambridge: Cambridge University Press.

Wilson, J., Williams, N., and Sugarman, B. (1967) *Introduction to Moral Education*, Harmondsworth: Penguin.

Wimsatt, W. K. (1954) *The Verbal Icon*, Lexington, Ky.: University of Kentucky Press.

INDEX